N

SWEDEN

Copenhagen

DENMARK

Baltic Sea

0 Miles 80

North Sea

Hamburg

Bremen

Schloss Kartzow

Berlin

NETH.

Amsterdam

Cleves

Hannover

Grasleben

GERMANY

Poznan

POLAND

Oder

Recklinghausen

Düsseldorf

Bernterode

Leipzig

Dresden

Siegen

Aachen

Marburg

Weser

Weimar

Cotta-Grosscotta

Koblenz

Merkers-Kieselbäch

BELG.

Rhine

Wiesbaden

Frankfurt

Main

Prague

LUX.

Trier

Offenbach

CZECHOSLOVAKIA

Metz

Heilbronn

Nuremberg

Ellingen

FRANCE

Stuttgart

Danube

Rhine

Munich

Linz

Vienna

Castle of Neuschwanstein

Berchtesgaden

Altaussee

AUSTRIA

HUNG.

Zurich

Campo Tures

SWITZERLAND

Inn

San Leonardo

Bolzano

Drau

Geneva

Adige

YUGOSLAVIA

Milan

Venice

ITALY

Po

Adriatic Sea

□ Major art repository

◇ Allied collecting point

Elbe

Oder

Gene Thorp

THE GREATEST TREASURE HUNT IN HISTORY

The Story of the Monuments Men

Monuments Man Lieutenant James Rorimer (center) at the castle of Neuschwanstein supervising the removal of paintings stolen by the Nazis.

THE GREATEST TREASURE HUNT IN HISTORY

The Story of the Monuments Men

by

ROBERT M. EDSEL

SCHOLASTIC

FOCUS

NEW YORK

All rights reserved. Published by Scholastic Focus, an imprint of Scholastic Inc., *Publishers since 1920*. SCHOLASTIC, SCHOLASTIC FOCUS, and associated logos are trademarks and/or registered trademarks of Scholastic Inc.

The publisher does not have any control over and does not assume any responsibility for author or third-party websites or their content.

Library of Congress Cataloging-in-Publication Data Available
ISBN 978-1-338-25119-7

10 9 8 7 6 5 4 3 2 1   19 20 21 22 23

Printed in the U.S.A.   23
First edition, January 2019

Book design by Abby Dening

To my wife and soulmate, Anna, whose unwavering support guided me in writing this book, as it does all that I do; and to our beautiful sons, Francesco and Rodney

CONTENTS

CAST OF CHARACTERS

WESTERN ALLIES

Serving in Italy

CAPTAIN DEANE KELLER
Age as of June 1944: 42.
Born: New Haven,
Connecticut.
Portrait painter; professor
of art at Yale University.

SECOND LIEUTENANT FRED HARTT
Age: 30.
Born: Boston,
Massachusetts.
Art historian.

Serving in Northern Europe

LIEUTENANT GEORGE L. STOUT
Age: 46. Born: Winterset,
Iowa. Art conservator at the
Fogg Museum, Harvard
University.

CAPTAIN WALKER HANCOCK
Age: 43. Born: St. Louis,
Missouri. Award-winning
sculptor.

CAPTAIN ROBERT POSEY
Age: 40. Born: Morris,
Alabama. Architect.

PRIVATE FIRST CLASS LINCOLN KIRSTEIN
Age: 37. Born: Rochester,
New York. Cofounder of
the New York City Ballet
(originally known as the
American Ballet
Company).

SECOND LIEUTENANT JAMES J. RORIMER
Age: 38. Born: Cleveland,
Ohio. Curator at The
Metropolitan Museum of
Art and The Cloisters.

ROSE VALLAND
Age: 45. Born: Saint-
Étienne-de-Saint-Geoirs,
France. Custodian of the
Jeu de Paume Museum
in Paris.

MAJOR RONALD EDMUND BALFOUR
Age: 40. Born: Oxfordshire,
England. Lecturer in
history at Cambridge
University.

CAPTAIN WALTER "HUTCH" HUCHTHAUSEN
Age: 39. Born: Perry,
Oklahoma. Architect.

PRIVATE HARRY ETTLINGER
Age: 18. Born: Karlsruhe,
Germany. Immigrated to
the United States when he
was thirteen years old.

AXIS POWERS

Leader of Fascist Italy

BENITO MUSSOLINI
Age: 60. Born: Dovia di
Predappio, Italy.
Dictator.

Leaders of Nazi Germany

ADOLF HITLER
Age: 55. Born: Braunau
am Inn, Austria. Dictator.

HERMANN GÖRING
Age: 51. Born:
Rosenheim, Germany.
Reichsmarschall.

Serving in Italy

GENERAL KARL WOLFF
Age: 44. Born:
Darmstadt, Germany.
Supreme leader of all SS
troops and police
in Italy.

ALEXANDER LANGSDORFF
Age: 45. Born: Alsfeld,
Germany. Accomplished
archaeologist.

Serving in Northern Europe

ALFRED ERNST ROSENBERG
Age: 51. Born: Reval,
Russia. Leader of the
ERR, the chief Nazi
looting organization.

COLONEL KURT VON BEHR
Age: 54. Born: Hanover,
Germany. Head of the
ERR in Paris, France.

BRUNO LOHSE
Age: 32. Born: Buer,
Germany. Deputy Chief
of the ERR in Paris,
France.

HERMANN BUNJES
Age: 32. Born: Bramsche,
Germany. Göring's
personal art agent in
France.

ABOUT THE
MONUMENTS MEN

The Monuments Men were a group of American and British men and women—accomplished museum curators, art scholars and educators, architects, archivists, and artists— who volunteered for military service during World War II combat operations to preserve works of art, monuments, and other cultural treasures from the destruction of war and theft by Adolf Hitler and the Nazis. Together, they made up the Monuments, Fine Arts, and Archives section, or MFAA, part of the Civil Affairs division of the Western Allied armies.

The MFAA was an extraordinary experiment. It marked the first time an army fought a war while comprehensively attempting to mitigate damage to cultural treasures. Those who served in the MFAA, known as the Monuments Men, were a new kind of soldier, charged with saving rather than destroying. Initially, they consulted with Allied air commanders to direct bombing away from cultural sites. As they entered the battered cities of Europe alongside combat troops, the Monuments Men, working without adequate transportation, supplies, or personnel, effected temporary repairs to hundreds of churches and monuments.

During the final months of the war, as the extent of Nazi looting became known, the Monuments Men served in harm's way as art detectives engaged in the greatest treasure hunt in history.

Prior to this war, no army had thought of protecting the monuments of the country in which and with which it was at war, and there were no precedents to follow . . . All this was changed by a General Order issued by the Supreme Commander-in-Chief [General Eisenhower] just before he left Algiers, an order accompanied by a personal letter to all Commanders . . . the good name of the Army depended in great measure on the respect which it showed to the art heritage of the modern world.

MONUMENTS MAN LIEUTENANT COLONEL
SIR LEONARD WOOLLEY, 1952

Dennis Posey, son of Monuments Man Captain Robert Posey, on the family horse.

Dear Dennis: Germany started this war by invading one small country after another until finally France and England had to declare war on her. We helped France and England but didn't start fighting. Then suddenly Japan attacked us and Germany declared war on us at the same time. And so we had to fight, painfully at first for we were unprepared. Now we are strong; England is strong; Russia, who was attacked by Germany is strong; Italy who fought with Germany has been defeated by us and has swung over to our side; France who was defeated by Germany but liberated by us is building a powerful army . . . And so, these are the reasons that I think we will soon defeat Germany and Japan and teach them such a lesson that when you and other little boys like you grow up you will not have to fight them all over again. And I hope no other country will start a fight to get its way for wars are bad.

MONUMENTS MAN CAPTAIN ROBERT POSEY,
IN A LETTER TO HIS SEVEN-YEAR-OLD SON

PRELUDE

In 1907, an eighteen-year-old aspiring artist named Adolf Hitler applied for admission to the Academy of Fine Arts in Vienna, Austria. He felt humiliated when a group of jurors, whom he believed were Jews, rejected his application. The memory of this experience never left him. It fanned the flames of an already burning desire to seek revenge against people who he believed had wronged him. For the remaining thirty-eight years of his life, Hitler continued to see himself as a gifted artist and architect, a creator, with an unyielding determination to prove his genius to the world.

As the leader of Nazism, Hitler used art as a weapon of propaganda to instill a sense of superiority in the German people at the expense of those he termed subhuman, particularly Jews. German

Aspiring artist Adolf Hitler.

Watercolor painted by Adolf Hitler in 1914.

art through the nineteenth century—"true art" in Hitler's view—was easy to comprehend, often depicting scenes of everyday life. Renderings of the human form evoked youth, strength, heroism, and sacrifice, the qualities of the "master race" that Hitler wanted to project at home and abroad.

Hitler believed that modern art, with its bold colors and distorted figures, could only be the product of sick minds. The Nazis labeled these works and the artists who created them "degenerate." In their view, such interpretive paintings and sculpture destroyed the more traditional concept of beauty and were incomprehensible to the viewer.

To avoid spoiling the minds of the nation's citizens, Nazi leaders ordered German museum directors to remove from their walls some sixteen thousand "degenerate" works of art by greats, including Pablo Picasso, Henri Matisse, Edgar Degas, Paul

Gauguin, and Vincent van Gogh. Some of these artworks were traded. Almost five thousand were destroyed in a Berlin bonfire as part of a fire department training exercise. Others were sold on the international art market. As one high-ranking Nazi Party official reasoned, "In so doing we hope at least to make some money from this garbage."

In May 1938, Hitler made his first official state visit to Italy. The trip began in Naples, where the people welcomed him with hundred-foot-long banners bearing Nazi swastikas hung from balconies overlooking the path of his motorcade. In Rome, he and other senior Nazi leaders walked through the Colosseum, retracing the steps of Roman rulers and gladiators. But it was the beauty of Florence, jewel of the Renaissance, with its extraordinary churches, bridges, and museums, that Hitler most wanted to see.

The German leader spent two hours walking through the art-filled rooms of the Pitti Palace and Uffizi Gallery, past masterpieces of the Renaissance, enjoying the splendor and richness of the collections. Hitler saw himself as an artist among artists. During his tour, an idea took hold, one with far-reaching consequences: Hitler, the visionary, decided to build a museum in his hometown of Linz, Austria, and assemble a collection of art and cultural objects that he believed would rival some of the world's most respected museums.

It had a formal name—Gemäldegalerie Linz—but it quickly became known as the Führermuseum. His idea had a major obstacle: Many of the masterpieces and other cultural objects that he would need for his Führermuseum were already in Europe's most important museums and private collections. That would soon change.

Hitler and Italian dictator Benito Mussolini (to Hitler's left, wearing cap) visiting the Florence museums in May 1938.

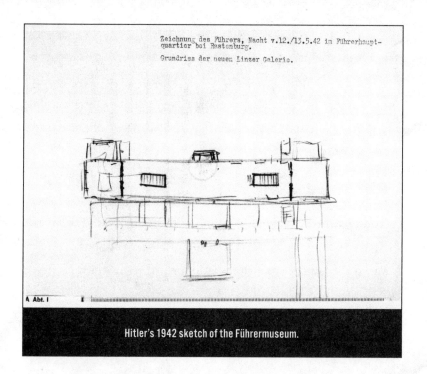

Zeichnung des Führers, Nacht v.12./13.5.42 im Führerhaupt-
quartier bei Rastenburg.

Grundriss der neuen Linzer Galerie.

A Abt. I

Hitler's 1942 sketch of the Führermuseum.

Nazi Germany invaded Poland on September 1, 1939, marking the formal beginning of World War II. The invasion also sounded the starter gun for the most premeditated looting operation the world had ever seen. Thefts are normally associated with speed—get in and get out quickly. However, the Nazi looting operation continued without interruption for nearly six years.

The occupation of Poland alone provided Hitler and his museum with treasures of immense rarity and value. Cracow, one of the most picturesque cities in all of Europe, suffered irreplaceable losses. From the Czartoryski Museum, the Nazis stole the only painting by Leonardo da Vinci in Poland, one of just sixteen paintings by Leonardo known to exist in the world. From Saint Mary's Basilica, they looted the most important object in all of Poland, the Veit Stoss Altarpiece. With these priceless pieces and riches from the private collections of Austrian Jews that had been confiscated the previous year, in particular from the Austrian branch of the Rothschild banking dynasty, Hitler and his art advisors quickly amassed a treasure that rivaled many of the world's major art museums.

Nazi Germany's invasion of the Netherlands, France, and Belgium in May 1940 pried open Western Europe's treasure chest. In contrast to their brazen looting of Eastern Europe, the Nazis wanted to pillage under a veil of legality in the West, so they simply changed the laws of conquered nations to strip Jews of their rights

Nazi Reichsmarschall Göring and Hitler admiring a painting.

to own private property. This created an avalanche of opportunities for Hitler and his agents, and also for the number two man in the Nazi Party, Reichsmarschall Hermann Göring, an art collector with an insatiable appetite.

The greatest theft in history was underway.

JUNE 26, 1939

Letter from Hitler directing Dr. Hans Posse to supervise the construction of the Führermuseum in Linz.

ADOLF HITLER'

OBERSALZBERG, den 26. Juni 1939

Ich beauftrage Herrn Galeriedirektor Dr.Hans Posse, Dresden, mit dem Aufbau des neuen Kunstmuseums für die Stadt Linz/Donau.

Alle Parte,t- und Staatsdienststellen sind verpflichtet, Herrn Dr.Posse bai Erfüllung seiner Aufgabe zu unterstützen.

"I commission Dr. Hans Posse, director of the Dresden Gallery, to build up the new art museum for Linz Donau. All Party and State services are ordered to assist Dr. Posse in fulfillment of his mission."
—Adolf Hitler.

NOVEMBER 5, 1940

Reichsmarschall Hermann Göring's order concerning distribution of Jewish art treasures.

In carrying out the measures taken to date for the safeguarding of Jewish art property by the Chief of Military Administration in Paris and the Einsatzstab Rosenberg (Chef OKW. 2 f 28.14. W. Z. Nr 3812/ 40 g), the categories of art objects moved to the Louvre will be established as follows:

1. Those art objects for the further disposition of which the Führer has reserved for himself the right of decision;

2. Those art objects which will serve to complete the collection of the Reichsmarschall;

3. Those art objects and library material which appear useful for building up the Hohe Schule and for the task of Reichsleiter Rosenberg;

4. Those art objects that are appropriate for turning over to German museums . . . will immediately be inventoried, packed and transported to Germany by the Einsatzstab with all due care and with the assistance of the Luftwaffe.

5. Those art objects which are appropriate for transfer to French museums and to the French and German art trade will be sold at auction at a date yet to be fixed; and the proceeds will be assigned to the French State for benefit of the French dependents of war casualties.

6. Further seizure of Jewish art property in France will be effected in the heretofore efficient manner by the Einsatzstab Rosenberg, in co-operation with the Chief of the Military Administration Paris.

Paris, 5 November 1940

I shall submit this suggestion to the Führer,
pending whose approval this procedure will remain
effective.

Signed: GÖRING

Hitler sketching preliminary concepts for the Führermuseum in Linz.

MAJOR BATTLE LINES AND ART REPOSITORIES IN ITALY

YUGOSLAVIA

Trieste

Fasano
Gardone
Salò · *Lake Garda*
Recoaro
Verona
Venice
Padua

Po

Parma

Marano sul Panaro
Oliveto
Bologna

A p e n n i n e s

SAN MARINO

Poggio a Caiano
Dicomano
Poppi
Gothic Line
Sassocorvaro

Pisa
Arno
Florence
Montegufoni
Montagnana
Incisa
Mensanello
Siena

Adriatic Sea

TUSCANY

M o u n t a i n s

I T A L Y

Tiber

Bernhardt Line

Monte Cassino
Jan. 17–May 18, 1944

Rome
Palestrina

Gustav Line

Valmontone
Velletri
⑥
Liri Valley

Barbara Line

Volturno Line

Hitler Line
Anzio
Fossanova
Itri

Tyrrhenian Sea

Terracina
Gaeta

Caserta
Naples

Salerno

◻ **Art repository**

Paris

GERMANY
AUST.

FRANCE
SWITZ.
ITALY
YUGO.

Bay of Biscay

Madrid
★
SPAIN

Rome
★

Med. Sea

Algiers
Tizi Ouzou

Oran
Timgad
Tunis

MORO.
ALGERIA
TUN.

0   200
Miles

N

0   *Miles*   40

Gene Thor

CHAPTER 1

LETTERS HOME

Palestrina, Italy: June 1944

The army jeep crept along the hillside road leading to Palestrina, a small Italian town about twenty miles east of Rome. Captain Deane Keller—artist, professor, husband, father, and newly assigned Monuments Man for U.S. Fifth Army—knew the path from his student days, when his painting and drawing talents had earned him the opportunity to study at the American Academy in Rome. No one was shooting at him then, but that was eighteen years ago. Recent reports detailing how German troops were using elevation and blind turns as part of their ambush-and-retreat tactics caused great concern. Determined to serve his country and return home to his wife, Kathy, and their three-year-old son, Dino, Keller and Giuseppe de Gregorio, an officer of the Carabinieri and also his driver, continued advancing up the hill, cautiously.

After rounding a bend in the road, Keller grabbed Giuseppe's arm and told him to stop. He was out of the jeep before it came to a halt. About one hundred feet ahead, lying facedown in the road, was the body of an American soldier. As Keller approached, he thought of a phrase he had once heard used to describe a corpse: "sweetish smell." There was nothing sweet in the air on this hot

Deane Keller and his son, Dino.

June day. Despite the overpowering and nauseating stench, he continued walking.

Those one hundred feet felt like a mile. With each step Keller thought about "the boys," as he referred to them in his letters to Kathy. They had been fighting their way up the Italian peninsula since landing at Salerno in September 1943, taking one hill after another. Some were the age of his art students at Yale University. He wasn't sure why he felt such paternal feelings of pride for them. Maybe it was a consequence of being forty-two years old. Maybe it was being five thousand miles away from his own son, unable to be the father that he had envisioned. Seeing the young men in uniform—"the boys" driving the tanks, the infantry soldiers crouching behind them, and this brave warrior lying in the road—reminded him of Dino.

As he knelt beside the young man's body, Keller noticed something in the overturned helmet. Wedged inside the helmet liner was an airmail envelope addressed to the soldier's mother. Keller wiggled the envelope out of the webbing. As best he could tell, the letter had been hurriedly written, perhaps before or even during battle. All he could do at this point was make sure it was posted.

Keller, like all the soldiers he'd met, relished receiving mail from home. Letters were the sole connective tissue—a lifeline of hope—for soldiers separated by time and distance from family and close friends. Even those containing the most dreaded news were preferred to the heartache and gnawing pain of no news at all.

Keller recalled a letter he'd received from his mother before beginning his assignment as a Monuments Man that filled him with pride and emboldened him for the difficult days he knew were ahead. Standing next to the body of this American soldier, caressing a letter to a mother that contained the last earthly thoughts of her son, was just such a day.

Military service "is a big sacrifice for you," he remembered his mother writing, "but I am thankful you can see beyond that to realize the great need for good men to help. I believe you will never regret it for your own sake and the sake of Dino. He says proudly now—'My Daddy's a sojer.' I don't know who told him that—but I suppose he saw you in that first uniform."

On the long dust-filled drive back to headquarters, with the dead soldier's letter inside his shirt pocket pressed against his chest, Keller closed his eyes for what seemed like just a few minutes, lost in thought about all that had happened since leaving his teaching position at Yale to get into the fight.

New Haven, Connecticut: May 1943

In May 1943, as the end of the semester approached, Keller finally received a reply from the Marine Corps. "Rejected: poor eyesight," or so they said. Admittedly, at 5 feet 7 and 170 pounds, with a grayish tint to his hair and the stereotypical wire-rimmed glasses of a professor, he was hardly the strapping figure of youth that so frequently passed through the recruiting office. Then a well-timed letter from a colleague, Tubby Sizer, the former director of the Yale University Art Gallery, mentioned a newly created art protection unit that would comprise soldiers charged with saving rather than destroying. In Keller's mind, that sounded just right. At the end of his letter, Tubby tried to preempt Keller's natural tendency. "Don't be so damned MODEST," he wrote. "Put it on thick." Keller did, and it worked.

By the time Keller reported to Fort Myer, Virginia, for active duty in late September 1943, circumstances in Italy had changed dramatically. Operation Husky, the successful invasion of Sicily by U.S., British, and Canadian forces that began on July 10, resulted in the removal from office of Benito Mussolini, known as "Il Duce," the leader of Fascist Italy and Adolf Hitler's most important ally.

The battlefield then shifted to the Italian mainland, and within days, Italy signed an armistice agreement with the Allies. Hitler was enraged that his former ally had surrendered. He immediately transferred one million German soldiers to Italy to build a series of defensive lines that stretched across the Italian peninsula between Rome and Naples, intended to slow the Allied advance and make it as costly and bloody as possible. The war was now going to be fought in a country that contained millions of works of art, monuments, and churches, placing some of the greatest masterpieces of Western civilization at risk of being destroyed. It was a recipe for disaster.

Following a month of orientation and training at Fort Myer, Captain Deane Keller boarded a Liberty ship bound for North Africa. Like his 550 shipmates, including many young soldiers headed into combat, he felt proud, excited, and scared. On December 2, 1943, after more than three weeks at sea, he reached his temporary home, an army Civil Affairs training school in the remote hillside town of Tizi Ouzou, Algeria.

The kaleidoscope of fall color of the Virginia countryside was just a memory now. Standing in this desolate Algerian town, all Keller could see were colorless clusters of half-finished buildings and an abundance of braying donkeys and bleating goats. The sound of a familiar voice over his shoulder caught him by surprise.

He turned around, shaking his head in disbelief, and smiled: Standing before him was Major Tubby Sizer, the man who had encouraged him to join the new art protection unit and become a Monuments Man.

Sizer had been among the first selected to serve as a Monuments Man. The army had created the Civil Affairs school, where Keller now found himself, to educate American and British officers about military government and how to run a town once combat troops moved on. With their training now complete, Sizer, fellow American Captain Norman Newton, and British Monuments Man Captain Teddy Croft-Murray were on their way to Naples, Italy.

Despite the obvious good intentions of leaders in Washington and the Monuments Men at Tizi Ouzou, everyone questioned whether the mission could succeed. Would Allied commanders listen to the recommendations of middle-aged art history professors or architects to direct artillery fire *away from* a church or monument when being fired upon? Would Allied troops respect signs the Monuments Men posted making churches and historical buildings off-limits, even if it meant sleeping outside in the rain? And how could just eight Monuments Men, in an army of more than two hundred thousand soldiers, protect even a portion of the works of art and monuments in culturally rich Italy? After eight weeks of training, Keller was on his way to Naples to find out.

Keller's initial duties involved inspections of nearby towns and villages. These experiences left him feeling sad, not because of the extent of destruction, but out of sympathy for what the Italian people had endured. As an artist, he had always admired the country's beauty and boundless creative achievements, but it was the

Italian people who had won his heart so many years earlier. "'*Buona gente, buonissima gente, ma bisogna saperla prendere.*' Good people, very good people," he always told his students and the soldiers he met, "but you have to know how to take them."

During one inspection, Keller visited a hospital where he saw a man without a nose. In its place were two holes. Before the war, had he seen someone in such sad condition, he would have looked away. But sights such as this were all too common during war. Now, each wounded child, destroyed home, and damaged town made him realize how sheltered and privileged his life had been.

The severity of fighting at the town of Cassino, about seventy miles northwest of their headquarters in Naples, had Allied forces pinned down and the Monuments Men waiting until the battle was over. The only practical route into central Italy, and the big prize, Rome, required passage through the Liri Valley. That meant contending with an impregnable mountain bastion overlooking the entire valley, the Abbey of Monte Cassino—and the Germans knew it.

Every effort had been made to avoid damage to the abbey, but General Dwight D. Eisenhower's December 29, 1943, order concerning the protection of cultural treasures made it clear: "If we have to choose between destroying a famous building and sacrificing our own men, then our men's lives count infinitely more and the buildings must go." On the morning of February 15, waves of Allied bombers severely damaged the abbey, but the fighting continued for three more bloody months.

Norman Newton was the first Monuments Man to reach the heavily mined and booby-trapped abbey, still under fire from enemy mortars, just hours after the remaining Germans had been

C O P Y

~~CONFIDENTIAL~~

ALLIED FORCE HEADQUARTERS

Office of The Commander-in-Chief

AG 000.4-1

29 December 1943

SUBJECT: Historical Monuments

TO   : All Commanders

Today we are fighting in a country which has contributed a great deal to our cultural inheritance, a country rich in monuments which by their creation helped and now in their old age illustrate the growth of the civilization which is ours. We are bound to respect those monuments so far as war allows.

If we have to choose between destroying a famous building and sacrificing our own men, then our men's lives count infinitely more and the buildings must go. But the choice is not always so clear-cut as that. In many cases the monuments can be spared without any detriment to operational needs. Nothing can stand against the argument of military necessity. That is an accepted principle. But the phrase "military necessity" is sometimes used where it would be more truthful to speak of military convenience or even of personal convenience. I do not want it to cloak slackness or indifference.

It is a responsibility of higher commanders to determine through A.M.G. Officers the locations of historical monuments whether they be immediately ahead of our front lines or in areas occupied by us. This information passed to lower echelons through normal channels places the responsibility on all Commanders of complying with the spirit of this letter.

/s/ Dwight D. Eisenhower

DWIGHT D. EISENHOWER,
General, U. S. Army,
Commander-in-Chief.

DISTRIBUTION:
"C"

CLASSIFICATION CHANGED
TO
By authority of CALA
By J. F. PAYSLEY
AGD
Date 4 AUG 1945

Restricted Classification
Removed For
Executive Order 11652

1   189

driven out. His damage assessment report painted a grim picture: "Reconstruction of entire Abbey is possible although much is now only heap of pulverized rubble and dust."

The far greater tragedy was the body count. Four months of fighting in grueling weather conditions had exacted a toll so great it hardly seemed believable: fifty-five thousand Allied soldiers dead, wounded, or missing; twenty thousand dead or wounded

Monuments Men approach the remains of the Abbey of Monte Cassino.

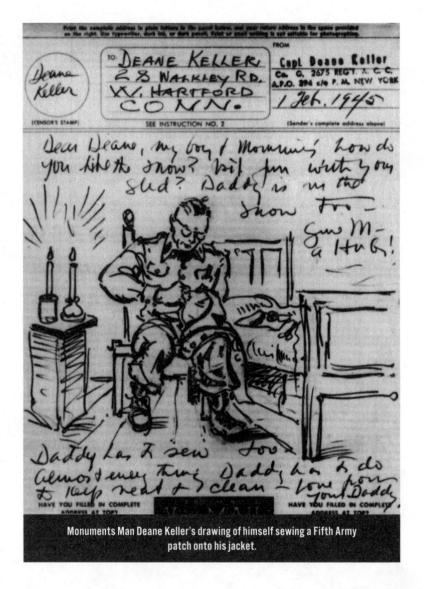

Monuments Man Deane Keller's drawing of himself sewing a Fifth Army patch onto his jacket.

Germans; and one historic but largely destroyed fourteenth-century Benedictine abbey.

With the stalemate at Cassino ended, Allied forces and the Monuments Men began their advance toward Rome. Several received new assignments. Keller's exceeded all expectations: He would be the first Monuments Officer attached to Fifth Army and its fighting force of eighty thousand soldiers.

On his last night in Naples, Keller held up the sleeve of his uniform to the small, dim lamp near his bunk. Needle and thread in hand, he began sewing onto his uniform the shoulder patch for Fifth Army, which he had purchased earlier in the day from a street vendor. "I haven't worn my ribbon or shoulder patch yet. Don't know when I will," he had written Kathy. "I feel the boys at [the] front are the ones to wear the stuff. Maybe some day I'll feel I earned it." That day had finally come.

About one week into his new assignment, things were going well for Monuments Man Captain Deane Keller. He had the job he wanted—a position of enormous responsibility—and a jeep, a rarity for the Monuments Men. He swelled with pride serving his country and helping the Italian people, but it came at a high cost. The bloodbath at the Battle of Monte Cassino served as a painful reminder to Keller and his family that he might not see them again, ever. Most of all, he missed being the dad that he had promised to be when Dino was born.

For now, he resigned himself to writing letters, lots of letters. Each letter to Kathy had a message for Dino, right up until the time he realized that his three-year-old boy couldn't yet read. A few weeks later, or perhaps months—war was like that, the blurring of time—he realized that the solution to communicating with his son wasn't through words but images. Every boy liked looking at cartoons, and after all, Keller was an artist and an art teacher.

One of Monuments Man Deane Keller's early drawings to Dino summarizing his experiences as a soldier.

One of Keller's earliest drawings summarized his journey, step by step, from his trip to North Africa and training at Tizi Ouzou— "Toozy Woozy," as he jokingly referred to it—to his work in Italy.

With Keller's assignment as a Monuments Man now underway, Dino would be receiving many more drawings.

Near Palestrina, Italy: June 1944

Somewhere on the road back to headquarters, Keller awakened and quickly checked the pocket of his shirt. The letter from the dead American soldier was still there. It prompted him to write to Kathy as soon as he reached his tent. He began his June 25 letter by recounting some of the experiences of his first few weeks as a Monuments Man. With the death of the young soldier fresh on his mind, the tone of his letter changed. He wanted to share with Kathy something he'd been thinking about. "The life of one American boy is worth infinitely more to me than any monument I know." Keller thought of it as a personal manifesto of sorts, one that would guide him in his work as a Monuments Man.

Rome, Italy: June 1944

Monuments Men Lieutenant Perry Cott, British Captain Humphrey Brooke, and Lieutenant Fred Hartt, who had joined the operation in late April, couldn't believe they were in Rome, not under these conditions. Like Keller, Cott and Hartt had each visited the city during their time as students, but those experiences couldn't compare with the exhilaration of accompanying Fifth Army troops into the Eternal City.

It had taken the Western Allies six months to blast through Monte Cassino before sprinting north to Rome. The first units fought their way into the city on the morning of June 4, liberating it by late afternoon. The sound of the deliriously happy throngs of people cheering as the tank column of a modern army motored past the almost nineteen-hundred-year-old Colosseum left Hartt, Cott, and Brooke speechless. But the appearance of the Arch of Constantine and Trajan's Column, and many of the city's other landmarks, wrapped in protective casing made of brick, sandbags, and scaffolding brought them back to the reality of the war—and their mission.

While Brooke and Hartt set out to conduct damage assessments, Cott began gathering information on the status of works of art. The Vatican and its collection, one of the most comprehensive and important holdings of art in the world, were safe. So, too, were the treasures of the Brera Picture Gallery in Milan, the Accademia in Venice, the Borghese Gallery in Rome, and those from many of the nation's most important churches, which Pope Pius XII had allowed to be stored for safekeeping within the Vatican's walls. Cott, a seasoned museum curator and art scholar, was astonished at the thought that, with these combined holdings, the Vatican was the richest museum in the world, at least for the moment.

Monuments Man Lieutenant Colonel Ernest DeWald, director of the MFAA in Italy, reached Rome several days later. After presenting his credentials to the Holy Father and explaining the purpose of the Monuments operation, he and Cott gained access to the Vatican storage areas. On June 26, they began their investigation into works of art belonging to museums in Naples that the

Hermann Göring Tank Division had delivered to Rome for safe-keeping. Suspicions abounded.

The media spectacle surrounding the Hermann Göring Tank Division's arrival was Nazi propaganda at its best—they seldom missed a chance to promote a good deed done. But when two trucks of this elite fighting unit mysteriously disappeared on the way to Rome with the artwork, it greatly concerned Italian art officials, especially since it involved a division named after Hermann Göring, the Nazi Party's second-most powerful man and the most prolific art collector in the world.

After a quick look at the crates that the Hermann Göring Division had delivered to Rome in January, DeWald and Cott began inventorying the contents, starting with crate number 1. A few minutes passed before DeWald looked at Cott, puzzled. Crate number 1, which according to their inventory schedule had been packed with three paintings, was completely missing. That hardly

Pieter Bruegel the Elder, *The Blind Leading the Blind*, 1568.

seemed an accident. Later they opened crate number 29, relieved to find one of the paintings that belonged in the missing crate number 1. A second of the missing paintings appeared in crate number 58. But they never found the third and most important painting: the world-famous masterpiece by Pieter Bruegel the Elder, *The Blind Leading the Blind.*

"There can be no doubt that the paintings were stolen by persons who knew just what they wanted," DeWald told Cott in disbelief. The thieves clearly had a shopping list. What else could explain that in several instances they had left behind paintings of far greater importance? Hiding the works that they didn't want in crates with extra space was a cover-up attempt as clumsy as the theft itself.

DeWald and Cott were gobsmacked by the audacity of the theft. In all, seventeen works of art from Naples and the ancient site of Pompeii were missing, a few of which were among the most recognizable works of art in the world. The Hermann Göring Division soldiers might as well have driven to Naples, backed up their trucks to the doors of the Museo Nazionale in broad daylight, and lifted the masterpieces off the wall. Both DeWald and Cott believed that the works of art were in Nazi Germany, probably recent additions to the ever-growing collection of Reichsmarschall Hermann Göring.

Reports of Nazi looting throughout Europe were hardly new, but the Vatican inventory provided the Monuments Men with their first hard evidence that the Nazis had looted art treasures in Italy. With German troops now retreating north toward Florence, the Monuments Men feared that this was just the beginning.

CHAPTER 2

INDEPENDENCE DAY

English Channel: July 4, 1944

George Stout loved being on the water. The ocean air reminded him of the summer he spent working with his uncle in Corpus Christi, Texas. One day each week, he would paddle a small wooden boat over the shallow waters of the Gulf of Mexico and spend the day fishing. For a young boy from landlocked Iowa, the vastness of the ocean created a fascination that never left him. But those carefree days were long ago. Now he was aboard the Liberty ship SS *Joseph Story* with hundreds of other soldiers, steaming from Southampton, England, to the bloodied beaches of Normandy, France.

Four weeks earlier, on June 6, 1944—"D-Day"—American, British, and Canadian forces had mounted the largest seaborne invasion in history. Almost 156,000 men crossed the English Channel that day, from safety into hell. With the British coastline now only faintly visible on the early-morning horizon, Stout closed his eyes and tried to picture the unimaginable: 7,000 ships crossing these same waters, all at the same time, headed into battle.

The D-Day landings proved successful, but the casualty figures were staggering. Enemy fortifications on the coastal ridgeline provided a clear killing field for German machine gunners on

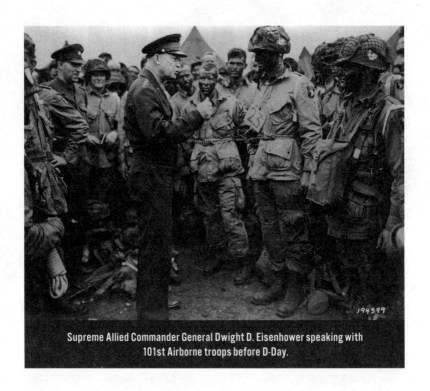

Supreme Allied Commander General Dwight D. Eisenhower speaking with 101st Airborne troops before D-Day.

beaches increasingly pockmarked by mortar and artillery shells. Many Allied soldiers never made it onto the beach; many who did never made it off. By the end of the initial operation, some twelve thousand American, British, and Canadian soldiers were dead, wounded, or missing.

In the thirty days of fighting that followed, Western Allied forces had their foothold in Europe, but progress proved agonizingly slow. Savage German resistance had limited the Allied advance to just seven miles inland. Berlin, the capital of Nazi Germany, was still 778 miles away. On the Eastern Front, the Wehrmacht was reeling. Just weeks earlier, the Soviets had hurled over one million Red Army soldiers at the center of the German line, inflicting catastrophic damage to Hitler's forces. The fall of

Rome to U.S. Fifth Army pressured German forces to the south. Now, with the successful landing of Western Allied forces on French soil, Hitler and his military commanders were fighting a three-front war.

Stout, like the other men on board, nervously wondered what he would confront once he reached France and beyond, and, of far greater concern, if he would be returning home. Those same thoughts had filled his mind when he crossed this stretch of water as a young U.S. Army private to fight in World War I, back when no one ever thought they would have to number them. Stout reminded himself that he had survived the carnage of that war; he was determined to survive this one, too.

June 6, 1944: D-Day landings at Omaha Beach.

Standing on deck, Stout gently swayed to the rhythmic motion of the ship. Being on the ocean was like being locked in a room with just your thoughts. The crossing would take about five hours—plenty of time to ponder how an idea of his had landed on the desk of the president of the United States, and, in turn, how he and a much too small group of men were going to save hundreds of thousands of the world's most precious art and cultural objects from the destruction of war.

Stout had only himself to blame for being on this troop transport in the first place. Had it not been for his idea to create teams of cultural preservation officers, he would have been in the safety of his conservation lab at Harvard University wearing a white over-coat instead of an army uniform. But President Franklin D. Roosevelt had approved his "brain child," as friend and former boss Paul Sachs, associate director of Harvard University's Fogg Museum, referred to it. As a member of the Roberts Commission, charged with the selection of Monuments Officers, Sachs had written him expressing hope that he would volunteer to become a Monuments Man, "because not only is this commission the result of your great thinking and clear statements at the time of the Metropolitan [Museum] meeting just after Pearl Harbor, but in a very true sense you seem to me the real father of the whole show . . . It is my deliberate opinion that the appointment of this Commission is due to your initiative, imagination and energy."

At forty-six years of age, Stout knew enough to be suspicious of such laudatory praise, even from someone he trusted. "You are kind to give me so much credit in getting this work under way," he remembered telling Sachs, "but you magnify it one hell of a lot. Something far below the average set of brains is needed to figure out what ought to be done. Getting it done is what counts." George Leslie Stout had defined his life by getting things done.

Paul Sachs had made a correct assessment, and Stout couldn't deny it. He possessed exactly the right qualities to lead the Monuments Men operation in northern Europe. He was unflappable under pressure. His methodical and reasoned approach would prove essential to solving problems. Everyone knew there would be plenty of those. He was a naturally charismatic man and a confident leader, the kind that men want to believe and follow. He even looked the part, with his pencil-thin mustache, combed-back black hair, and movie star good looks.

No person in the United States had spent more time pondering how to protect works of art and other cultural treasures during war than George Stout. Years of experiments and research at the Fogg Museum led him to develop a set of scientific principles for the evaluation and preservation of cultural treasures. He was an avid believer in sharing information with fellow conservators. Gradually, Stout and his colleagues had guided the profession of conservation from an art form to a science.

Stout watched as the storm clouds of war gathered over Europe once again. Technological developments introduced during the Spanish Civil War added a sense of urgency. In October 1936, incendiary bombs landed near El Escorial, the imposing monastery-museum thirty miles northwest of Madrid. Two weeks later, high-explosive bombs blew out the windows of Spain's national museum, the Prado. The implications were clear: Massive aerial bombardment and the consequent fires instantly created a new threat to museums, libraries, and other monuments that would require a whole new way of thinking about how to protect them.

By the time of America's entry into World War II, following the December 7, 1941, Japanese sneak attack on Pearl Harbor, Hawaii, Stout was ready. Acting on his own initiative, he had prepared instructional pamphlets addressing the need he had anticipated years earlier. More important, he made an eloquent and compelling case for why the governments of the United Nations had a responsibility to take every measure possible to protect the world's shared cultural heritage. He argued why the work had to be done. He wrote the book on how to do it. Then he put his career on hold and volunteered for military service, leaving his wife, Margie, and their two boys behind.

The Monuments operation had begun in earnest in 1943, when President Roosevelt ordered Captain Mason Hammond, a classics professor at Harvard—and the first Monuments Man—to Sicily, but not until three weeks *after* the invasion of Italy had commenced. An army of one Monuments Officer was better than none at all. While Paul Sachs and other officials in the United States and England scrambled to get more Monuments Men into treasure-laden Italy, Hammond hitchhiked his way from town to town conducting inspections and posting OUT OF BOUNDS signs. Somehow, working without a jeep, and on his own for four weeks before other Monuments Men began arriving, Hammond found a way to get the job done.

Stout arrived in Shrivenham, England, at the United States–British Civil Affairs training center in March 1944, now a lieutenant in the U.S. Naval Reserve. Others soon followed . . . very

RESTRICTED
TO ALLIED FORCES

NATIONAL MONUMENT

OUT OF BOUNDS
OFF LIMITS

IT IS STRICTLY FORBIDDEN TO REMOVE STONE OR
ANY OTHER MATERIAL FROM THIS SITE

SOUVENIR HUNTING, WRITING ON WALLS OR
DAMAGE IN ANY FORM WILL BE DEALT WITH AS

MILITARY OFFENCES

DWIGHT D. EISENHOWER,
GENERAL,
Supreme Commander,
Allied Expeditionary Force

By order of
J. E. DIXON-SPAIN
Sqdn Ldr.,
MFA - A. Spec. offr.
20352

RESTRICTED

DECLASSIFIED
Authority NND 750148
By ___ NARA, Date 4/5/81
21st ARMY GROUP.

An OUT OF BOUNDS sign posted by the Monuments Men.

few others. His original plan had called for a new class of specially trained conservators who would be attached to each of the U.S. Army's three army groups in Europe. Each conservator would have a minimum staff of ten people that would include skilled packers, movers, taxidermists, secretaries, drivers, and photographers. They would be provided with jeeps, covered trucks, field radios, crates, boxes, packing materials, rope, cameras with film (the army was notorious for providing one without the other), aerometers to check air quality, and hygrometers to check humidity levels. But army bureaucracy had slowed the approval process to a crawl. Stout realized he would be lucky to begin the operation with ten Monuments Men total. Staff support per his recommendation? Not a chance.

Several British Monuments Men had already begun their training at Shrivenham, including Stout's roommate, Captain Ronald Balfour, a historian at King's College in Cambridge, whose pride and joy was his personal library containing some eight thousand volumes. Balfour was a slightly balding forty-year-old bachelor who had dedicated his life to history and ecclesiastical studies. Stout took an instant liking to Balfour. His expertise with books, archives, and religious objects would make him a valuable addition to the team; so, too, would his military upbringing.

Others in the British contingent included Lieutenant Colonel Geoffrey Webb, one of England's most distinguished art scholars, and the senior ranking officer among the initial group of Monuments Men in northern Europe; Major Lord Methuen, an accomplished artist; and Squadron Leader Dixon-Spain, a noted architect. The latter two were veterans of World War I.

The American side included Captain Marvin Ross, a Harvard graduate and expert on Byzantine art, who was second in command to Webb. Captain Ralph Hammett and Captain Bancel LaFarge, both renowned architects, would be immensely important to the operation in determining which damaged buildings could be salvaged and which were beyond repair. Captain Walker Hancock, the most decorated member of the group, was a forty-three-year-old award-winning sculptor. His knowledge of Europe and expertise with languages would be an invaluable asset. More than that, Stout admired Hancock's relentlessly optimistic and easygoing demeanor, prized personal attributes at any time, but doubly so during periods of stress.

Second Lieutenant James Rorimer, at just thirty-eight years of age, had risen through the ranks of the museum world to become curator of medieval art at The Metropolitan Museum of Art in New York City and its newly opened Cloisters Museum. Rorimer, a true Francophile, spoke the language fluently. He was an ambitious man, a hard charger. Nothing and no one was going to get in his way. The Monuments Men would need those skills in the months ahead. Sachs had made a great choice selecting him.

Then there was Captain Robert Posey, an outsider to the group of art scholars and museum men, but very much an insider when it came to the military. Posey loved soldiering; it was in his blood. Stout didn't know much about him other than he wasn't a member of Paul Sachs's Harvard circle. Posey was an architect, however, and that skill plus his military training made him invaluable to the group. Stout did know that they shared one very important thing: young sons at home whom they missed very much.

Stout had retraced the situation in his mind countless times. There were just eleven men, including him—at least initially, and for who knew how long—responsible for protecting the accumulated artistic and cultural wealth of Western civilization located in northern Europe from the destruction of war and theft by the Nazis. But the "brain child" he had envisioned and what the army provided him were worlds apart. With eleven men—one Monuments Man for every eighty thousand U.S. Army soldiers—how were they going to get it done? *Could* it even be done? Stout didn't want to use the word "impossible," but "unlikely" seemed about right.

For the operation to have any success, they would certainly need some breaks along the way, especially from combat commanders in the field. Three early assets provided hope. First, the Monuments Men went to war with a priority list of what needed to be saved. Volunteers in the United States, skilled in the arts, had compiled a Monuments, Fine Arts, and Archives List of Protected Monuments for each western European country, with maps indicating the locations, which were then forwarded to the Monuments Men serving in Italy and those training at Shrivenham. They had also overlaid this information onto aerial reconnaissance photographs, providing pilots with critical imagery that would hopefully spare those sites from damage.

The second asset wasn't a thing but a person: Captain Mason Hammond, the very first Monuments Man. Hammond's five months of experience in Sicily and the Italian mainland supplied insightful examples for General Eisenhower and his staff on what worked and what hadn't. Adjustments had already been made to the invasion plans for northern Europe that they hoped would provide a critical edge for Stout and his team, assets that Hammond did not have in Italy. With Hammond in London, attached to Eisenhower's staff, the Monuments Men in the field had someone in their corner who was reliable, trustworthy, and experienced in what they were about to do.

General Eisenhower himself was the third source of encouragement. "Ike," like Hammond, had struggled with how to fight a war in a country that, for all practical purposes, was a museum.

Initially, Eisenhower did not believe that the Monuments Men needed any special endorsement of their mission from the senior commander. By December 1943, he realized he had been wrong. The order that he issued on December 29, 1943, transformed the Monuments operation in Italy from that point forward by providing the explicit backing of the senior military commander, but it came late, after six months of combat. Not wanting to repeat the same mistake, and no doubt a consequence of Mason Hammond's admonitions, Eisenhower issued a similar order to all commanders eleven days *before* D-Day.

Beads of saltwater dripping off the rim of his helmet awakened him. George Stout wasn't sure how long he had been dozing, but he remembered thinking about Eisenhower and his order. Reaching into his leather jacket pocket, he pulled out the order and, with a great sense of pride in their mission, read the first paragraph again:

Shortly we will be fighting our way across the Continent of Europe in battles designed to preserve our civilization. Inevitably, in the path of our advance will be found historical monuments and cultural centers which symbolize to the world all that we are fighting to preserve. It is the responsibility of every commander to protect and respect these symbols whenever possible . . .

The sight of hundreds of anchored ships with a canopy of protective barrage balloons overhead confirmed for Stout and the others on board that they had reached their destination, Utah Beach. Getting ashore involved more waiting. Since being in the army, he had taken to heart a soldier's saying: "Hurry up and wait." Around 11:00 a.m., Stout stood on deck and watched as vessels at anchor began a makeshift fireworks display. Even war wasn't going to interrupt the chance to celebrate the Fourth of July. After all, the navy had plenty of explosives.

The Normandy landing beaches.

A Rhino barge carried them the rest of the way. Not once did Stout take his eyes off the sand wall overlooking the exposed beaches. Like everyone who set foot on any one of the D-Day landing beaches, Stout felt anguish for the soldiers who had made this same journey on June 6 into a torrent of gunfire. He couldn't imagine what it must have been like on Omaha Beach, where Germans high above on cliffs could shoot down on the American soldiers scrambling to safety. It reminded him of the nightmarish trench warfare and the scenes of carnage he had witnessed during World War I.

Lieutenant George Wilson, who had reached Normandy the same week as Stout, made observations universal to the soldiers who had seen those beaches:

> *I'm sure much of the horrific results of that battle had been cleared away, and all the dead and wounded were gone. Still, the terrible scars of war seemed to shout at us. Burned-out vehicles, sunken landing craft, ships, tanks, guns, pillboxes lay twisted and still. It hardly seemed possible anyone could have survived, yet men had waded in and driven the Germans back, now some seven or eight miles inland in most places.*

Like many arriving soldiers, Wilson had freedom of movement the first few days and used them to wander around the battle area. What he saw sickened him:

> *The ghastly stories we had heard about the fierceness of the fighting were true. German war prisoners were*

digging up the partially decomposed bodies of their own
dead—buried in neat rows in mass graves about three
feet deep—for movement to a new location. Working
with shovels and bare hands, the prisoners stuffed the
corpses into mattress covers and piled them on trucks in
rows, like cordwood. Some of the bodies were badly
mangled and very difficult to pick up. Stern-faced men
turned white, and many had to turn away to vomit at
the sight and smell.

Later that evening, after reporting to First Army headquarters, after laying out his bedroll on the sand of Utah Beach under a star-filled sky, and after the excitement of a German plane passing overhead spraying the beach with machine-gun fire, Stout thought about the irony of his day. This was the second time he had set foot on French soil during war. It happened on the 168th anniversary of the day when 13 American colonies renounced British rule and declared their independence as a newly formed nation. Now, those two nations, once at war with each other, were united in their determination to defeat Nazi Germany. And France, the nation that had provided early critical support to those united states, would at some point be the first country in northern Europe to be liberated and regain its own independence with their assistance.

With first light at 6:00 a.m., Stout needed to get what sleep he could. It would be one of many precious commodities in the busy days ahead.

CHAPTER 3

"LITTLE SAINTS, HELP US!"

On the road to Siena, Italy: July 4, 1944

As his jeep made its way north from Rome to Siena, Deane Keller marveled at the beauty of the Tuscan countryside. Vast golden wheat fields accented by groves of green cypress trees covered undulating hills as far as the eye could see. Six-hundred-year-old bell towers emerged from the distant ridgelines, set against an endless blue sky. The tranquility of the drive made it easy for him to forget about the war, but it was always just one gunshot, one destroyed building, one dead American boy away from smothering any other thought.

Keller entered Siena on the Fourth of July, one day after the city's liberation by Fifth Army troops, who had been charging north since taking Rome. To avoid a catastrophic fight in the center of a medieval art–filled town, the German commander, Generalfeldmarschall Albert "Smiling Al" Kesselring, so called because of his effortless and ever-present grin, had declared Siena an "open city." Under this arrangement, Allied troops refrained from attacking while German forces withdrew. Only two hours separated the opposing armies. Keller pulled out his field journal and noted that despite minor damage, Siena had been "artistically bypassed."

After making sure OUT OF BOUNDS signs had been posted on the fifty buildings and churches on the MFAA List of Protected Monuments, Keller wanted to check the status of the city's legendary works of art. First he had to figure out where they were.

Just one week earlier, Monuments Officers DeWald and Cott had conducted their inspection of the Naples treasures. During their walk through the Vatican storage area they saw thousands of crates from museums in Milan, Venice, and Rome, but none from the art-rich cities of Tuscany, in particular Florence and Siena. Officials in Rome did have lists indicating the locations of the various Tuscan repositories, but they considered them outdated. No cause for worry, they said. Superintendent of Florentine Galleries Giovanni Poggi had no doubt relocated the art treasures back into the cities out of the way of the coming ground battle.

On July 8, Keller and his Carabinieri driver, Giuseppe, pulled up to the Bishop's Palace in Mensanello—the most important of the three major Sienese art repositories—caked in dust. Tuscany was beautiful, but driving on the roads was a punishing experience, like wading through talcum powder. While the "open city" declaration had spared Siena from war, it hadn't extended as far as Mensanello, about eighteen miles outside the city. Allied forces had just wrenched control of the area from German troops. French-manned artillery batteries, part of Fifth Army forces, pounded German positions nearby.

After dusting himself off and trying to adjust for the deafening boom and vibration of the howitzer cannon, Keller entered the palace to discover a makeshift first aid station. Boom! A French military doctor was treating three wounded French colonial soldiers. Keller attempted to make an introduction and explain why he was there, but continuous artillery fire drowned out his words. He could barely hear himself. Boom! Sizing up the scholarly middle-aged Fifth Army officer standing before him, the French doctor assumed it had something to do with the two large crates leaning against the wall, so he pointed to them. Boom!

Keller walked over to the crates for a closer look. Someone had cut helmet-sized holes in the sides of both crates and then removed the packing material and flannel wrapping to see what was inside. What person wouldn't have been curious, he thought; he certainly was. For a moment, as he crouched down on one knee to peer inside the hole, Keller was oblivious to the sound of the artillery, the blood on the floor, and even the injured soldiers. His eyes needed a few seconds to adjust to the diminished light, and then time stopped. Staring back at him was an old friend—the Madonna and Child panel of the *Maestà*, Siena Cathedral's high altarpiece and the city's most iconic work of art. He'd last seen the seven-by-thirteen-foot double-sided wood panel painting, now disassembled, as a student almost two decades earlier.

The Sienese artist Duccio di Buoninsegna created the exquisitely refined painting of the Madonna and Child, surrounded by angels and saints, between 1308 and 1311. Duccio used vivid colors to paint his figures with delicacy and tenderness, a style that influenced two centuries of artists who followed. And now Keller had found it, 633 years later, in the middle of a war zone. The altarpiece appeared safe and, from what he could see, undamaged.

Duccio di Buoninsegna, *Maestà*, 1308–1311.

Other smaller paintings, about forty in all, lay hidden inside the palace chapel. Keller examined each one before individually wrapping them in blankets to create a measure of protection against the constant vibration. Nearby he noticed a protected-monuments sign posted by order of the German commander Kesselring. In this instance, it appeared that German troops had respected it. For now, unable to post guards, all Keller could do was notify art officials in Siena that the *Maestà* had come through the battle safely.

Florence, Italy: late July 1944

With Fifth Army giving chase, German forces continued their strategic retreat north to the Gothic Line, intending to make a stand in the Apennine Mountains. Directly in their path lay Florence, the capital city of Tuscany—and the single greatest concentration of art in the world. Siena and Rome had been lucky. Would Florence, with its magnificent churches, beautiful bridges, and irreplaceable works of art, be so fortunate? And where were the city's paintings, sculptures, and other artistic treasures? Had they been moved back into the city as officials in Rome believed, or were they still in the various countryside villas surrounding Florence, at risk of being stolen, or worse, destroyed?

Second Lieutenant Fred Hartt, Regional Monuments Officer for Tuscany, was determined to find the answer.

Hartt was an impassioned, at times impetuous, and immensely talented art historian who had spent more than half of his life studying Italian artists and their works. His gift for the arts was apparent from an early age. While most of his schoolmates longed

Monuments Man Second Lieutenant Fred Hartt.

to be on the athletic fields, Hartt was lost in a world of French Gothic cathedrals, Italian Renaissance sculpture, and Oriental silk screens. At thirty years of age, he was at least ten years younger than the other Monuments Men, which spoke to the level of respect for his ability. His gangling appearance, accented by dark, heavy-rimmed glasses, masked a brilliant scholar with a photographic memory and boundless energy.

The obliterated courtyard of Sa[...]
The Last Supper is covered

When he arrived in Italy in mid-January 1944, Hartt had been assigned to a photographic interpretation unit assessing collateral damage to nearby monuments caused by Allied bombing. He hated his job. Volunteering for military service had been a personal quest to help save the art of Italy. Instead, he found himself confirming its destruction. Restless and impatient, he looked for ways to wrangle a transfer into the Monuments section. On April 6, he

ria delle Grazie Church in Milan.
oden scaffolding (center left).

wrote Ernest DeWald, director of the MFAA in Italy, pleading for a transfer. His orders came through two weeks later.

Shortly before departing for his new assignment as a Monuments Man, Hartt prepared a report summarizing bomb damage in sixteen Italian cities. After checking and rechecking one of the photographs, adjusting the overhead lamp with one hand while repositioning his magnifying glass with the other, he was sure. On the night of August 15, 1943, a British high-explosive bomb had completely obliterated the courtyard of the Santa Maria delle Grazie Church in Milan, and all but the northwest corner of its dining hall. Hartt couldn't be certain, but as best as he could tell, given the resolution of the photograph, the wall containing Leonardo da Vinci's greatest masterpiece, *The Last Supper*, may have been reduced to rubble. It was a bitter realization that he and the other Monuments Men feared might be repeated in the Tuscan capital.

On July 27, Hartt pulled up to British Eighth Army headquarters in a battered army jeep with worn tires, defective shock absorbers, and a shattered windshield. Unlike most military vehicles, his had a name. At some point in its storied existence, whether in North Africa or Sicily, no one knew, someone had painted "Lucky 13" across the metal riser that once contained a windshield. Hartt knew that just having a vehicle was a stroke of luck, even one as beat up as his. Like Keller, he guarded his jeep like a cowboy did his horse—it was that important.

Hartt and the other officers and soldiers of Eighth Army were eager to get into Florence and begin inspections. He'd first visited Italy in 1936 and dreamed of returning ever since. The thought that German forces would use his beloved city as a defensive fortification, risking damage to hundreds of years of beauty, sickened him.

Several days later, while eating breakfast in the officers' mess at British Eighth Army headquarters, Hartt heard a stunning announcement broadcast by BBC Radio. Wynford Vaughan-Thomas, a veteran correspondent, accompanied by Major Eric Linklater of the British Royal Engineers, had stumbled upon an art repository in the middle of a major battle zone just outside Florence. It contained masterpieces from two of the city's most important museums, the Uffizi Gallery and the Palatine Gallery, housed inside the Pitti Palace. Rome officials had been grievously wrong: The Florentine treasures had not been moved back into the city. Hartt felt exhilaration and horror, all at once. Mind-jarring images of unprotected, art-filled villas dotting the Tuscan countryside filled his head.

Castle of Montegufoni.

Never one to sit still, Hartt immediately sought authorization to drive to the art repository—the Castle of Montegufoni—to secure it and report back as quickly as possible. Permission in hand, Hartt, "armed and helmeted," jumped into Lucky 13 and headed out. Heavy artillery fire blocked portions of the route, forcing him onto alternate roads so small they didn't appear on his maps. Stops at numerous military checkpoints chewed up more time. Throughout the journey, the night sky flickered from the constant flashes of artillery. Exhausted after spending almost twelve hours driving a mere eighty-three miles, Hartt decided to spend the night at Eighth Army press camp at San Donato in Poggio.

That evening Hartt met with Vaughan-Thomas and Major Linklater, who had just returned to camp after spending the day checking on three additional art repositories nearby. Did they ever have a story to tell! Linklater, who had been commissioned to write the official history of the Eighth Army campaign, had been eager to visit the 8th Indian Infantry Division, just one of the many multinational components of British Eighth Army. He and Vaughan-Thomas had arrived at the Castle of Montegufoni on the afternoon of July 30. Enemy forward positions were now just a little more than a mile away from the castle. While waiting to interview the senior commander, Linklater and Vaughan-Thomas had wandered through the cavernous building and noticed various groups of panel paintings leaning against the wall. Hartt couldn't believe what he was hearing, especially the fact that the paintings were not in crates and that the painted surface was visible rather than facing the wall as an added measure of protection.

Hartt found these paintings from the Florence museums inside the Castle of Montegufoni.

"But they're very good! They must be copies!" one of the men recalled saying. Then Linklater told Hartt how he had entered another room filled with paintings—a few crated, most not—and heard Vaughan-Thomas shout, "The whole house is full of pictures. They've come from the Uffizi and Pitti Palace!"

Fred Hartt sat stunned, speechless at what he'd just heard. The two men ran down a list of the paintings they had seen. Hartt shook his head in disbelief. Some of the most important works of art in the world, each priceless, lying on the floor of a villa, unprotected, covered in dust, in a war zone . . . It seemed too incredible to believe.

The following day, August 1, Hartt, accompanied by Linklater and Vaughan-Thomas, drove the short distance to Montegufoni. Cesare Fasola, librarian of the Uffizi Gallery, who had walked seventeen miles from Florence through a combat zone to watch over the collection, greeted them. British artillery encircling the castle continued firing their thunderous rounds. Enemy shells passed overhead and exploded in the distance, but not far enough away to be of any comfort to the four men.

The scene inside the castle was no less bizarre. Hartt immediately recognized each painting, a mind-jarring assembly of works by world-class artists of the Renaissance, including Raphael, Rubens, Giotto, Cimabue, Andrea del Sarto, Pontormo, and Uccello. It wasn't just the importance of the artists whose works had been stored there; many of these paintings were the most famous and important work ever created by the artist. Botticelli's tour de force, *Primavera*, the sight of which stunned Vaughan-Thomas, was just one example. Seeing so many works of art that he had studied and admired, leaning against the walls of the castle, unprotected, left Fred Hartt feeling overwhelmed.

Deane Keller standing beside Botticelli's masterpiece, *Primavera*.

While Hartt tried to gather himself, Fasola described recent events. After leaving Florence ten days earlier, he'd stopped at another repository, the Villa Bossi-Pucci in the tiny town of Montagnana. German troops had already taken 291 masterpieces belonging to the Uffizi and Pitti Palace museums. Only those objects too large to fit in their trucks were left behind. The villa was a mess: doors pried off their hinges, windows left wide open, and books tossed from the library strewn about the grounds, many bearing soldiers' boot marks.

With nothing more to do at Villa Bossi-Pucci, Fasola then walked to the Castle of Montegufoni, fearful he would discover a similar scene. While those paintings were still inside the castle, German troops were, too. "The packing cases had all been opened, the pictures taken out and flung about," he explained to Hartt. As the days passed, he tried to befriend the soldiers to keep them away from the paintings, especially after discovering that they were using a dark corridor containing eight fifteenth-century paintings by Fra Angelico as a latrine. When Fasola pleaded for them to remove their bottles and glasses from the surface of *Adoration of the Magi*, a fifteenth-century tondo by Ghirlandaio, a German soldier pulled out a knife and threw it at the wooden panel, piercing an area of the sky.

Lacking any authority, Fasola defensively told Hartt that all he could do was accompany the castle custodian on his nightly rounds. It was a helpless feeling, but not hopeless. One evening, Fasola recalled, he watched as the custodian stared at a group of religious paintings and whispered to himself, "Little Saints, help us!" It was an incredible story, Hartt thought, by a man who had done more than anyone could have expected to preserve objects that in so many ways defined the history of Florence—a man who was a true hero.

It took several hours, but when finished, Hartt confirmed that the inventory count was correct. All 246 paintings that Florentine officials had placed at the castle were accounted for and undamaged. But the Castle of Montegufoni was just one of the art repositories housing treasures from Florence. Many others were located behind enemy lines. The Allies could only wonder about their fate.

Hartt sounded the alarm in a blunt and to-the-point cable to Ernest DeWald: "Five deposits located. Reference BBC broadcast. Situation in hand. All safe save for damage to Pontormo *Visitation* and Bronzino *Portrait*." He then prepared a memo to Lieutenant General Oliver Leese, commander of British Eighth Army, marked SECRET, which contained map references, a list of twelve other deposits, and a terse summation of the situation: "The fate of these priceless treasures lies in the hands of the Eighth Army."

CHAPTER 4

THE MEETING

Saint-Lô, France: August 1944

George Stout entered the town of Saint-Lô in a state of disbelief. Exactly one month had passed since setting foot on Utah Beach, and in that time, he'd visited dozens of small villages and towns on daily inspections and witnessed every kind of damage possible, including some that seemed impossible. But nothing compared with the panorama of devastation that now lay before him.

All that remained of the skyline of Saint-Lô, a thousand-year-old walled town about thirty-five miles from the Normandy landing beaches, was a series of saw-toothed structures that resembled fields of densely packed stalagmites. No building had escaped damage. Rubble piles reached twenty feet high. Most streets—if you could even locate where the street had once been—were impassable. Stout couldn't find an unbroken piece of glass in any building or home. Fully mature trees in bloom had been decimated, leaving lonely twigs, void of any greenery, rising to the sky. War had killed the town of Saint-Lô, and perhaps as many as twelve hundred of its twelve thousand inhabitants.

It wasn't intended to be this way. On the evening of the D-Day landings, in an effort to create transport bottlenecks and cut off German reinforcements, Allied naval guns and air forces

The smashed French town of Saint-Lô.

relentlessly pummeled the Saint-Lô rail station and power plant. Leaflets dropped the day before warning townspeople that a raid was imminent were blown off course. The strikes hit their targets, but they also killed innocent people, shattered historic buildings, and pulverized the entire town. Ten days later, a fierce ground battle began for control of the ruins, but not before yet more bombers dropped their payloads over the city in support of the assault forces. Once American boys of the 29th Infantry Division entered Saint-Lô, the Germans returned the favor and began raining shells down on them, smashing the rubble into dust. Twice the number of American boys were killed taking Saint-Lô than during the carnage of the D-Day landings. Fire consumed the Hôtel de Ville—the city's town hall—along with its library of rare manuscripts. The eight-hundred-year-old Church of Sainte-Croix survived largely intact, but almost nothing was left of the town museum.

Stout maneuvered his way around piles of stone fragments to inspect the heavily damaged fifteenth-century Gothic-style Church of Notre-Dame, one of the few buildings still standing, but military police refused to let him enter. After explaining his orders—to conduct inspections of historic structures, place OUT OF BOUNDS signs, and effect temporary repairs where possible—the MPs explained theirs: No one was to enter the church by order of British Monuments Officer Dixon-Spain, who had already inspected the church and posted the MPs. Stout knew that Dixon-Spain was in the Normandy area, but without field radios, one Monuments Man had no idea what a fellow officer had inspected, or where he might be headed next. That was a major problem.

The MPs shared one other piece of news: The Germans had mined the church pulpit and altar, and they had also connected a stick of dynamite to a piece of stone near the entry, which an unsuspecting priest or soldier was sure to move and trigger an explosion. Stout flipped the page of his field diary and added it to a growing list of booby traps he'd come across in other inspections.

The Monuments Men were supposed to stay behind combat troops, but in the Normandy area, Allied and German soldiers were so densely packed together that it was tough to tell where the lines of one side ended and the other's began. Like a summer storm that suddenly appears and just as quickly vanishes, the war came to small towns and then moved on, only to reappear. Proximity to the fighting lines, added to the countless number of booby traps hidden near altars, underneath dead animals, and behind doors, meant that the Monuments Men were in constant danger.

Standing in the rubble of Saint-Lô, Stout realized that a meeting with the other Monuments Men was now urgent. Inefficiencies were irritations in civilian life, but Stout knew that they could lead to deadly mistakes during war. The likelihood that one or more of his group might not make it home—perhaps even he himself—was something he'd considered while at Shrivenham, and each day since. But tempting fate by driving through combat zones for an inspection that another Monuments Officer had already conducted was negligent. Mistakes like that had to end immediately.

The Monuments Men were doing their jobs, but they weren't working in a coordinated manner. In fairness, without field radios, how could they? They were already woefully understaffed and largely on their own. Without command authority, they had to assess each situation and consult with each combat commander before using the only weapon they had—the power of persuasion. That took time. Stout had to hand it to his friend Paul Sachs, whose selection of middle-aged Monuments Men with extensive life experiences and teaching backgrounds had proven a stroke of genius. Still, despite their expertise and planning, the Monuments Men were frustrated about the lack of army support.

Stout took a moment to look down the list of the men he'd trained with at Shrivenham. Webb and Ross were always destined to spend most of their time in London advising General Eisenhower's command staff. Balfour, the lifelong historian, and Hancock, the award-winning sculptor, were, much to his frustration, victims of army bureaucracy, stuck in England waiting on orders just when he needed them most. Trying to get the two World War I veterans—British Monuments Men Lord Methuen and Dixon-Spain—across zones for a meeting would involve even more army red tape and delay. Better to just gather the Americans: Rorimer, the hard-charging curator; distinguished architects LaFarge and Hammett; and Posey, the dedicated soldier.

Near Saint-Lô, France: August 13, 1944

The meeting took place on August 13, at a First Army supply center just outside the ruined city of Saint-Lô. It had taken a few days, but Stout managed to get confirmations from everyone. Rorimer, who had walked ashore on Utah Beach just nine days earlier, hitched a ride from headquarters with Hammett, and the two arrived first. LaFarge followed in a small British vehicle. Some minutes passed before Stout pulled up, to everyone's great surprise, in a captured German Volkswagen Kübelwagen, which he had been assigned just a few days earlier. It was a wreck of a car, without a top or windshield. But bad as it was, it was his. He was grateful to not be dependent on cargo trucks and other military vehicles to do his job. Wheels meant independence.

The fifth American, Monuments Man Robert Posey, was unable to secure a ride, so they had to begin the meeting without him. Stout chuckled. Long ago he'd learned to find the humor in difficult situations, even if just a wince—part of his unflappable approach to life. After all, who couldn't appreciate the irony of this situation: The lack of transportation prevented all the Monuments Men from meeting to solve, among other problems, the lack of transportation.

Even though LaFarge, the first Monuments Man to set foot in France, outranked the others, everyone deferred to George Stout and his quiet confidence. Besides, five weeks in and out of the front lines conducting inspections had earned him seniority in the field. Far from being a complaint session, the purpose of the meeting was to share their individual experiences, then apply their collective resourcefulness to find solutions to each problem. Stout repeated what he had said so many times in letters to Paul Sachs, and to each of the men at Shrivenham: What matters—all that matters—is getting the job done.

Jim Rorimer, the determined curator who had impressed Stout from the outset of their training at Shrivenham, quickly spoke up. "There's so much to do it's difficult to know where to begin. Trying to cover my sector is like trying to clear the woods of acorns." With so many historic churches and monuments in the Normandy region of France, any "attempt to record this damage effort amid the many gaping craters and fire-swept hulks of buildings would be like trying to scoop up wine from a broken keg." Stout agreed; Rorimer's metaphors aptly described what he had seen in Saint-Lô, Caen, and many other destroyed towns along the Normandy coast.

Rorimer then recounted how German soldiers had made a mockery of the Hague Convention's rules of land warfare by regularly using church steeples as observation posts and sniper nests. Allied forces overcame the problem by firing an artillery round at the steeple: no more German observer or sniper, but also no more steeple. The others all nodded, somewhat impatiently: They had each seen plenty of damaged churches.

Of course you have, Rorimer acknowledged, but that's not the point. Whether or not Allied commanders were looking at the MFAA List of Protected Monuments he couldn't be sure, but somehow they instinctively knew that if it was possible to kill the enemy and only damage but not destroy a church or other historic landmark, that was the right choice. It then fell to the Monuments Men to determine if the damage could be repaired or if it was so great that the building was at risk of collapse. In those situations, combat commanders ordered the precious remains of the churches, hundreds of years old, scooped up for use as road base to keep their heavily mechanized armies on the move. Rorimer described several confrontations with citizens who had begged for their churches to be spared. But when he explained that there was no other way, that this was the price of freedom, they usually understood.

On his visit to the severely damaged Abbey of Saint-Sauveur-le-Vicomte, Rorimer found American GIs sharing their rations with the children and nuns who had miraculously survived the Allied air raids. At the Abbey of Cerisy-la-Forêt, an American general had ordered his troops to vacate their dry quarters and head outdoors, well aware of the cultural importance of the building. Right actions like that were going to win the respect of the French, and, Rorimer believed, the war.

"How are we supposed to know what one another are doing without field radios?" someone asked. That would have to be presented to the higher-ups, Stout replied. It was no easy task getting someone to listen. Twelfth Army Group, after all, had over one million men. Until then, everyone should provide duplicate copies of their daily field reports to Advance Section headquarters and circulate them among the group, including the two British World War I veterans, Lord Methuen and Dixon-Spain.

"What about the shortage of OFF LIMITS signs?" Stout had an answer for that, too: The army has commandeered a printing press in Cherbourg. Stout looked at Rorimer and asked him to arrange for five hundred signs to be printed immediately. Until then, they would improvise and make them by hand. If that didn't work, they would wrap white engineering tape around important locations. They knew that no soldier, no matter how curious, would wander into a site marked DANGER: MINES!

Transportation—as in, "There isn't any!"—was the most pressing problem. LaFarge had his beaten-up car and Stout his topless Volkswagen, which had already broken down once. But Rorimer and presumably Posey were wasting precious hours hitching rides. This, too, was on the list of needs that Hammett and Stout would discuss at their meeting with the duty officers of Twelfth Army Group on August 16.

Many things had indeed gone wrong, but Stout paused for a minute to focus on all that had gone right. He didn't need to reach for his notebook for prompts; that list he had memorized. There were the close calls, including the bombing of his encampment outside the town of Valognes, when a bomb landed just three hundred feet from his tent. Only in the morning did he learn that a medical corpsman had been killed. Yet, as exposed as they all were, especially to booby traps, no one in their small army of seven had been injured or killed. They had inspected hundreds of structures on the MFAA List of Protected Monuments and had posted many more OUT OF BOUNDS signs. Somehow they had also managed to dislodge American and British troops and French citizens from the comfort of being indoors in protected buildings without making enemies. In fact, Stout believed that the respect they had shown for these old structures had in some instances won over the support of the local people and even some Allied troops, despite the added hardship.

Even acknowledging that they had been lucky a time or two, Stout considered their mission thus far a success. Army bureaucracy was an impediment, but the commanders on the ground had been largely respectful of their work, so far at least. This came as a welcome surprise. The reports from Rorimer, LaFarge, and Hammett, and his meeting with Posey several weeks earlier, confirmed what Stout believed from the outset: With so little help from the army, the only way this mission had a chance of working was by winning over Allied commanders and the troops in the field, face-to-face, one by one.

CHAPTER 5

PRICELESS DUST

Florence, Italy: August 1944

On August 13, the same day that the American Monuments Men in France—all five of them—were meeting near the gutted city of Saint-Lô, Monuments Man Fred Hartt was making his way into Florence. Sporadic gunfire, perhaps from snipers, crackled ahead. Shellfire reverberated in the distance. Hartt's driver, Franco Ruggenini, maneuvered Lucky 13 through Porta Romana, the southern entrance to the city, past the Boboli Gardens, before turning left toward Villa Torrigiani, Allied Military Government (AMG) headquarters. But Hartt was oblivious to the sounds and the chaos, lost in thought about a city he considered his own.

Florence had in some ways saved his life; at least that's how Hartt saw it. His passionate study of the Renaissance provided an escape from memories of an unhappy childhood. Understanding the greatness of Michelangelo, Giotto, Masaccio, Botticelli, Donatello, Leonardo da Vinci, Raphael, and others who lived and worked in Florence required a thorough knowledge of the city's history. Hartt specialized in it.

The origin of Florence stretches back to the first century BCE, when the well-developed Etruscan society began to move down to the Arno River, which in time became the lifeblood of the city. The

Romans arrived during the time of Julius Caesar. By the 1400s, Florence had emerged as a center of international commerce. Its currency, the gold florin, and the banking dynasty it produced, the Medici family, became European powerhouses. The Medici wealth funded the artists of the Italian Renaissance, Western civilization's most prolific period of artistic achievement since the days of Greek democracy in Athens.

Hartt marveled at the genius of Filippo Brunelleschi, who applied mathematics to ancient architecture in order to design and construct the world's largest cupola atop the Florence cathedral, the Church of Santa Maria del Fiore. He admired the tenderness of Lorenzo Ghiberti's work, which magically wrought from bronze perfect expressions of human anatomy to produce for the cathedral's baptistery doors panels so beautiful that Michelangelo admiringly referred to them as the "Gates of Paradise." And now, filled with anguish, Hartt worried about how many of these things of beauty had survived.

A fortuitous meeting at AMG headquarters with Professor Filippo Rossi, Director of the Galleries of Florence, provided Hartt with an escort for his meeting with city art officials. Hartt and Rossi jumped into Lucky 13 for the short drive to the Pitti Palace, once home to the Medici family. Hartt knew the elegant palace and its stunning collection of art so well that a person could be forgiven for thinking he had once lived there himself. But the grandeur of *that* Pitti Palace and its expansive Boboli Gardens had given way to the emergencies of war. Now it provided refuge for more than six thousand Florentines who had been dislodged from their homes by German forces. From a distance, Hartt thought it resembled a crowded slum in Naples more than a royal palace. Clothing hung from nearly every balcony.

The engine of Lucky 13 moaned as it made the steep approach. Hundreds of people filled the sun-soaked piazza, including what turned out to be an informal welcoming committee of art superintendents and museum officials excited to meet the American Monuments Man. As he entered the building, Hartt could see people wandering aimlessly; others sat on the ground huddled in groups. Babies were crying. A few injured people nearby were moaning. But he also heard laughter and could see children at play. Try as they might, Hartt thought, the Nazis didn't break the spirit of the Florentines. These people were tired, filthy, hungry, and thirsty, but they were still alive.

The Florentine superintendent, Giovanni Poggi, and Dr. Ugo Procacci, an art official of the Tuscan museums, had, like the other citizens, been trapped in their city for nine days, worried about the fate of the treasures stashed in villas around the Tuscan countryside and eager for information. Hartt had precious details to share. He had just completed inspections of the Castle of Montegufoni, with its priceless paintings; the Villa Bossi-Pucci in Montagnana, which German troops had thoroughly looted; and several other Florentine repositories.

As the officials listened to Hartt explain the mission of the Monuments Men and discuss what he had discovered on his inspections, they couldn't believe their good fortune. The American had military authority, a jeep, and extraordinary knowledge of the city's monuments and works of art. The best chance of protecting the other repositories, Hartt explained, depended on him having a complete list of all the Tuscan repositories and their locations. Poggi and Procacci quickly complied.

Hartt took a moment and hurriedly scanned the list, making a running tally in his head of the number of art repositories. When he reached the last page, the magnitude of the problem nearly knocked him off his feet. Thirty-eight villas in all, located amid constantly shifting battle lines, housed many of the world's greatest art masterpieces. Making matters worse, about one-third of the works had no protective crates or wrapping. Hartt was frustrated—and angry. His most dreaded nightmare had now become a reality. How many masterpieces had already been destroyed in battles or stolen by fleeing German forces, he wondered. He could and would inspect the remaining repositories in Allied-controlled areas, but there wasn't a thing he could do about those located behind enemy lines other than wait. Hartt abhorred waiting.

Their meeting at an end, Hartt asked Dr. Procacci to show him how to reach the most damaged portions of the city. As they set out on foot, moving very slowly over smashed stone and broken glass in the direction of the Ponte Vecchio, Procacci began recounting the dying days of the beautiful city.

Toward the end of July, German commanders had issued a proclamation ordering everyone living along the Arno to evacuate their homes. On July 31, civilians were prohibited from crossing any of the city's six main bridges. This divided Florence into northern and southern halves. While German sappers laid their cables and explosive devices beneath the bridges, soldiers went house to house along the Arno, ensuring that everyone had complied with the evacuation order. When they found a locked door, they used grenades to open it.

Several days passed, followed by a new decree ordering all citizens to remain in the lower floors of their homes, away from all windows. Clearly the German commanders didn't want any witnesses to the Wehrmacht's evil deeds. By this time, thousands of people had crammed themselves into the Pitti Palace, seeking any safety they could find. The first in a series of thunderous explosions came on the evening of August 3, each so forceful that the ground shook. Terror seized the crowd, then someone cried out, "The bridges, the bridges!"

The destroyed bridges of Florence.

Explosions continued until dawn, when an eerie quiet descended upon the city. Under the cover of darkness German forces had retreated north, to the relative safety of the Gothic Line, leaving behind smoldering ruins. Five of the six bridges no longer crossed the Arno but lay in it. In an absurd effort to spare the Ponte Vecchio—Hitler's favorite bridge, Procacci pointed out—German forces deliberately destroyed entire city blocks of buildings and medieval towers hoping to create impassable rubble piles.

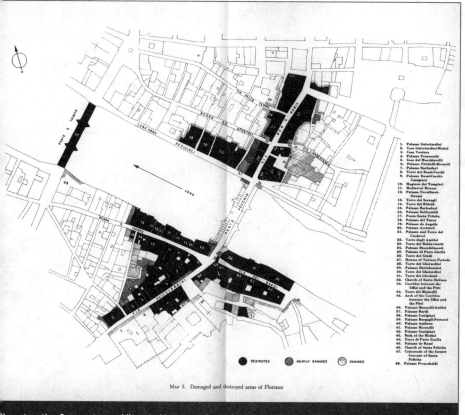

Map 3. Damaged and destroyed areas of Florence

The retreating German trops obilterated large sections of medieval Florence (in black) to block Allied passage across Hitler's favorite bridge, the Ponte Vecchio (center).

By the time Hartt and the superintendent reached a small piazza near the Arno, Hartt no longer needed anyone to describe the destruction; he could see it for himself. It was worse than anything he could ever have imagined, "one gigantic trash pile together, spilling into the Arno." In an instant, centuries of beauty and history had been reduced to priceless dust.

Conditions elsewhere in the city were abysmal. The intense heat of August had cooked human waste from the broken sewers and decaying corpses buried under collapsed buildings to create a suffocating smell. Hartt pulled out his handkerchief, but it did little good. Barefoot women stood shoulder to shoulder preparing spartan meals on outdoor stoves. Children sat in circles on the ground, devouring their meager suppers. No one indulged in vanity. Young women looked thirty years older, with their once well-coifed hair

Rubble piles are all that remained of the medieval towers that once flanked the Ponte Vecchio.

standing on end, caked with grayish dust. Men patched and repatched their ragged clothes.

There were shortages of everything except dust, bullets, and the dead. Snipers randomly picked off civilians. German artillery shells intermittently rained down on the city, claiming even more lives. Men, armed with picks and shovels, hacked away at the thirty-foot-high mounds of medieval stone to clear paths so workers could begin rebuilding. Women searched through the pieces for heirlooms. A cluster of people usually indicated the location of one of the city's temporary clean water supplies. Such oases were rather easy to discover by following someone carrying straw-covered wine jugs or gasoline cans in each hand. It was a pitiful sight. All the destruction would take months to clean up and years to repair, and even then, Hartt sighed, the city would never look the same.

With the complete list of repositories in hand, Hartt wanted to resume his inspections, but the situation in the city center was desperate. Florence needed as many Monuments Men as possible to protect the remains of historic buildings that had any chance of being salvaged and to recover what they could of rare books and works of art buried in the debris. The search for the stolen Florentine treasures would have to wait.

Near Pisa, Italy: September 1944

Hunkered down on the outskirts of another destroyed Italian town, Deane Keller flipped through the pages of his field diary and made some calculations in his head. Maybe he was off by a few hundred miles here or there, but in the nearly four months since becoming a Monuments Man, Keller figured he'd driven about eight thousand miles, over dusty, bomb-cratered roads, inspecting hundreds of damaged towns. The scenes of misery and hardship were always similar; only the names of the places changed. But from what he was hearing from the boys of Fifth Army, the situation in the city of Pisa might be the worst of all. Compounding matters, half of Fifth Army's strength had been depleted in just a couple of months, partly the result of combat losses, but mostly because General Eisenhower had siphoned units for an invasion of southern France, called Operation Dragoon, which began in August.

As German shells continued to fall, Keller pulled out his regional map, its folded edges now as soft as tissue paper. Pisa was located fifty miles west of Florence, and as the seagulls overhead confirmed, just eight miles inland from the Tyrrhenian Sea. The ancient city owed its early development to the Romans, who understood the importance of its strategically positioned port. The Arno River, flowing east to west, divided the city center just as it did in Florence. This fate of geography also meant the river was a barrier the Allies would have to cross in their offensive that continued to grind north.

Allied leaders had declared Florence off-limits to bombing due to its historic, art-rich city center. But Pisa, a city with a rich artistic and cultural history of its own, had no such exemption and was subjected to continuous punishing bombing raids that caused immense destruction. Fifth Army artillery then targeted any German-occupied buildings that the bombers had missed. After six grueling weeks of battle, Keller hoped there was still something left to liberate.

The following day, September 2, Keller and a small team of AMG specialists entered the south side of the city and crept along in their jeeps until the volume of debris forced them to abandon their vehicles and walk. They climbed over ruins, jumping at the occasional rat in the rubble, all the while looking for mines. With four months of experience walking through destroyed Italian towns, Keller instinctively assumed that German forces had booby-trapped every building and pathway. After walking just a few blocks in Pisa, he was sure of it.

The going was slow and tedious, but by the end of the day he and the other officers finally reached the old city hall near the banks of the Arno. To celebrate their harrowing journey, Keller and Captain McCallum, the engineer on his reconnaissance team, decided to hang the Stars and Stripes and the Union Jack from a balcony that overlooked the river. As he looked out over the destroyed city and its demolished bridges, Keller realized that he had gone the entire day and seen just two citizens in a city with a prewar population of seventy-two thousand people.

Early the next morning, Keller had to use the remains of a narrow streetcar track like a jungle gym just to cross the Arno on his way to inspect the heart of the city, the Piazza dei Miracoli—Square of Miracles. The growth and prosperity of Pisa from the eleventh through the thirteenth centuries had funded construction of the piazza and its duomo (cathedral), *battistero* (baptistery), campanile (bell tower—known as the Leaning Tower of Pisa), and *camposanto* (cemetery). But a cruel siege in 1406 by Pisa's most fierce rival, Florence, signaled an end to the maritime republic's power. Pisa had lived in the shadow of the Tuscan capital ever since.

Piazza dei Miracoli in Pisa. The Camposanto Monumentale, with its missing roof, can be seen at the upper right.

Entering the piazza, Keller noticed that the baptistery had sustained hits. He could see several holes in the roof of the Duomo and one on a facade column, but none looked too serious. A quick glance to his right confirmed that the Leaning Tower of Pisa was undamaged . . . and still leaning. But as he emerged from between the baptistery and the Duomo, he froze. The roof of the city's famed cemetery, the Camposanto Monumentale, was gone. Keller could see a few stubs of charred timber emerging above its walls, but nothing more. In this war, even the cemeteries were dying.

The architectural curiosity of the Leaning Tower of Pisa had for centuries drawn steady crowds, but Keller knew that the real jewel of the Piazza dei Miracoli was the Camposanto, constructed in 1278. The building consisted of two rectangles, one inside the other. The outer rectangle, about the size of an American football field, was covered; the interior rectangle, which contained a grass courtyard in the style of a cloister, was not. Separating the two rectangular spaces were Gothic marble arcades open to the grass courtyard from all four sides. The exterior walls and the Gothic marble arcades supported a wooden A-frame roof covered with lead.

Keller knew that the Camposanto glorified local memory stretching back to the medieval era. The marble pavement was interspersed with tombs, each marking the burial spot of a city luminary. Adding to the veneration, fourteenth- and fifteenth-century artists had then blanketed the interior walls with vibrantly colored frescoes. The Camposanto contained more painted surface than the entire Sistine Chapel at the Vatican, twenty thousand square feet in all. But Keller's overriding memory as a student wasn't of the building's frescoes, tombs, or history: It was the serenity of the space, a welcoming respite for the living, a solemn resting place for the dead.

Keller reached into his pocket and pulled out his field diary and, like a pathologist preparing to conduct an autopsy, started recording the damage:

> *On the floor next to the walls [are] thousands of pieces of fresco which have fallen to the ground either from the heat [or] the concussion from the jarring of the great beams as they fell to the floor. These [are] mingled with myriads of pieces of broken roof tiles, carved chunks of all sizes from the tombs, blackened embers and nails. All the*

sculptures [are] covered on the upper sides thoroughly
with the molten lead from heat and the running lead [is]
to be found on tombs and paintings alike.

"Thousands of pieces" wildly understated the volume of fragments. As Keller thought about it, they numbered into the millions. The floor of the Camposanto was now the world's largest jigsaw puzzle.

Out of the corner of his eye, Keller saw a man rushing toward him speaking Italian so hurriedly that it took a few minutes to calm him down before asking him to begin again. Bruno Farnesi, technical assistant—and witness to the fire—had quite a story to tell.

The roofless Camposanto Monumentale.

Five weeks earlier, on July 27, a violent artillery barrage had shaken the Piazza dei Miracoli. A few shells hit the massive structure. The Americans seemed to be aiming at a German observation post in the bell tower, Farnesi explained, but he doubted the Allies were trying to destroy it. German soldiers had established a position there to call in target coordinates to artillery batteries located far away from the Square of Miracles. Several other rounds struck the Duomo. Farnesi knew the cathedral was strong. It could take a dozen blows. But when the shelling stopped and the sky cleared, he saw a thin column of smoke rising from the Camposanto.

Even from the ground, flames were clearly visible on the northern side of the roof. Farnesi said he would have doused them, but the city had been without water for days. The only weapon to fight the fire was a tall ladder, which he had placed inside the Camposanto two months earlier.

A small group of volunteers, armed with nothing more than shovels, clubs, and poles, followed him up the ladder, but the wind off the Tyrrhenian Sea was pushing the fire across the roof faster than the men could fight it. The day was dying, but the fire was gathering strength. Farnesi watched as it ran along the great wooden support beams and wrapped its fingers around the lead roof. The beams snapped and crashed to the ground, causing the lead to run in rivulets down the walls. Farnesi urged the men forward, despite the blistering heat.

A shell whistled in, hitting the Duomo, but the great building held. Soon a volley of shells was raining down on the complex. The crowd scattered. The men struggled down the ladder and huddled behind the walls of the Camposanto. The shellfire seemed to be coming from the south, where the Americans were encamped. While the wall offered no protection from artillery, it was the only spot sheltered from the heat of the flames. Another explosion less than one hundred feet away knocked one of the men to the ground. This time, the small group ran for the safety of the cathedral.

Sometime later, maybe ten minutes or an hour—it was impossible for Farnesi to determine—the artillery fire stopped. Farnesi told Keller what happened next:

> *In the night, the Piazza dei Miracoli seemed to bleed in*
> *the vermilion color of the flames; the Duomo, the*
> *Baptistery, and the Campanile . . . were there, solemn,*
> *almost tinted with blood, to witness the tragic destiny of*
> *their brother, minor in age but not in beauty, who was*
> *perishing and was irredeemably consumed.*

It was a sad story, Keller admitted, and he'd heard plenty of them from all the Bruno Farnesis in each town that he had inspected.

Without another word, Keller turned and walked away, his head dropped and shoulders slumped. As he slowly crossed the lawn, his mind raced through a jumbled mix of memories . . . of Kathy and Dino, who never left his thoughts . . . of driving eight thousand miles inspecting dead cities . . . of the women in Naples, carrying buckets of rubble while their babies sat in the ruins . . . of San Miniato, on the hills outside of Florence, where twenty-seven civilians were killed when a mine detonated inside the cathedral into which they had been herded by the Germans . . . of Fred Hartt's preliminary report on Florence, with its bridges and medieval towers now reduced to dust and hundreds of its master-pieces stolen.

And during those four months, he wondered, what meaningful thing had he done other than inspections and advising others? "My assignment is MFAA officer, AMG Fifth Army," he had written his parents just weeks earlier. "I am not supposed to step out of my role. I would have no authority at all. The way I help is to talk with people, serve as interpreter—give help to any of the others who need it, and once in a while interject something in a meeting."

His thoughts drifted again, to the first dead American soldier he'd seen, and the letter the GI had tucked in the lining of his helmet for his mother. That American boy had become every soldier. That village had become every place he'd visited. But Keller also recalled other memories besides death and destruction, moments that had provided him with encouragement to go to the next place, and the next, like his time in Sezze Romano, where fifty towns-people had followed him to his jeep, offering prayers and thanks; and his stop in Monte Oliveto Maggiore, where the monks had hidden Allied personnel amid the artwork of Siena.

He also remembered the joy of hearing that Rome had been liberated virtually unharmed, and the excitement of finding Siena's most prized painting, Duccio's *Maestà*, safely inside its wooden crates. But this situation in Pisa was different, a chance to actually *do* something, something good, something permanent. Keller knew that Fifth Army didn't have the resources for the exhaustive and time-consuming project that he had in mind, but ignoring the problem would draw the scorn of the press and alienate Italians. One rainstorm would wash away the remains of centuries of history. Something had to be done. Keller was convinced that if the Monuments Men operation ever stood for anything, this was the moment to prove it.

A few minutes later, his body stiffened, and with a bounce to his step, he started back across the lawn of the piazza toward Farnesi and instructed him to bar entry to anyone who had not first obtained his permission. He then wandered off again, looking for a unit with a field radio; he had to make an emergency call.

CHAPTER 6
OBJECTIVES

Paris, France: late August to September 1944

The convoy of Allied troops lumbered into the outskirts of Paris—the City of Light—on August 25, snaking around barricades and an occasional burning vehicle. Sporadic gunfire crackled along the route. After four years of Nazi tyranny, the day of liberation had arrived and Monuments Man Jim Rorimer, part of the advance team entering the city, was in the thick of it.

German forces were fighting a desperate retreat everywhere. On the Eastern Front, the Soviets routed another Wehrmacht army group—five hundred thousand soldiers—in Ukraine and eastern Poland. While the Germans weren't hemorrhaging as much territory in Western Europe, the loss of Paris was a symbolic blow. German General Dietrich von Choltitz had surrendered his forces just hours earlier, but danger still lurked. Enemy snipers crouched in their hiding places, taking aim at the approaching military vehicles and curious civilians emerging to feel freedom once again. Rorimer could see signs of the fight for the city everywhere, including pickets and barbed wire on the streets, sandbag barricades in front of buildings, abandoned tanks and other military vehicles scattered about, smoldering embers of fires recently extinguished, and German artillery pieces still warm to the touch.

After spending the night in a hotel room that some German officer had occupied just twenty-four hours earlier, Rorimer put on his chocolate OD shirt (which was really dark green in color), fastened the buckles on his once-brown suede combat boots, grabbed his garrison cap, and walked across the Tuileries Garden to the cultural heart of the city, the Louvre Museum. Second Lieutenant—and former museum curator—Jim Rorimer knew practically every inch of the Louvre, one of the largest and most frequently visited art museums in the world. The paintings and sculpture that covered the walls and filled its rooms were as recognizable to him as his oldest friends. But that was a different time. War had a way of making familiar ground feel unfamiliar.

An unsettling silence had replaced the hustle and bustle of tourists. As Rorimer ascended the grand entry stairwell, he was shocked by the absence of one of the Louvre's signature pieces, a work that for decades had towered over all who climbed the steps: *The Winged Victory of Samothrace*, a second-century BCE Greek sculpture. At the top of the staircase he turned right, then right again into the main gallery. The paintings were also gone. In their place, someone had handwritten in chalk the names of artists and inventory numbers of their work. The Louvre was empty: no visitors, no works of art, just a lone Monuments Man armed with dozens of questions, striding with purpose—Rorimer always walked with purpose—down the Grande Galerie of the museum on his way to an appointment.

As he approached the museum's offices, Rorimer glanced out the window. U.S. Army soldiers were herding hundreds of German prisoners into the courtyard. In the distance, more GIs were

Empty frames that held Louvre masterpieces before their evacuation.

positioning antiaircraft guns around the perimeter. Nothing about this visit to the Louvre was normal until he rounded a corner and saw Jacques Jaujard, Director of the National Museums of France.

Being in the Louvre with a valued colleague provided a brief but welcome return to the world of normal. Rorimer admired Jaujard for helping museum colleagues in Madrid relocate to Switzerland art masterpieces at risk of being damaged during the Spanish Civil War. Jaujard's role in protecting the Louvre treasures bordered on magical. *How* he had done it was a mystery Rorimer wanted his friend to explain.

The experience in Spain contributed, Jaujard said, but it was advance planning that won the day. Rorimer leaned forward in his chair like a young boy eager to hear a great tale. When the Louvre, like other museums across Western Europe, closed in late August

1939, staff and volunteers worked around the clock to protect France's cultural heritage. Paintings, drawings, sculpture, and other precious objects, requiring thirty-seven convoys of five to eight trucks each, were taken to countryside châteaux. Vast quantities of centuries-old stained glass were removed from cathedrals in Paris, Chartres, and other cities, then packed and stored. The concern at that stage was getting everything to the countryside to protect it from bombing and the consequent fires. Rorimer, having walked through the ruins of fire-damaged cities in Normandy, recognized all too well what would have happened to the Louvre treasures had Paris suffered the same fate.

Knowing *The Winged Victory of Samothrace* weighed several tons, and, contrary to appearances, was not one solid piece of marble but thousands of shards painstakingly reassembled, Rorimer was eager to learn how Jaujard and his team moved it down the stairwell. Simple, Jaujard explained. They built a pulley that enabled them to mount the sculpture on wooden skids, then lowered it down the steps like a skier on a downhill slope—but at a snail's pace.

Rorimer also wanted to know the fate of the *Mona Lisa*, the most famous painting in the world. "*La Joconde*," Jaujard sighed with a smile, using the French name of Leonardo's masterpiece. With great satisfaction, he explained how his team had evacuated it on an ambulance stretcher in the dead of night, into a waiting van. A museum curator accompanied the masterpiece on its journey. To maintain a stable climate for the painting, the doors of the van were sealed. The painting arrived at its destination safely, but the curator had nearly suffocated. This was just the first of five moves. In the end, it found safety lying on a floor in Château de

Evacuation of *The Winged Victory of Samothrace*, second century BCE, from the Louvre Museum.

Montal, in southwestern France, inside its custom-made red-velvet-lined wooden case, next to the bed of a fifteen-year-old girl.

The conversation took on a more serious tone when Jaujard began describing the challenges of protecting other treasures from the French museums during the four-year-long Nazi occupation. Realizing the importance the Nazis placed on creating an appearance of legality in their transactions, Jaujard had converted French

Monuments Man James Rorimer (right) in front of the wall where Leonardo da Vinci's most famous work, *Mona Lisa*, once hung.

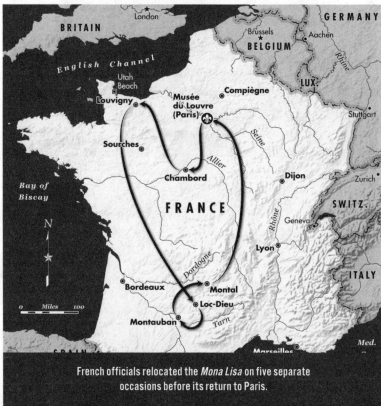

French officials relocated the *Mona Lisa* on five separate occasions before its return to Paris.

bureaucracy into a weapon by waging a paper war to prevent, or at least slow to a crawl, any effort to steal works of art from the national collections. The strategy for the most part worked. Covert connections with the French Resistance, his virtual eyes and ears when tracking German activity, also proved important.

But there were notable failings, Jaujard lamented. While the French museum collections had largely been saved, the Nazis' premeditated and systematic looting of Jewish-owned collections, especially the preeminent dealer-collector dynasties, was a loss of immeasurable proportion. Jaujard estimated that one-third of the French private collections—perhaps as many as twenty thousand works of art—were now in Germany. Rorimer listened as his friend ran down the list of prominent collectors who had been looted, including Rothschild, Rosenberg, and David-Weill. He knew them all. Unfortunately, so did the Nazis. These enormously rich, museum-quality private collections contained treasures by Old Master artists, including Johannes Vermeer and Rembrandt van Rijn, the great Postimpressionist painter Vincent van Gogh, and twentieth-century master Pablo Picasso. Museum directors hoped someday to acquire them. The Nazis had a simple and more certain plan: just steal them.

This initial visit with Jaujard was meant to be more of a social call than a briefing session, but Rorimer considered it a welcome beginning to his first day of duty as the MFAA Specialist Officer for Paris. As Rorimer said his goodbyes, he realized that perhaps only a fellow museum man could fully appreciate Jaujard's herculean achievements during the Nazi occupation. Rorimer knew that his friend was far too modest to ever lay claim to an act of bravery, but there was no question that Jacques Jaujard was a hero, not just to France, but to all those who loved the arts.

Exiting the museum, Rorimer passed several U.S. Army tanks parked in the Tuileries Garden, a Paris landmark that he believed as worthy of protection as any historic building. The tankers gathered around small fires where they were preparing a hot breakfast and coffee. Others were shaving.

Rorimer wasn't focused on the tanks, or the soldiers, or possible billeting violations; his thoughts centered on opportunity. Jacques Jaujard had provided the Monuments Men with key information about priceless paintings that the Nazis had stolen from French collectors and then shipped to Germany. *He did say one-third of the private collections in France, right?* Someone had to find those treasures and return them to France, but where to begin? Jaujard mentioned that some museum employees had lists of what was stolen and some idea of where it had been taken, but Berlin was still 655 miles away and Rorimer clearly had his hands full of work in Paris. Still, it wouldn't hurt to dig deeper. Perhaps Jaujard would be willing to arrange a meeting with his museum employees?

Bruges, Belgium: mid-September 1944

On September 16, three weeks after the liberation of Paris, British Major Ronald Balfour, George Stout's roommate at Shrivenham, reached the Belgian town of Bruges. Four days earlier, the First Canadian Army had taken the city in a dash along the Channel coast. Army bureaucracy had delayed his departure from England until the last week of August, but now, attached to First Canadian

Army, he was finally at work as a Monuments Man, following leads on a brazen theft by the Nazis.

Sitting on a pew inside the Church of Our Lady, with a few minutes to spare before his meeting with the dean, Balfour reached into his field pack, pulled out a stack of typed notes, and began shuffling through the pages. He was constantly revising his thoughts about how to explain to the fighting men why cultural preservation mattered. As he scanned the pages he found the paragraph of interest.

"We do not want to destroy unnecessarily what men spent so much time and care and skill in making," he whispered. "These examples of craftsmanship tell us so much about our ancestors." The echo of footsteps caused him to look up from the page, but it was just a parishioner. After watching the local woman light a candle, he resumed. "If these things are lost or broken or destroyed, we lose a valuable part of our knowledge about our forefathers. No age lives entirely alone; every civilisation is formed not merely by its own achievements but by what it has inherited from the past. If these things are destroyed, we have lost a part of our past, and we shall be the poorer for it." He'd found the right words; of that he was sure. Now he needed to find more opportunities to share them with the men.

Moments later the church sacristan tapped him on the shoulder. The dean, Reverend René Deschepper, was ready to meet with him. As they walked past parishioners on the way to Deschepper's office, Balfour could see that the euphoria of two days earlier, when British troops liberated the city, had already given way to the reality of the difficult road ahead. The hardships of Nazi rule had created short-ages of everything. Despite that, the dean had thoughtfully arranged for his assistant to bring them tea. Field journal in hand, Balfour began taking notes as the dean shared the events of September 7.

Sometime around midnight, two German officers appeared at the locked doors of the church demanding entry. In the street behind them were twenty or more armed sailors from the local barracks and, curiously, several trucks marked with Red Cross insignias. "We're taking the Michelangelo. To protect it from the Americans," one of them said. Reverend Deschepper, anguished from just recounting the story, explained to Balfour, almost defensively, that there was nothing he could do to stop them. He then handed the British Monuments Man a postcard containing a photo-graph of what the Germans had stolen.

Even before taking it, Balfour knew that the dean was speaking about the Bruges *Madonna*. It was priceless, famous for being the only sculpture by Michelangelo to leave Italy during his lifetime. The nearly life-sized master-piece, carved out of white marble in 1504, when the Florentine master was twenty-nine years old, depicted the ten-derness between a very young virgin mother and her Christ child. As he looked at the image, Balfour marveled at how Michelangelo had transformed a

Michelangelo, Bruges *Madonna*, 1501–1504.

rigid, heavy piece of stone into a work that revealed the softness of human skin and the lightness of fabric folds. His genius had breathed life into both figures. Beyond the protective pose of a young boy standing between his mother's legs and her flowing robes, their fingers interlocked, Michelangelo subtly foreshadowed the painful fate of Christ. Balfour put down the postcard, adjusted his glasses, and asked the dean to continue.

The two German officers posted several sailors at the doors and ordered others to the north aisle of the church, where the sculpture had been placed in 1940 as a protective measure. In near darkness, using only flashlights to continue their nefarious operation, they positioned a bed mattress on the floor in front of the sculpture. And this, the dean said with emphasis, revealed the true evil of their actions.

Four days earlier, a Dr. Rosemann had personally delivered the mattresses, offering them as additional protection from Allied bombing. Rosemann was the senior official in Belgium of the German art protection unit, known as the Kunstschutz. When the two German commanders in charge of the looting operation specifically asked for the mattresses, the dean realized that far from being a last-minute thought, the Germans had devised a plan to loot the church of the Michelangelo sculpture long before the actual theft. The only spontaneous aspect of their operation was the theft of eleven valuable paintings that had hung inside the church for centuries.

The dean and sacristan watched as a group of sailors inched the sculpture forward and then tilted it toward the mattress on the floor. It took nearly a dozen sailors to lift and carry it toward the door. Once there, they laid a second mattress on top of the sculpture, tied it into place, then loaded it into one of the Red Cross trucks. The paintings were put in the second truck. The two German officers and remaining sailors departed in the third. It took them five hours, but when done, the Germans had looted a work of art that had been in Bruges for 440 years. The Church of Our Lady was missing its centerpiece; Belgium was missing a national treasure.

Reverend Deschepper had no idea where the sculpture was, or how the Germans intended to transport it, presumably back to Nazi Germany. But he pleaded with Balfour to find it and see that it was returned to its home in Bruges. He then handed him the stack of postcards on the off chance that someone who might have seen the sculpture would come forward with information. It seemed unlikely, but that—and prayer—were his only hope.

After thanking the dean for his good wishes and the stack of postcards, Balfour exited the church, positioned his beret, and found a nearby bench to supplement his interview notes. That the Germans had looted was hardly news. But the fact that they were *still* looting, at a time when Allied soldiers were less than a week away from Bruges, when human nature should be screaming for a person to flee, not hang around and steal something as iconic as Michelangelo's Bruges *Madonna*, indeed *was* news. He reached into his field pack once more, pulled out one of the postcards the dean had given him, and took a long look. Reverend Deschepper was certainly right about one thing: Someone somewhere knew something about the whereabouts of the Michelangelo. Balfour was determined to find him.

Near Verdun, France: late September 1944

Robert Posey, the lone American Monuments Man unable to attend the August 13 meeting near Saint-Lô, pushed the most recent package from Supreme Headquarters Allied Expeditionary Force (SHAEF) out of the way, trying to find the calendar in his pup tent. With a towel wrapped around his neck and dog tags, he was about to take his first hot shower in two months, in a captured German barracks no less. The timing of it made him laugh. Just days earlier, he had written his wife, Alice, pointing out how "things that seem luxuries in the field would seem to be the most meager of items" in civilian life. The "meager" items—a home-cooked meal; a bed, preferably indoors; and yes, even a hot shower—were always things to savor, but not knowing when the next opportunity to experience them might come made Posey all the more appreciative.

As Monuments Officer for General George S. Patton's U.S. Third Army—well, it wasn't really Patton's army, but try and convince anyone serving under him of that—Posey was sure he had the best assignment in the whole army. For a guy from a poor family, raised on a dirt farm outside the small town of Morris, Alabama, population five hundred, he'd done well for himself. Besides, what he and his family lacked in money they more than made up for in patriotism.

Serving in the military was in his blood. A Posey had fought for the British crown during the colonial period, in the French and Indian War; served as a minuteman in the South Carolina militia during the Revolutionary War; and battled against the Creek

Nation in the War of 1812. Eight Posey brothers fought in the Civil War; only one survived. Now, Robert Posey was in eastern France, a captain in the U.S. Army, continuing that proud tradition of service to the nation.

Family tradition wasn't the only reason he'd joined the military. The army's Reserve Officers' Training Corps—the ROTC—was his ticket out of Morris, Alabama, and into Auburn University. With scant family finances, there was no other way he could have attended college. Architecture became his interest, and that, in turn, helped him get a job and provide for his family. He figured he owed the army a lot.

After his shower, back in his tent and dressed, he opened the package from SHAEF. Reports . . . directives . . . those were the norm . . . but the inclusion of photographs of works of art? They looked interesting! A detailed description of each work of art accompanied the photographs, all Belgian treasures, and summary information about their history right up until the time they went missing. Missing? They haven't gone missing, he thought. The Nazis have stolen them.

Two of the objects were so iconic he recognized them immediately: Michelangelo's Bruges *Madonna*, whose theft had been reported by Monuments Man Ronald Balfour one week earlier, and the Ghent Altarpiece, certainly the most important painting in Belgium and perhaps among the five most important works of art in the world. The sculpture by Michelangelo was valuable, but the Ghent Altarpiece dwarfed it in importance. With no further obligations that afternoon, Posey lay down on his cot and started reading through the materials.

The Adoration of the Mystic Lamb—its formal name—belonged in Saint Bavo's Cathedral in the town of Ghent, about thirty miles east of Bruges. The double-sided wood panel painting, measuring twelve feet high and sixteen feet wide, was completed in 1432 by Jan van Eyck and his brother, Hubert. From the outset, the painting was considered a towering achievement in the development of art. The use of oil-based paint to create lifelike renderings of people, not the idealized forms of centuries past, astonished viewers. The minute attention to detail—whiskers and beards, fabric on gowns, brightly illuminated landscapes, jeweled embroidery, and even individual strands of hair—demonstrated an artistic ability unlike anything anyone had ever seen.

Jan and Hubert van Eyck, Ghent Altarpiece, 1432.

To Adolf Hitler and the Nazis, the Ghent Altarpiece was Germanic in style and therefore belonged in Germany. Six of the twenty-four panels had been owned by a German museum for nearly one hundred years, until 1919, when the surrender terms of the Treaty of Versailles that ended World War I forced Germany to relinquish them as war reparations. Those six panels were taken to Belgium and united with the other panels, leaving Germans, and Adolf Hitler, with a bitter, festering wound.

Germany's invasion of Western Europe in May 1940 provided Hitler with a chance to get even and right the perceived historic wrongs of Versailles. Belgian officials knew exactly what that meant. While German Wehrmacht troops were advancing west into France, three trucks carrying the Ghent Altarpiece were on the road to Italy, desperately hoping to reach the Vatican and safety. By the time the trucks approached the border, Italy had declared war on France. Closed borders forced the drivers to change direction. They headed west, eventually finding an art repository at the foot of the Pyrenees, in the southwestern French town of Pau. At that point the safety of the Ghent Altarpiece became the responsibility of the French government.

German officials knew where the Belgian treasure had been hidden, but why rush to take it? By 1942, Hitler, unable to resist temptation any longer, ordered a secret delegation to France with instructions not to return to Germany without the van Eycks' masterpiece. French art officials, including Jacques Jaujard, protested vigorously; so did Belgian officials. But it was all too little, too late. The painting disappeared into Nazi Germany and had not been seen since.

After finishing the report, Posey dropped it on the wood pole floor of his tent and grabbed his map. He figured that, at the speed of Third Army's advance, they should be crossing the border into Germany, now less than sixty miles away, in no time at all. It was anyone's guess what they would find on enemy soil, but hiding something that important without anyone knowing about it seemed unlikely. Posey felt sure of one thing: If the Ghent Altarpiece was hidden somewhere in Third Army's area of operations, it was as good as found—assuming the Nazis hadn't destroyed it.

With his work duties complete, Posey poked around in his field pack for some writing paper and a pen. Each envelope he mailed home contained a letter for his wife, Alice, and a separate one for his seven-year-old son, Dennis, whom he often called "Woogie." Army censors limited what he could say about his work and forbade any reference to where he was, or where he was headed. But he always made sure to let Alice know how much he missed her and Woogie, and that his time away from them, though painful, was worth it. He was happy in his job and honored by what he was doing. Letters to Woogie always asked about "the Zoo," a growing menagerie of animals that were part of their family. Most recently Woogie had added a bunny rabbit. His son didn't just love animals; he was a born zookeeper.

There wasn't much Posey didn't like about the army other than missed opportunities with his son, like seeing his first ride on a horse and being at his side to comfort him when he got the measles. But coming from such a poor family, Posey knew the value of the little things he seldom had as a child and made a point of surprising Woogie by including souvenirs with his letters. Sometimes it was a postcard from one of the cities Third Army had liberated, or foreign stamps and currency. Occasionally he sent home some war booty like a Nazi swastika belt buckle.

This night, as he thought about what to write his boy, he remembered that Alice had mentioned some problems Dennis was having with bullies. Pen in hand, he got out a piece of U.S. Army stationery and started writing:

> *Dear Dennis: I am sorry that you have so much trouble with the kids fighting around town. That is the price one pays for being a bit more civilized than the people about him. I think the best way to handle it is to develop a good uppercut. When you get a bit older you can take boxing lessons . . . Until you learn some fist fighting ways it is probably better to avoid them.*

After rereading what he'd written, Posey realized it likely wouldn't be much help. Advice was always a distant second to the magic of a hug. Trying to be an engaged dad from afar was the toughest part of war.

CHAPTER 7

RESURRECTION AND TREACHERY

Pisa, Italy: September to October 1944

Monuments Man Deane Keller knew there was risk in making the call. The office of Brigadier General Edgar Hume, commander of Allied Military Government in Italy, was already being bombarded with requests for help, made worse by the devastation to medieval Florence being reported by Fred Hartt. It would be easy for the general's staff to ignore his request and write off the Camposanto as another casualty of war. But Keller knew that Hume, who had served on General Eisenhower's command staff in North Africa, had spent one year of graduate school in Rome. Perhaps the general's knowledge of Italy and its cultural heritage would work in his favor.

The following morning, September 4, a small convoy of military jeeps pulled into the Piazza dei Miracoli. Keller could barely contain his smile. His call had worked. General Hume hadn't just sent his staff—he'd come himself, accompanied by the archbishop of Pisa. It was a hopeful beginning. As they approached the medieval structure, Keller, serving as translator, pulled some tourist postcards of the Piazza dei Miracoli out of his pocket and passed them to General Hume and the archbishop. The two stood outside the entrance holding the photographs of the undamaged Camposanto, with its lead-lined timber roof, at arm's length, juxtaposed against the now-bare cemetery walls.

Seeing that the postcards were having the desired effect, Keller led the small group into the burial site. Even five weeks after the inferno, the smell of smoke lingered in the air. The crackling sound of shoes crushing tiny fragments of hundreds-of-years-old plaster and debris jolted his visitors. Millions of pieces of fresco fragments blanketed the floor of the Camposanto. Ancient tombs and urns, shattered by the intensity of the fire, lined the interior walls. Charred remains of frescoes still affixed to the wall had the consistency of dust after being baked by thirty-eight days of exposure to the intense Tuscan sun. The sight and smell of so much fire-damaged beauty created a somber but fitting mood. After all, Keller thought, they were in a cemetery.

As the visitors emerged from the remains back into the Piazza dei Miracoli, Keller realized his gamble had paid off. The presence of the archbishop of Pisa pleading the case for emergency intervention had certainly helped. But providing General Hume with an opportunity to see and feel the damage to this once-great monument proved the decisive factor. Something could be done, the general told Keller. Something *must* be done.

Seven days later, Keller walked the floors of the Camposanto, cleared of most of the fresco remains and debris. Overseeing a small army of engineers, Italian military personnel, and fresco specialists from Florence and Rome that General Hume's staff had somehow located and transported to Pisa, provided a sense of accomplishment not present in his previous inspection work. Each day presented new challenges, but he loved the opportunity to be "doing" something. No lumber? No problem, Keller told his team. A midnight "requisition" from an overstocked ship in nearby Livorno would suffice. All the while, German shells rained down on the area, killing one woman in a nearby building.

By October 12, the job was complete. Army engineers and Italian volunteers put the finishing touches on a temporary roof made of tarpaulin and tarpaper. The interior walls of the Camposanto and what remained of the once-great fresco cycle would now be safe until a new roof could be constructed. Keller had used much of that time to supervise the gathering and storage of the detached pieces of frescoed plaster that had littered the floor of the cemetery when he first arrived, in anticipation of the day when the tedious work of reassembling the pieces could begin. The Camposanto would get the second chance that so many damaged churches and historic structures in Italy would not.

Exhausted but proud, Keller returned to his tent to write Kathy and share the good news. "The job is done, works perfectly. The frescoes were dry as a 15th-century tibia in the last downpour." In another letter he put the achievement into perspective. "This is the biggest job I have had of its kind," he told Kathy. "It has been interesting all through, though fraught with unforeseen troubles. I wonder if this whole story will ever come out for people to know about and to realize—I doubt it."

Florence, Italy: September to October 1944

Fred Hartt scrolled another piece of paper into his typewriter to complete his initial damage assessment report on Florence.

Deane Keller "supporting" the Leaning Tower of Pisa.

Michelangelo's towering achievement, the sculpture *David*, had come through the battle unscathed, but the images of other cultural treasures far less fortunate paraded across his mind, leaving him feeling like a grief-stricken family member identifying a deceased loved one.

The sweltering heat of August had not helped his mood.

Having addressed the destruction of five of the city's six bridges and made mention of the one that had survived, the Ponte Vecchio, another thought came to mind. "The destruction may not have held up the war in Italy five minutes," he typed, "but it paralyzed the city. This had been the heart of Dante's Florence. These were the streets and squares scarcely altered since Giotto and Masaccio walked them." Now everything Hartt saw, "houses, towers, palaces with all they contained and with all their glorious memories, lay collapsed in mountainous heaps of rubble."

Flipping the pages of his field journal, the name of a church that he'd inspected caught his eye. It didn't have the importance of the city's duomo, or the beauty of Santa Maria Novella, but something notable had taken place there that Hartt wanted to add to his typed report.

> *Santo Stefano is gravely damaged. The 13th-century*
> *facade is split from top to portal, the roof tiles are gone,*
> *and the interior full of rubble. The 93-year-old parish*
> *priest, Padre Veneziani, refused to leave his church, and*
> *died from the concussion of the mines. His body was*
> *removed only 18 August, from the sacristy where it had*
> *lain since 3 August.*

Michelangelo, *David*, 1501–1504.

Florentine craftsmen entombed the *David* (background)
and other Michelangelo sculptures (foreground) to protect them from Allied bombing.

The death of the parish priest put a face to his mission, but more than that, it reminded him of something Deane Keller had said several months earlier. Hartt couldn't remember Keller's exact words, but the point of his remark was this: Being a Monuments Man required balancing the dramatic with the mundane. Saving works of art or a building was important, but so were the essential tasks of securing supplies and writing reports. Despite the focus on *things*, the job existed to help *people*.

By early September, with Fifth and Eighth Armies' long-awaited assault on the Gothic Line underway, Hartt resumed his inspections of the other repositories on the list provided by Florentine art officials Poggi and Procacci. Shifting battle lines still prevented access to some of the villas used to store art, but on September 5, Hartt and his driver were able to reach a royal villa in the small town of Poggio a Caiano. Days earlier, the Allies had received a bizarre telegram from Swiss officials conveying a German request that Allied forces *not* bomb Poggio a Caiano because of the art treasures being stored there. The message explicitly stated that there were no German troops in that particular area. Something didn't add up, Hartt thought. Was it a trick of some kind? Had German forces laid booby traps throughout the villa expecting the Allies to rush to the scene? Without a firsthand inspection it remained a mystery.

Gaining access to Poggio a Caiano was not easy. The destruction of a key bridge forced Hartt and his driver, Ruggenini, to take a back route, then wade across a canal before inching up a steep embankment. Hartt wanted to laugh at how goofy they must have looked, crawling hand over foot like two children mimicking monkeys, but he was too winded to spare the extra breath. They emerged from the gully to be greeted as liberators by villagers excited to see their first Allied officer.

Hartt found the custodian and wasted no time in getting to the bottom of what had taken place. Had German soldiers been here? Did they take any of the works of art that had been stored in the villa? The custodian, although nervous, seemed relieved for a chance to share what he'd seen with somebody of authority.

A Major Reidemeister, a representative of the Kunstschutz, the German art protection unit, had arrived toward the end of August, the custodian explained. He had with him trucks, men, and an order to remove certain items. Determined to prevent the removals, the custodian had informed the German major that the villa and its contents were under the protection of the Holy See in Rome, and that Generalfeldmarschall Kesselring, the senior German military commander in Italy, had also issued a protective order for the works of art.

Hartt, increasingly anxious, pressed again. The details were important, but what he wanted was a yes or no to his question. Did the Germans take any of the works of art that had been stored in the villa? Yes, the custodian replied.

Overwhelmed by anger and impatience, Hartt barked more than asked: What precisely *did* the Germans take? Flustered, the custodian sputtered, "Bargello Museum!" Hartt wanted to cry out in pain. The Bargello housed the most important collection of Gothic and Renaissance sculpture in the world, including masterpieces by Michelangelo and Donatello that had, over centuries, come to define the city.

The dates of the theft corresponded precisely to the German government's message to Swiss officials. Clearly the request for the Allies to avoid bombing Poggio a Caiano was a feint to buy time for German troops to empty the villa. Speechless at the involvement of German government officials and the deceptiveness of the theft, Hartt immediately wrote Ernest DeWald, director of the MFAA in Italy:

> *Dear Ernest, This is what they stole. I retain the original hand written document which the custode [sic] made out . . . They started stealing the stuff two days before they broadcast to us not to bomb it. God knows where it is now. If I were you I would call in the correspondents & make a big story out of this. Maybe that will save other stuff from being stolen.*

In early October, with the inspections of all but one of the thirty-eight Tuscan repositories now complete, Hartt gathered his interview notes and field journal to write a summary report of his findings. The thieves had acted on specific orders from the German military commander of Florence, Colonel Metzner, and SS Colonel Alexander Langsdorff, recently appointed head of the Kunstschutz operation in Italy. General Karl Wolff, the SS commander for all of Italy, had issued orders that provided Langsdorff with the trucks and gasoline that he needed for the operation. Each theft involved either subterfuge or threat. At least one—the looting of Palazzo Pretorio in the town of Poppi—took place at gunpoint.

Michelangelo, *Bacchus*, 1496–1497.

Typing what had been stolen left Hartt feeling like a father listing the names of his missing children. There were masterpieces by foreign artists acquired by the Medicis hundreds of years earlier: the pioneering Dutch and Flemish painters Rembrandt and Rubens; German masters Dürer and Cranach; and the greatest Spanish painter to ever hold a paintbrush, Diego Velázquez. The Italian artists that Hartt had long studied and dearly loved followed, including Michelangelo, Raphael, Caravaggio, Titian, Botticelli, and Donatello.

Looking over the list of missing masterpieces, Hartt felt sick to his stomach, like he had six months earlier when he realized the

Donatello, *Saint George*, 1417.

peril to Leonardo da Vinci's bomb-damaged masterpiece, *The Last Supper*. But as he quieted his emotions, he started thinking about what the Germans could have stolen but didn't. Two of Leonardo's paintings, the *Annunciation* and the *Adoration of the Magi*, had been left behind along with Michelangelo's *Doni Madonna*, one of only four known paintings by the Florentine master and certainly his most important. While there was no masking the loss to Florence, and to all those who loved art, plenty of masterpieces had survived the German looting operation and were now safe.

Hartt tallied what the Germans had stolen and then resumed typing. "A grand total of 529 paintings, 162 works of sculpture and minor arts, 6 large cartoon drawings, and 38 pieces of medieval and Renaissance textiles have been taken from the public collections of Florence, in all 735 objects." He stumbled for a few minutes trying to find the right words and then they came to him: Florence "had suffered a robbery on a scale to dwarf the depredations of Napoleon."

Writing reports wasn't going to get the Florence treasures back home, though. Waiting for something to happen wasn't an acceptable alternative, either, not for a restless art historian. Determined to act, Hartt ran down his list of the most influential people in Florence. One name came to mind: the archbishop of Florence, Cardinal Elia Dalla Costa. Perhaps he would be willing to use his extensive connections with the Vatican to make inquiries about the whereabouts of the stolen masterpieces.

CHAPTER 8

SEARCHING FOR CLUES

Outside Aachen, Germany: October 1944

Walker Hancock, the award-winning sculptor, appreciated the irony. He'd spent most of his forty-three years as an artist creating beauty. Now, as the Monuments Officer for First Army, he passed each dreadful day watching beauty—entire cities—be destroyed. Aachen was under siege, the first German city to experience the wrath of Allied ground forces. Plumes of dense smoke by day and the glow of fires on the horizon at night served as marker beacons for a battle that still raged after nearly ten days of house-to-house fighting.

First Army's task was to break through Aachen and drive into Germany's industrial heartland, the Ruhr Valley. Since the city was part of the Siegfried Line, the defensive fortifications that protected Germany's western border, Hitler knew that a breach there would quickly be filled with Western Allied forces steamrolling their way to Berlin. Aachen had to hold or Nazi Germany was doomed.

As the wind picked up carrying the first blast of winter chill, Hancock lifted the collar on his field jacket and thought about all that had happened since leaving the comfort of his art studio in the village of Lanesville, Massachusetts. News of the Japanese sneak attack on Pearl Harbor had rearranged his priorities, like it had for so many millions of Americans. The decision to volunteer for U.S. Army Air Forces Intelligence had come easily, but he failed the physical examination and was rejected. Determined to serve, he signed up for Naval Intelligence and passed their physical, only to be drafted by the army and sent to basic training. Hancock considered it a near-perfect lesson in the ways of the military: Sometimes nothing made sense.

Hancock crossed the English Channel on September 26, the last of the group who trained together at Shrivenham to set foot on the European continent. He spent his first night in Paris, in a comfortable apartment with fellow Monuments Man Jim Rorimer. Neither of them slept much as Rorimer passed the hours recounting many of his experiences since landing on Utah Beach six weeks earlier. Hancock listened closely, treating each of Rorimer's stories as a tutorial for Monuments work. "Safeguarding" came up several times in conversation, a word the Nazis regularly used to describe their good deeds removing cultural treasures from war zones. But Jacques Jaujard, Director of the National Museums of France, had counseled Rorimer not to be fooled. "Safeguarding" was nothing more than a Nazi synonym for "theft."

From Paris, Hancock hitched a ride to his first official assignment inspecting monuments near the rear of First Army territory, only to discover that George Stout had already inspected many of the sites. With sun-drenched skies and beautiful countryside, Hancock felt more like a tourist on holiday than a soldier during war, but that began to change after reaching First Army headquarters in Verviers, Belgium, just twenty-five miles from the dark storm clouds of war gathering over Aachen.

The early skirmishes around Aachen had begun in mid-September. Hancock knew that the city had very little military value, but what it lacked in industry it made up for in historical importance. It had been the capital of Charlemagne, the first ruler in nearly three centuries to unite much of Europe. On Christmas Eve in the year 800, Pope Leo III crowned Charlemagne the Holy Roman Emperor. Over the next six hundred years, the Palatine Chapel, part of Aachen Cathedral, served as the coronation hall for more than thirty kings. In Hitler's view, a German city so rich in history and so important in symbolism had to be defended to the death.

A forced evacuation of the city sent all but 20,000 of the 165,000 inhabitants fleeing east. German troops then fought a desperate battle, using every nook and cranny, including the sewer system, to defend the city. The Allies responded with flamethrowers, igniting everything and everyone inside. Allied tanks flattened any target that bombing and long-range artillery had missed. The sturdiness of hundreds-of-years-old stone buildings frustrated U.S. commanders. Aggrieved at the loss of their troops, they wheeled artillery into position and fired point-blank at the defiant walls. Periodically, dazed citizens who had ignored the evacuation notice rushed out of hiding, pushing baby carts and wheelbarrows overflowing with personal belongings. The casualty figures on both sides were horrendous.

Wehrmacht troops surrendered at noon on October 21. The

The gutted streets of Aachen, Germany.

following morning, Hancock and Monuments Man George Stout hitchhiked their way to Aachen in a jeep with war correspondents. On the way into town they passed minefields, defensive fortifications made of concrete pylons, pillboxes outfitted with machine guns, and barbed wire. The city was deathly quiet. The smell of battle still hung in the air. Most street markers were missing. Mangled vehicles, twisted trolley lines, and craters the size of small buses had turned the streets into an obstacle course. Bombs had sheared off entire sides of buildings. Hancock caught a glimpse of one, six stories in height, with the kitchens on each floor exposed to view.

Aware the city had been conquered, German military commanders unleashed a barrage of artillery fire that sent Hancock racing from one doorway to another seeking cover. Inspections would have to wait, Hancock thought. This day was going to be spent just trying to survive. Maneuvering through the city center, Hancock heard a rhythmical but out-of-place sound. Looking over his shoulder he did a double take as a U.S. soldier wearing a Native American headdress atop a horse galloped down the cobblestone street. The whistle of another incoming artillery shell and the near-simultaneous explosion sent him dashing for yet another doorway. He had to laugh at the absurdity of it all, the American Old West meeting medieval Germany, all in the middle of a war zone.

The oldest part of Aachen was a labyrinth of narrow streets that never seemed to meet at right angles, which made it difficult to get a line of sight on his objective, the Palatine Chapel. Suddenly, as the smoke from another round of artillery faded, the chapel appeared, undamaged. Surprisingly, the double doors were wide open. One sprint later, Hancock felt the safety of the chapel's large Byzantine-influenced octagonal space that for centuries had provided peace and refuge for pilgrims and worshippers. The stone construction of Charlemagne's time, now more than eleven hundred years old, felt more like a blast-proof bunker than a chapel. Hancock paused and gave thanks for both.

As his eyes adjusted to the darkness, his other senses compensated. Glass crackled as he stepped on it. The stench of soiled mattresses and blankets strewn on the floor wafted in the stale air. The refugees who had occupied this space had obviously left in a hurry, perhaps when the Allied bomb, which he could see resting beneath one of the vaults of the apse, came crashing down through the ceiling. While the impact of the bomb had demolished the

Inside the battle-damaged Aachen Cathedral.

high altar, it miraculously had not exploded. Providence had looked with favor on the cathedral that day.

A nearby voice startled Hancock, causing him to crouch as he swung around. The figure motioned him forward with one hand; the other held a small lantern. The young man's face didn't appear threatening—more worried than anything else. One by one they climbed a narrow spiral staircase. When they reached the top step, the man turned and introduced himself. "I am Father Erich Stephany, the church vicar." The man trembled constantly. Hancock pitied him. Shelling and confinement indoors had taken a visible toll on his health.

Hancock quickly explained his mission. The Aachen Cathedral, famed for its treasury, contained one of the rarest collections of late-medieval art objects in the world, including a Gothic silver-gilt bust of Charlemagne and the eleventh-century jewel-encrusted processional Cross of Lothair. Hancock wanted to see the treasury objects and confirm that they were safe.

Father Stephany also had a request for Hancock. American GIs had detained six boys, ages fifteen to twenty, all members of the church fire brigade. Together, these boys had successfully extinguished five separate fires caused by incendiary bombs. The church is defenseless without them, the vicar explained. No one else is able to operate the pumps and hose should disaster strike again. They are good boys, the vicar pleaded, who in their adolescent enthusiasm joined the Hitler Youth even though they didn't feel it in their hearts. The vicar asked if Hancock could take civilian clothes to the boys and have them released and brought back to the church. Hancock looked at the vicar and saw a face consumed with worry. Clearly he feared that some GI might mistake the Hitler Youths for Wehrmacht soldiers because of the similarity in uniforms and shoot them.

After writing down the names in his field diary, Hancock promised to do what he could to find the boys. Having responded to the vicar's request, he returned to his own. Where are the objects that belong in the treasury? The vicar said he didn't know; the last time he saw them, German soldiers had packed the most important

Bust of Charlemagne, 14th century.

Cross of Lothair, 11th century.

Fire Guard for Cathedral

		approximate age
Hans	Dürnholz	20
Helmut	Jansen	17
Georg	Stockem	17
Nikolaus	Geurten	17
Karl	Pirotti	19
Willi	Minartz	15

Monuments Man Captain Walker Hancock's list of the fire brigade boys.

items, including the two Hancock had specifically asked about—the Bust of Charlemagne and the Cross of Lothair—and taken them deeper into Germany.

Paris, France: late November 1944

Three days after Thanksgiving, Jim Rorimer crossed the sixteenth-century Tuileries Garden. With the war now on Germany's doorstep, more than 150 miles away from Paris, some semblance of normal life had returned with people strolling through the gardens enjoying a brisk November afternoon. Rorimer smiled. Just two months earlier, he'd prevented the army from converting the Jeu de Paume Museum into a post office. That turned out to be relatively easy. Then he'd managed to get the army to remove hundreds of jeeps, troop carriers, and ten-ton trucks from the historic garden. That had proved the greater challenge.

Seeing the citizens of Paris resume some semblance of normal life following four years of Nazi occupation and knowing he had played a part left Rorimer feeling good, but now he feared progress had stalled. The urgency in the Parisian air during those initial weeks of liberation had faded. French bureaucracy mixed with army regulations slowed everything down even further, adding to his frustration.

As he neared the Louvre Museum, Rorimer zeroed in on what was bothering him the most. If Jacques Jaujard was correct, and more than twenty thousand works of art had indeed been stolen from French private collectors and dealers, where was the paper trail? Where were the leads? After weeks of digging, he had found only dead ends. Someone knew something, but clearly he hadn't identified who that "someone" was, not yet at least. Parisians just wanted to put the horrible memories of occupation behind them and move on with their lives. That greatly impeded his efforts.

The scene inside the Louvre looked very different than it had when Rorimer first visited in late August. Visitors! Noise! Paintings hanging on the walls! Rorimer paused to take it all in and smiled. The Louvre had reopened several weeks earlier, but Rorimer thought only of the twenty thousand works of art still missing— and the fact that he had no leads to pursue.

He arrived in Jaujard's office as a friend in need. When Rorimer began to ask for information, the director rose from his desk, went to his office door, and shut it. Jaujard intended for this to be a private conversation between two trusted friends and colleagues who shared a common objective. Rorimer began by expressing his frustration, almost disbelief, about the lack of leads, especially given the size of the theft. He knew that the French museum establishment had formed the Commission for the Recovery of Works of Art to address this problem, but that was two months ago, at the end of September. As far as Rorimer knew, the commission hadn't made much progress.

Jaujard, seeing an opportunity, looked at his friend and said just two words: Rose Valland. Sensing confusion, Jaujard reminded him that he'd met Valland in passing during one of his previous visits to the director's office. Rorimer apologized; he hadn't really paid her much attention. Jaujard smiled: neither had the Germans.

As Rorimer leaned forward in his chair, Jaujard opened up with details and descriptions that sent the Monuments Man hurriedly flipping through his notepad to find a blank page. He wanted to take down every detail.

Soon after occupation, the Einsatzstab Reichsleiter Rosenberg, or ERR, the Nazi looting organization dedicated to the confiscation of Jewish-owned property, converted the Jeu de Paume Museum into its looting operation headquarters. The museum's central location and proximity to the Louvre made it the ideal clearinghouse for thousands of works of art that the Nazis were stealing from Jews and other private collectors. They informed Jaujard that they needed one person familiar with the facility who could keep the building operational. He had asked Mademoiselle Valland, the custodian and, for all practical purposes, the curator of the museum, to remain at her position to assist the Germans—and to spy for him.

Hearing the word "spy" stunned Rorimer. He knew that Jaujard had performed heroically to save the national museum collections from the Nazis, but the risks he must have taken, not to mention those of his spy, Rose Valland, exceeded anything he had imagined.

The risks were quite real, Jaujard acknowledged, but the opportunity to have someone trusted inside the Nazi looting headquarters, someone who also understood German, was too great to ignore. In October 1940, shortly after the Nazis took control of the Jeu de Paume, Jaujard had taken Valland aside and ordered her to remain at her post, "no matter what." She accepted this new responsibility without hesitation; in fact, she considered it an honor to have been asked. Take my word on this, Jaujard implored his friend: Valland's commitment to saving the art of France should be questioned by no one.

While Jaujard described the forty-six-year-old Valland, Rorimer furiously scribbled down bullet points of his comments. "Middle-age; simplicity in her manners; self-reliant [sic]; independent; strong willed manner; indefatigable; never complained about her own personal grievances or discomforts."

All this information fascinated Rorimer, but his characteristic impatience got the better of him. With a heavy tone of skepticism in his voice, he asked Jaujard why, if Valland had all this information, had she not turned it over to the French commission? And why was Jaujard being so forthcoming with an American? Both were good questions, Jaujard said. Valland *had* turned over to the commission important lists of locations used by Nazi officials and warehouses where they had stored stolen objects in Paris until

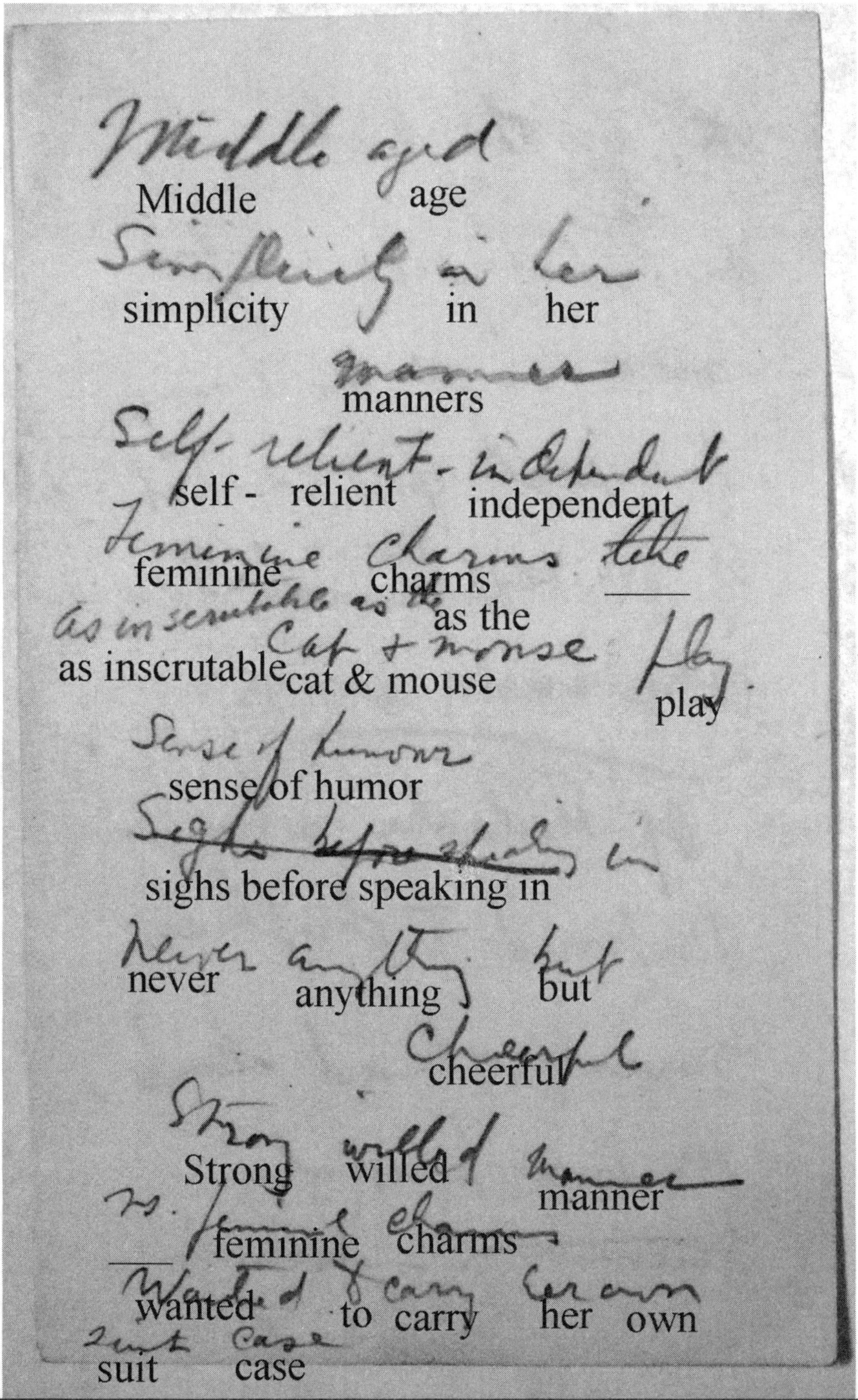

Middle age
simplicity in her
manners
self - relient independent
feminine charms ____
as the
as inscrutable cat & mouse
play
sense of humor
sighs before speaking in
never anything but
cheerful
Strong willed
manner
____ feminine charms
wanted to carry her own
suit case

Rorimer's notes about Rose Valland. [Please note: The typed annotations have been added by the author.]

shipment to Germany. But of course the Nazi officials, like the stolen objects, were no longer there. However, Valland had not provided other essential information to the commission about where the objects might be now. Jaujard acknowledged that Albert Henraux, head of the French commission, had asked him to encourage Rorimer to speak with Valland. Perhaps by getting to know her he could earn her trust and find out more details about what she knew.

Rorimer wanted to know why this woman, a complete stranger, would trust *him*, when she wouldn't trust her own countrymen on the commission? He also had another concern: Suppose she didn't really have what Jaujard thought she had. Maybe her information, if any, was worthless. The wily museum director reasoned that Valland would trust Rorimer precisely because he was *not* French. The problem of collaboration with the Nazis did not end with their departure. One of the city's newspapers, *Le Figaro*, printed a daily feature titled "Les arrestations et l'épuration" (Arrests and purges) that detailed the previous day's developments in the pursuit of collaborators. Beneath the article appeared two lists: *les exécutions capitales* (death sentences) and *les exécutions sommaires* (summary executions). Not certain who could be trusted, Valland was reluctant to turn over all of her information to the French commission, or anyone else. Seen in that light, her hesitation made sense to Rorimer.

It is true, Jaujard continued, that many people do not believe that Valland has any information of substance. He knew otherwise. She had confided some of it to him; much she had not, though, and he agreed with her decision because even he could not guarantee that her information would remain confidential. Rorimer, it seemed, was in the best position to gain access to the valuable information gathered by Rose Valland and use it to find France's stolen treasures.

Jaujard, seeing that his friend didn't appear entirely convinced, reminded him that when the U.S. Army had wanted to convert the Jeu de Paume Museum into a post office, it was Rorimer who had taken action to prevent it. Valland was never one to say much, but she didn't miss anything. In her mind, Rorimer had saved "her" museum from suffering through yet another occupation. That had made quite an impression on her, and indeed on everyone in the Paris museum community.

At that moment Rorimer's head was spinning with thoughts, doubts, possibilities. Suppose Jaujard was right? Valland certainly was in a position to have gathered critical information. Somehow she had managed to avoid being caught or killed. And if she did have lists of what was stolen and where it was . . . twenty thousand works of art? There really wasn't anything to think about. If Jaujard or others on the French commission would help with another introduction, he would of course be pleased to meet with her.

CHAPTER 9

GETTING HELP

Florence, Italy: November 1944

Throughout a wet Tuscan fall, Fred Hartt continued salvaging all he could of his beloved Florence. Nearly every building in the city center needed terra-cotta roof tiles at a time when torrential rains created a new threat to the city's cultural heritage. Each day brought progress, but Hartt felt frustrated that it was always measured in increments, not giant leaps. The same was true for the boys up in the mountains north of Florence, who were fighting relentless rain and boot-sucking mud as much as they were the German defenders they often could not see. Although preoccupied with his work addressing problems in the city, Hartt never stopped thinking about the 735 missing Florentine masterpieces. In mid-November, he received news that sent his spirits soaring.

Two months had passed since he and Giovanni Poggi, Superintendent of Florentine Galleries, had met with Archbishop of Florence Cardinal Elia Dalla Costa to seek the Vatican's assistance in locating the works stolen by German troops. Hartt had hoped for a quick reply, but with the passing of days, then weeks, he assumed that Vatican officials had decided not to use their extensive network of contacts to pursue the matter. A phone call from Poggi rekindled his hopes. The archbishop had finally received a reply from the Vatican.

Hartt nearly burst with excitement. If Vatican officials knew nothing, they probably wouldn't have wasted time writing a letter, or responding at all. They must know something! He wanted Poggi to blurt it out, and he did. According to the Vatican secretariat of state, "the works of art were stored in the [Alto] Adige, in a place called 'Neumelans in Sand.'" Finally, a name! A place!

Hartt quickly grabbed a map of northern Italy. The Alto Adige region, a mountainous German-speaking portion of Italy that shared borders with Switzerland and Austria, was a perfect hiding spot. At a moment's notice the works could be spirited across the Italian border into Nazi-controlled Austria. But despite his best effort, Hartt couldn't find "Neumelans in Sand" on the map, or in any Italian guidebook, which meant the Monuments Men were right back where they had started.

Five days later Hartt received new information from an Italian freedom fighter. At the end of July, two German trucks loaded with the stolen works of art taken from Florence arrived at a villa near the town of Modena. Wehrmacht troops offloaded many of the paintings and used them to decorate the villa for a large party that German military officials had hosted in early August. Mid-month, they reloaded their war booty back onto the trucks and headed north, destination unknown.

Hartt's emotions were a roller coaster of news: one minute hopeful that someone would at least confirm the works were safe, regardless of where they were located, the next dejected at not knowing anything. He slept only slightly better on December 9, when Nazi-sympathetic Italian officials announced that they had been allowed to inspect the works of art. But for slight damage, the works of art were safe. They made no mention of where the stolen art was hidden. For all Hartt knew, it might very well be in Nazi Germany.

With the Allied armies digging in for winter, mired in the central mountains hundreds of miles from northern Italy, there wasn't much Hartt could do about it anyway. Finding the Florentine treasures, to Hartt's great frustration, would have to wait until spring, when offensive operations resumed.

Brussels, Belgium: November 1944

The British Monuments Man for First Canadian Army, Ronald Balfour, spent much of October and November at various harbors along the Belgian coast searching for clues about the whereabouts of Michelangelo's masterpiece the Bruges *Madonna*. The concentration of Allied troops on the ground and Allied superiority in the sky would have made an overland route far too risky. The sailors who stole the priceless sculpture and paintings at gunpoint must have loaded it onto a ship that then steamed through the North Sea to reach Germany. If the ship hadn't departed from a Belgian port, it must have sailed from one in the Netherlands.

Balfour never made it, though. On November 29, disaster struck when his vehicle crashed. He suffered a broken ankle and other cuts and bruises. Doctors at the hospital in Eindhoven insisted that he be sent back to England for care, but he refused. He would be of no use to the MFAA there, so he finagled a transfer to a Brussels hospital instead. Being hospital-bound meant suspending his search for the Bruges *Madonna*, but it didn't prevent the search from continuing. Each day for three weeks, British Captain George Willmot, a recent addition to the expanding group of Monuments Officers, stopped by the hospital to see Balfour, not as a visitor, but as a student.

Working from his bed, Balfour shared his field experiences with Willmot, including details about the theft of the Bruges *Madonna*. On that last day, he reached into his field pack, rummaged around for a few seconds, pulled out one of the postcards given to him by Reverend Deschepper at the church in Bruges, and handed it to Willmot—just in case the newcomer needed it.

Aachen, Germany: November 1944

In late October, Monuments Men Walker Hancock and George Stout began their search for the six boys in the fire brigade in Brand, a suburb of Aachen. Walking door-to-door making inquiries seemed fruitless until an old woman pointed to a nearby home. Hancock pulled the list of names out of his pocket as he approached the residence, then knocked on the door and asked to see Helmut Jansen. After a bit of commotion, a frightened but composed boy came to the door. Hancock thought he looked about seventeen years old. One by one the other boys appeared.

Hancock introduced himself and told the boys that they were needed in Aachen to resume their work protecting the cathedral. With that, he handed them the civilian clothes Father Stephany had provided and told them to change. The local combat commander who had accompanied the two Monuments Officers watched in disbelief. "Well, I'll be damned," he said to himself as much as to Hancock and Stout. "Here they are, at least safe, and when you tell them they can go back into that hell-hole they act as if you'd given 'em a thousand dollars apiece. I can't figure it out." But the two Monuments Men understood perfectly well. The cathedral, Aachen's most important monument, had defined the city since its construction. It hadn't survived centuries of war and turmoil by accident. The fire brigade boys proudly continued the tradition of preserving it for future generations, even at the risk of their lives. In fact, they considered it an honor.

In early November, a new threat emerged that Stout believed would marginalize his skills and disrupt the MFAA at a time when it was gaining traction. Some army planner had issued new orders transferring him out of First Army to a new position with army groups fighting in the Netherlands. In the four months since arriving in France, Stout had survived bombs and booby traps. He wasn't about to succumb to the army's bureaucracy.

Stout didn't complain; he never complained. Instead, he immediately went to work using army regulations to press his case. He formally requested reconsideration of the order. The response came back quickly: request denied on grounds he was specifically qualified for the assignment. Stout agreed that he was qualified, but he believed that his present assignment with First Army in Germany, where most of the stolen objects would likely be found, was the optimal use of his skills.

First Army's Acting Chief of Staff for Civil Affairs concurred and forwarded Stout's request up the chain of command all the way to General Omar Bradley's headquarters at Twelfth Army

Group. On November 6, Stout received new orders containing another surprise. The previous orders transferring him to the Netherlands mission were rescinded; Stout would now be the emergency inspector for Twelfth Army Group (which included First, Third, Ninth, and Fifteenth Armies). Monuments Officers assigned to these armies would be in the lead with the combat troops, identifying situations needing special attention, including, everyone anticipated, discoveries of stolen works of art. Stout would be the man "on call," like a trauma doctor ready to respond to emergencies.

Despite the distraction caused by the series of orders, Stout continued his inspections. He also made a day-trip to Paris, where local authorities discussed information indicating that much of what had been stolen from France had been shipped to southern Germany. Stout found this only mildly helpful. Southern Germany covered a vast amount of territory with extensive mountainous areas. What he and the other Monuments Men needed were detailed leads, captured German documents, and luck if they were to find the loot.

On November 18, Stout met Hancock in Aachen, still under bombardment by German artillery, to resume their search for treasures missing from the city's major art museum. The battle for Aachen had been waged from the air, in the streets, and from room to room. Every building had some battle scar. While the facade of the Suermondt Museum building had suffered minor damage, the interior spaces had been trashed. Shattered glass and debris littered the floors. Soldiers, or perhaps displaced persons, had rifled through the museum records. The place was a wreck.

Sifting through the records looking for clues was painstaking work, even for a sculptor and artist like Hancock who measured progress over months and years. Too little light and too much dust forced him to use his flashlight, but reading documents through the floating silvery particles illuminated by the beam strained his eyes. He coughed constantly. Then came a breakthrough.

Hancock found a list of schools and courthouses where the Suermondt's less valuable holdings had been stored for safety. Further digging led to a copy of the official museum catalogue. A note on the cover explained that objects marked in red had been moved a second time for safety to Siegen, a town about 110 miles east of Aachen. Hancock quickly unfolded his map while pondering a new problem. Somewhere in the town of Siegen, 104 paintings and 48 pieces of sculpture—and who knew what else—belonging to the Suermondt Museum in Aachen lay in hiding, but where? And when would U.S. troops force a German retreat sufficient to allow the Monuments Men to enter Siegen?

Hancock felt certain about one thing: If the ferocity of the battle for Aachen was indicative of the fight ahead, any art repository in Siegen might not survive, even if they could find it. But at last, their detective work had paid a dividend. The Monuments Men had a name, a target: Siegen, Germany.

Near Aachen, Germany: early December 1944

Captain Walter Huchthausen, one of two new additions to the Monuments Men, reported for duty to Ninth Army in early December. Army bureaucracy was only partly to blame for the six-month delay in getting him into service. In mid-June 1944, just

Monuments Man Captain Walter Huchthausen.

days after arriving in London, Huchthausen was seriously injured during a V-1 rocket attack, German retaliation for the successful D-Day landings at Normandy. Even while recuperating, he worked each day preparing a glossary of commonly used German terms for English-speaking soldiers.

Having studied in prewar Germany, Huchthausen knew the country and the language, both valuable attributes for the challenges ahead. His experience as an architect was an essential skill to aid in the salvation of damaged but repairable buildings, especially as the amount of enemy territory under Allied control increased. The Monuments Men who had met with him—Rorimer over dinner in Paris, Stout during a field inspection, and Hancock when First Army turned over responsibility for Aachen to Ninth

Army—all liked this handsome, boyish-looking thirty-nine-year-old architect. To the man, they considered Huchthausen a great addition to their small army, with just one caveat. Everyone had a difficult time pronouncing "HUCK-towzen" correctly, so they immediately gave him the nickname "Hutch."

Even in the early weeks of his first assignment in Aachen, Hutch demonstrated the kind of initiative that earned the respect of his more experienced peers by converting the Suermondt Museum into a safe house for works of art being found in dozens of locations in and around the city. Hancock couldn't figure out if Hutch's popularity with soldiers or some magical touch was responsible for his ability to procure transportation, but it was certainly a skill that he admired.

Near Nancy, France: December 1944

In December, after six months of waiting in London, Lincoln Kirstein, another new recruit to the Monuments Men, finally arrived in Europe, none too happy about all the delays. Most of the Monuments Men knew Kirstein, a towering figure in the arts. He'd authored six books; cofounded the American Ballet Company, Harvard Society for Contemporary Art, and *Hound & Horn* literary magazine; and been a successful art critic, all before his thirty-seventh birthday. Simply put, Kirstein was a polymath, exceptionally gifted in multiple fields.

George Stout had instructed Kirstein when he was a graduate student at Harvard. Jim Rorimer, the hard-charging curator, had befriended him when they both lived and worked in New York City. In Germany, Kirstein was just another soldier in uniform, at

Monuments Man Private First Class Lincoln Kirstein.

least to Robert Posey. Like any new soldier, he would have to prove himself.

As Posey looked over the new man's résumé and thought about what he'd heard others say about Kirstein, he realized just how different they both were, an odd-couple pairing extraordinaire. Posey loved being a soldier and understood life in the military; Kirstein found the experience dreadful. Posey knew the rules and followed them; Kirstein preferred to write his own. Posey approached problems logically; Kirstein trusted his instinct and liked to improvise. Posey tended to be stable in demeanor; Kirstein was manic-depressive.

The Posey family had been so poor that Robert's mother gave his sister to an aunt after his father died because there wasn't enough food for three children. Kirstein, the son of a wealthy self-made businessman, never experienced poverty. Posey knew a lot about architecture, but not a great deal about works of art, and it was at that moment that he realized why someone, probably Stout, had paired the two of them. Kirstein knew a lot about everything, including art and architecture. No wonder Stout, Rorimer, and other Monuments Officers had pleaded with the Roberts Commission and the army to get Kirstein into the MFAA.

One other distinction couldn't be missed. Every Monuments Man in northern Europe served as an officer but one, Lincoln Kirstein, who held one of the lowest ranks in the army, private first class. Some arcane army rule prohibited privates from serving in the MFAA. Only repeated pleadings by the Roberts Commission resulted in the army relenting and making this exception.

Kirstein wouldn't officially begin his position until January. Until then, Posey had plenty of reports to write, including an update on the Ghent Altarpiece. That's a laugh, he thought. With no leads of any sort, that particular report will be a blank page. Posey also had letters to write, especially with Christmas fast approaching. A rather large package from home, marked "with love from your family," had arrived a few weeks earlier. He'd wanted to save it for Christmas Day, but on December 16, a mixture of excitement, curiosity, and loneliness prevailed.

Alice had really packed this box well, far better than all the others, he noticed, which forced him to slow down and savor the moment. There seemed no end to the material she used. Finally he reached something firm—a package within a package—that he pulled out of the box. Snuggly taped between two protective layers of cardboard he found a phonograph record. The absence of a note made him even more curious. With his helmet in one hand and the record in the other, he dashed out of his tent to Special Services, where a sergeant manning the radios motioned Posey into an adjacent room while he put the disc on the record player.

After an agonizingly slow few moments, he heard something, not music, but a voice—one absent from his life for more than a year—emerge from the nearby speaker. Alice spoke first, prompting Woogie to "say anything you want." As Posey thought about it, speaking into a microphone to your dad when you can't see him must have been a weird experience for a seven-year-old boy. Then came his son's voice, and Christmas greetings, and more comments from them both, followed by a song. During war, surprises were rarely welcomed. Posey considered this an extraordinary exception, a single moment that would sustain him as long as necessary and serve as a lifelong reminder of the importance of family.

That evening, still basking in the glow of the Christmas greeting from his family, Posey heard a radio report about a new German offensive in the Ardennes Forest. U.S. troops had tried to absorb the blow but were falling back. First reports were often suspect, so Posey decided to hang around Special Services to find out more.

CHAPTER 10

LONGINGS

Paris, France: Christmastime 1944

Blowing wind mixed with record low temperatures did nothing to dampen Jim Rorimer's enthusiasm. Jacques Jaujard had wanted him to meet with Rose Valland. Now, just a few days before Christmas, this matronly-looking woman wearing small wire-rimmed glasses was standing next to him, chain-smoking, while they shivered outside waiting for the manager of the Warehouse for Enemy Property to arrive with the keys.

The process of earning Valland's trust began six days earlier with Rorimer's discovery of several paintings and engravings inside a U.S. military facility. Following protocol, he promptly delivered them to the Jeu de Paume Museum, now the headquarters of the French Commission for the Recovery of Works of Art, and its secretary, Rose Valland. The artworks weren't terribly important, but the act of turning them over to the commission surprised Valland. "Thank you," she had told him. "Too often, your fellow liberators give us the painful impression they have landed in a country whose inhabitants no longer matter."

Being at the Jeu de Paume Museum that day provided Rorimer with a chance to visit with the leader of the commission, Albert Henraux, who, like Jaujard, suggested Rorimer and Valland cooperate to find France's stolen treasures. But Henraux had gone one step further, handing Rorimer a list containing the addresses of nine buildings in Paris, mostly apartments and one warehouse, used by the ERR. After scanning the list, Rorimer wondered aloud who had compiled the information. Henraux smiled: "Mademoiselle Valland, of course." Henraux then nudged the persistent curator, suggesting that he enlist the help of Valland to inspect each address.

Rorimer and Valland visited six of the nine locations several days later. Their search produced little, but the time they spent together proved invaluable. Over coffee between stops at the ERR apartments, Valland gradually revealed some of what she had seen during her four years as Jaujard's spy. Rorimer soon had no doubt that Jaujard and Henraux's suspicions were true. Rose Valland *did* know much more than she had told the commission.

It all made sense. Every day for four years, Valland had entered the den of thieves, observed their operation, and compiled secret notes about the day's activities. With German soldiers watching her by day and the Gestapo trailing her at night, she somehow avoided being caught. It was hardly surprising that she guarded her notes so closely. More than just pieces of paper, they defined her life.

Since arriving in Paris, Rorimer had gathered every piece of information he could about the Nazi looting operation. Although the ERR took its name from Nazi Party ideologue Alfred Rosenberg, it was Nazi Reichsmarschall Hermann Göring, the second-most powerful man in all of Germany, who quickly commandeered the operation. ERR operatives served as dealmakers loyal to him and his burgeoning art collection. Now Rorimer had an opportunity to hear from the only person who could describe these events as they had happened. Rose Valland had much to say.

Within months of the invasion of France in May 1940, the Nazis had converted the Jeu de Paume Museum into a concentration camp for works of art. "The atmosphere around me changed immediately with the arrival of the German trucks loaded with stolen works of art," Valland explained to Rorimer.

> *The rooms and offices were immediately occupied. The Luftwaffe soldiers carried in the crates that they had been escorting . . . The unpacking started the next morning. Paintings by Old Masters were passed from hand to hand until the human chain ended at a support wall. Some of them were dropped and ended up underneath the boots, but the order was to proceed as quickly as possible.*

The sheer volume of paintings, sculpture, drawings, and furniture that passed through the doors of the museum was one thing; the quality of it was different. Valland, with her nearly photographic memory, made mental lists of incoming masterpieces by some of the most famous Old Master painters, including Vermeer, Raphael, and Velázquez. Hours later, German troops would barge through the door with another group of priceless paintings by the most revered Impressionist artists, such as Monet, Renoir, and Degas. Although Hitler had declared works by the Impressionists "degenerate," they might still prove valuable in trades. With her teeth gritted in anger, she watched Nazi officials mishandle these degenerate works and place them in a rear area of the museum, a room Valland referred to as the "room of martyrs."

After a long drag on a cigarette, Valland looked at Rorimer and summed up the scale of the problem. "France and its art world represented for the Nazi leaders a vast and inexhaustible hunting reserve, jealously guarded and managed." When Rorimer mentioned that Jaujard had estimated, during one of their visits, that the Nazi looters stole more than twenty thousand works of art from private collectors in France, Valland responded with a wry smile. They took far more than twenty thousand objects, she said. France was powerless to stop them from taking all that they wanted. What more could the French have done? What could anyone have done when the Nazis issued decrees stripping French Jews of their right to own private property? How do you protect private collections from the greed of Reichsmarschall Göring, who is willing to use his position and influence to do anything to add to his personal art collection? *C'était une situation impossible.* Rorimer agreed; it was an impossible situation.

Each time Bruno Lohse, one of Göring's art buyers; Hermann Bunjes, a corrupt Kunstschutz official; and Colonel Kurt von Behr, commandant of the Jeu de Paume and local leader of the ERR, appeared at the museum, a flurry of activity quickly followed. They began by displaying the most recent arrivals—paintings, furniture, and tapestries that had been seized from Jewish collectors. Chilled champagne and hand-rolled cigars were at the ready. A period of calm followed. Everyone waited.

The sound of car tires crushing gravel, the squeal of brakes, car doors opening and closing, and the echo of heavy boots confirmed

Göring's arrival. While his Luftwaffe was flying nightly bombing missions over London, trying to knock Britain out of the war, Göring decided to add to his art collection. The scene was repeated with slight variation on each of his subsequent nineteen visits. Rorimer shook his head in disbelief. Twenty visits by the master thief, and Rose Valland had been there to witness each one of them.

Göring would slowly approach each work of art with the arrogance of an emperor, sometimes jingling loose emeralds in his pocket as normal people do coins, speaking in hushed tones to his group. Occasionally a painting or piece of furniture was so famous, such as Vermeer's masterpiece *The Astronomer*—assigned the ERR inventory code "R-1," the first object stolen from the Rothschild collection—that Göring had no choice but to reserve it for Hitler and the Führermuseum. The next best he took for himself. Once he made his choices, the items were crated, packed on trucks, and driven to his personal train to accompany him back to the Fatherland.

A final spasm of looting occurred in August 1944, during the final days of Nazi occupation, with the loading of 148 cases of stolen art onto 5 railway boxcars. Each day, the departure of the art train was postponed because of delays in loading 46 other boxcars filled with furniture and personal belongings stolen from the homes of Paris's Jews as part of a separate looting project known as M-Aktion. As the Allies approached Paris, Valland secretly met with Jaujard. With the train number, destination of the art crates, and their contents all in hand, she pleaded with Jaujard for French Resistance fighters to sabotage the train engines, or simply reroute

Nazi Reichsmarschall Göring examines a painting.

Johannes Vermeer, *The Astronomer*, 1668.

Göring admires two stolen paintings by Henri Matisse during one of his visits to the Jeu de Paume. Bruno Lohse, one of the Reichsmarschall's art buyers, is holding the paintings.

it. The Resistance did their job well. Train number 40044 and its contents remained trapped in Paris.

The 5 boxcars containing the 148 crates of art were unloaded and taken to the Louvre and the Jeu de Paume museums. But the contents of the other 46 boxcars, eventually offloaded and stored at the Warehouse for Enemy Property, went largely ignored. Now Rorimer and Valland had come to inspect it.

After a brief introduction, the manager invited them inside the warehouse. Within the cavernous space, wooden crates, one stacked upon another, towered forty feet into the air, as far as they could see. Uncrated chairs and tables rested on top, taken in such haste that the thieves hadn't had time to pack them. As they walked

Inside the Warehouse for Enemy Property, Paris.

through the warehouse, they saw pianos, radiators, mirrors, pots, pans, children's toys—even ladies' nightgowns—all that remained of Paris's once-vibrant Jewish community.

Rorimer felt gut-punched. The Nazi theft of priceless works of art had involved stealing from the rich, for the most part. This discovery evidenced quite the opposite; petty thievery of personal belongings on an industrial scale, priceless in their intrinsic value, looted from thousands of France's most vulnerable citizens. But the sick feeling in the pit of his stomach went deeper than just his role as a Monuments Officer. Decades earlier, his father had changed the spelling of the family name from "Rorheimer" because of his concerns about anti-Semitism in American life. Like the people whose possessions were stacked in rows before him, Jim Rorimer was also a Jew.

The warehouse was a likely place to find at least a few of the works of art stolen from France. Finding none, Rorimer felt disappointed. He struggled to make sense of not finding anything. Valland's lack of surprise convinced him that she'd known all along what was inside the warehouse—and what was not. Then another realization hit him: While he had been inspecting the nine apartments and one warehouse, Valland had been inspecting and watching him. What was this cat-and-mouse game she seemed to be playing?

As they exited the building, Rorimer decided to press Valland for specific information about where the Nazis had taken the art masterpieces, even as she quietly walked ahead of him. When she didn't respond, he asked again, this time with an edge to his voice that caused her to stop. Slowly she turned, faced him, and curtly said, "I'll tell you where, when the time is right."

Near Metz, France: Christmastime 1944

It didn't take long for Robert Posey, and everyone else who heard that first radio report, to realize that the German incursion into the Ardennes Forest was a major offensive. The attack succeeded in catching General Eisenhower and his commanders by surprise. Hitler had gambled that his troops could split two of Eisenhower's armies and mount a lightning-fast charge to the Belgian port of Antwerp, a crucial source of supplies for U.S. and British forces. Horrific fighting in the harshest possible winter conditions created mounting losses and a need for additional forces and replacement troops. Robert Posey immediately volunteered. His instructions were simple: "Keep firing until you can't fire anymore." And that's exactly what he did, right up until the time he stepped in a snow-covered hole and broke the arches on both of his feet.

Liège, Belgium: Christmastime 1944

Walker Hancock spent Christmas Day in Liège, Belgium, trying to enjoy a bath. War respected no holidays though. When a nearby explosion shook the building, he leapt out of the hot water, got dressed in record time, and hurried toward the bomb shelter, but by then the attack had ended. Dressed for the day, he decided to attend Mass in Saint Paul's Cathedral. Another bomb attack cut the service short. He did manage to get a haircut without interruption and catch a quick meal before heading to the bomb shelter to try and sleep. Despite the danger and disruptions, Hancock knew he had it far better than the boys on the front line, trying to find safety from German bullets, and winter weather just as lethal, in some shallow, rock-hard foxhole.

As he shifted back and forth trying to get comfortable on the cold, hard floor, Hancock's thoughts drifted to his wife, Saima, as they did every night. It seemed impossible to believe that they had been apart for more than eleven months, especially after twenty years of friendship. Then he thought about the Polish soldier bunked next to him days earlier. That poor fellow hadn't seen his family for *six* Christmases. "He's discouraged," Hancock had written Saima, "but we are guaranteeing him this will be the last away from home." Hancock hoped that would prove true, but who knew?

Florence, Italy: Christmastime 1944

After more than fifteen months away from home, Deane Keller needed a friend. While standing in line for mail in Florence, he found one. T/5 Charley Bernholz had just completed an assignment as driver for a senior officer relieved of duty. Keller liked his easygoing manner and considered his experience driving on Italian roads an asset. Within days, he arranged for Bernholz to become his driver.

Bernholz had another quality that Keller admired: He was a quiet hero, one of the boys. Before becoming a Monuments Man, Bernholz had pulled a severely wounded soldier from a burning truck filled with ammunition. He could have called it quits after dragging the man to safety. Instead, he went back to the truck again to check for other survivors. It was all there in his personnel file, along with a copy of his Bronze Star citation signed by Lieutenant General Mark Clark.

As Christmas neared, Keller and Bernholz used their jeep to

Deane Keller and his friend and driver, T/5 Charley Bernholz.

transport the poor children of Florence and their parents to the Allied Forces Christmas program. Each trip pulled at Keller's heartstrings; each little boy reminded him of Dino. But the program provided a temporary escape from the hardships of war for the people of Florence and the soldiers helping to rebuild the city, and for that he was grateful.

Reading in *Stars and Stripes*, the American military newspaper, about the tough fight the boys were having in the Ardennes Forest tempered any holiday celebration. Keller tried to compensate for his second Christmas away from Kathy and Dino by drawing scenes of Santa Claus delivering gifts and Dino, his face alight, opening them on Christmas morning. Somehow, seeing an image of Dino holding an oversized present made him feel a bit closer to home, even if it was a sketch of a make-believe scene that he had drawn.

On Christmas Day, Keller sat down to write Kathy and their son. He spent a while searching for the right words. Allaying her concern about his safety was always at the top of the list, especially with the news of the Ardennes Offensive filling the headlines. Censors limited what he could say about his work. A thought crossed his mind, one that seemed just right, and he began to write:

> *Today is Christmas and my first thoughts are with you*
> *and Deane . . . As I write the roar of tanks and heavy*
> *vehicles is in the air . . . Some boys will eat a turkey leg*
> *in a pup tent or in a foxhole. Some will die this day . . .*
> *Downstairs the radio has just come on and someone is*
> *singing a Carol . . . This is my Christmas—a big one*
> *filled with the highest ideals man is capable of . . .*

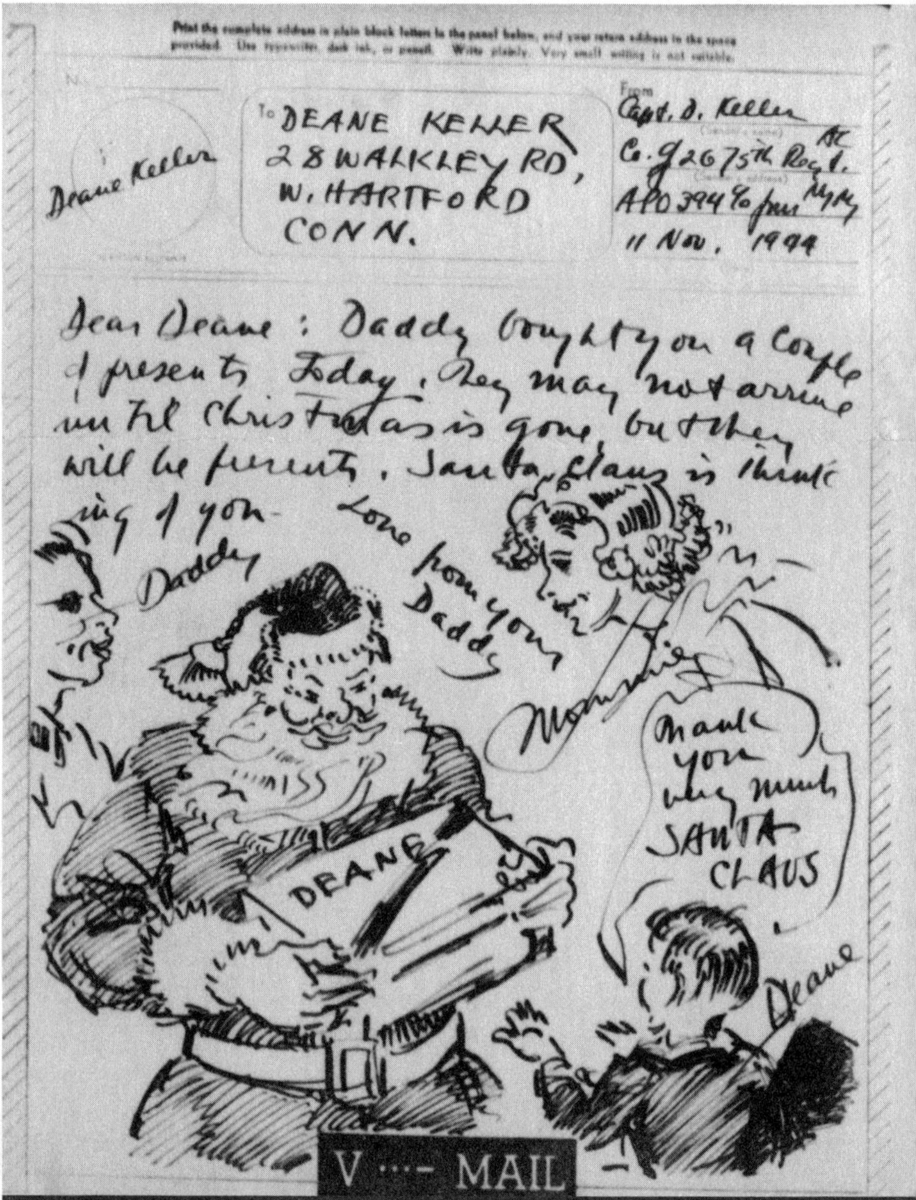

One of many Christmas drawings Keller sent to his son.

HAVE YOU FILLED IN COMPLETE ADDRESS AT TOP?

REPLY BY
V----MAIL

HAVE YOU FILLED IN COMPLETE ADDRESS AT TOP?

CHAPTER 11

SMALL VICTORIES

Near Givet, France: January 1945

By the end of January, the fight in the Ardennes Forest, dubbed the "Battle of the Bulge," had ended. Hitler had gambled that in one bold move he could force the Western Allies out of the war. If only he could blast through the Allied line and then get behind them, he would surround enough of Eisenhower's forces to convince American and British leaders to negotiate a peace. If he could do that, it would free his hands in Western Europe and allow him to concentrate on the Soviets in the east.

German forces did push a large bulge in the front line, but Western Allied forces quickly recovered, ending Nazi Germany's offensive capability. The cost was horrifying. Almost twenty thousand American boys lay dead; perhaps as many as eighty thousand were wounded or missing. Casualties meant the fighting armies needed replacements, and that's where nineteen-year-old Private Harry Ettlinger and twenty-five hundred other American soldiers were headed.

The trucks filled with replacement troops provided no real protection from the record cold temperatures. Only the bodily warmth of twenty-five soldiers crammed shoulder to shoulder inside each of the one hundred trucks made any difference, and even then, it was slight. But the bitter weather concerned Harry far less than figuring out how to stay alive. Soon they would be in battle on German soil, where the speed of the previous month's advances had ground to a crawl and every yard gained would cost some Allied soldier his life. Harry had been born in Germany, but he certainly didn't want to die there.

For centuries, Ettlingers had lived in the town of Karlsruhe, in southwest Germany. In fact, their last name derived from the nearby town of Ettlingen, where Harry's ancestors had been born. Harry grew up in a prominent family of retail and wholesale merchants who had built successful businesses despite anti-Semitic laws that prevented Jews from owning farmland and barred them from trade guilds.

Harry didn't see himself as being different from other boys until he was banned from the local sports association in 1933, the year Adolf Hitler rose to power as chancellor of Germany. Even then, the politics of hate and intolerance didn't mean much to a seven-year-old boy. But that changed two years later, at the start of fifth grade, when Harry's grades dropped precipitously. One of only two Jews in his class of forty-five students, Harry had been forced to sit in the back of the classroom, not because of some new regulation, but due to the prejudice of his teachers.

In 1937, a nationwide boycott of Jewish-owned enterprises, which had started four years earlier, finally forced the Ettlinger family business into bankruptcy. Harry didn't understand a lot about business, but he certainly remembered the time he had a bicycle accident and reached the hospital only to be denied admission. Even nine-year-old boys couldn't escape the hatred of the times. Nazi Germany had effectively declared war on its own people if they were Jews, immigrants, gay, or mentally ill. Harry's parents, like so many of their family friends, realized the time had come to leave their homeland, but where could they go? Many countries did not welcome the sudden increase in immigration requests from German Jews. Switzerland, Great Britain, France, and the United States had each denied the Ettlingers' applications. Still they tried again. In early May 1938, Harry's parents received notification that their second request to immigrate to the United States had been approved. But before leaving, Harry had to celebrate his bar mitzvah, a rite of passage ceremony for thirteen-year-old Jewish boys when they publicly become accountable for their actions.

With the drums of war beating more loudly, waiting until their son's thirteenth birthday presented too great a risk, so Harry's parents advanced the date of his bar mitzvah several times. At the end of September 1938, Harry entered adulthood in Karlsruhe's beautiful Kronenstrasse Synagogue. The family departed Germany for the United States the following day, and just in time. In less than two months, the Nazis used the assassination of a German diplomat as an excuse to declare open war on Germany's Jews. On November 9, *Kristallnacht*—the "Night of Broken Glass"— stormtroopers and Hitler Youth destroyed seven thousand Jewish-owned businesses and two hundred synagogues, including the one in Karlsruhe that had welcomed Harry Ettlinger into adulthood, the last bar mitzvah celebrated in the city during the Nazi era.

A Jewish-owned storefront, one of thousands damaged during *Kristallnacht*.

Before Hitler's rise to power, the Ettlingers were a well-to-do and respected family in their hometown. In America, a country with unfamiliar language and customs, they entered the growing ranks of poor immigrant families seeking little more than a chance to begin anew. Life was difficult. Harry's father spent three years looking for work before securing a job as a night watchman in a luggage factory. Harry learned to speak English, but with a thick German accent that made him stand out from the other boys in his class. Each day he took a commuter bus from his home in Newark, New Jersey, to his high school downtown. After school, he worked in a factory to help support his family.

Once America entered World War II, more and more boys joined the fight. By late spring 1944, only one-third of Harry's classmates attended graduation ceremonies because the other two-thirds either had volunteered for military service or had been drafted. Harry's draft notice arrived shortly after graduation. In mid-August, he joined a long line of army recruits headed off to basic training at Camp Wheeler in Macon, Georgia. Day after day, they drilled, marched, and disassembled and reassembled their M1 rifles until they could do it in their sleep.

In mid-October, near the end of training, a drill sergeant barked Harry's last name during morning roll call and pulled him aside.

"Private Ettlinger, are you a citizen of the United States?" he asked.

"No, sir. I'm a German Jew."

"Not for long. Come with me."

Harry found himself standing before a local judge, swearing an oath of allegiance to his new country, the United States of America.

Two months later, the warm feeling he felt the day he became an American citizen was a distant memory in the bone-chilling cold of France. The rumble of a hundred idling truck engines created a trail of exhaust that wafted in the freezing air and infiltrated the back of the deuce and a half's cargo area where Harry and the other replacement soldiers were sitting on benches. Let's get going, he thought. The smell was sickening. Waiting just created more anxiety. But get going to where? Harry didn't know. He looked at each of the eight buddies in his unit; none of them knew either. All anyone did seem to know was that the convoy of new recruits would link up with the mauled 99th Division, jokingly nicknamed the "Battle Babies," somewhere along the front lines.

Muffled voices and whistles outside, followed by the sound of engines revving, signaled the convoy was underway. The truck carrying Harry and his buddies lurched forward. This is it, Harry thought, a German-born American Jew on his way into battle.

Suddenly, Harry and the others heard someone running past their truck yelling "Stop, stop!" It took a minute for the convoy to grind to a halt, but once it did and the noise died down, they could hear the sound of crunching snow as someone marched by each truck yelling the same message over and over: "The following three men get your gear and come with me." Harry sat there trying to stay warm until one of his buddies elbowed him and said, "Hey dummy, that's you!"

After tossing his gear out of the truck and climbing down, the shouting started again. "Okay, let's get going!" someone yelled. Harry barely had time to turn and wave goodbye to the eight men who had been with him from the start, the guys who had become his family all the way through boot camp.

Harry had no idea why he and the other two soldiers had been ordered off the convoy or where they were headed, other than it wasn't to the front. But this much he knew for certain: Being pulled off that truck on January 28, 1945, his nineteenth birthday, was the best gift ever.

Spa, Belgium: February 1945

Walker Hancock had studied the situation map at First Army headquarters in the Belgian town of Spa so frequently that he knew it as well as the area back home. Although the German offensive in the Ardennes had failed, it did penetrate Allied-controlled territory, including towns Hancock and George Stout had already inspected. These places would have to be inspected again.

Hancock was particularly interested in the tiny village of La Gleize, Belgium, which he had visited just seventeen days before the Battle of the Bulge. The kindness of a young lady, Mademoiselle Geenen, and the beauty of a late-fourteenth-century sculpture of a Madonna had been on his mind ever since. Advance reports described the village as a "complete wreck," including the church housing the Madonna, but somehow the statue survived. Armed with a letter from the Bishop of Liège offering to provide shelter for the Madonna, Hancock arranged for a car and driver and set out for La Gleize on February 1.

Icy roads to the hilltop village turned a simple eight-mile drive into an adventure. The early reports proved correct; the village was in shambles. Hancock entered the church through a gaping shell hole in the wall near the front doors, which, strangely, were locked. The sight inside the church was a microcosm of war: overturned pews used as barricades by the German defenders, ammunition and shell casings, empty food ration cans, and shredded uniforms that in desperation had become makeshift bandages. Freezing cold weather mercifully muted what would otherwise have caused wretched smells. Hancock suspected that snowdrifts hid corpses of the defenders.

Despite the destruction and gruesome scene, the Madonna of La Gleize stood exactly where she had been when Hancock first visited the church in early December. The three-foot-high wooden

The Madonna of La Gleize, 14th century, inside the shell-damaged church.

sculpture lacked a certain refinement, but its grace and beauty overshadowed any shortcomings of the unknown artist. The Madonna, with her left hand resting across her heart and the right raised as if to offer a blessing, was mounted on a stone pedestal in the center of the church.

Hancock couldn't find the curé—the parish priest—but a Monsieur George offered to help. Monsieur George's bandaged head and weary look made Hancock think he might be in greater need of assistance than the Madonna. Upon hearing Hancock's intent and reading the bishop's letter, Monsieur George resolutely stated that the Madonna was going nowhere. The battle had passed and the sculpture had survived. It was safe inside the church, he insisted, and that's where it would remain.

In an effort to appease the Monuments Man, Monsieur George convened a meeting of the dozen or so villagers in what remained of his home and proposed that the sculpture be relocated to his cellar. Two men objected to that idea. The village mason stated with certainty that moving the sculpture was a physical impossibility. He had personally cemented the wooden sculpture to its stone base in such a way that the two were inseparable. After taking all this in, Hancock raised the possibility that perhaps the sculpture and stone base could together be freed from the wooden floorboards. The mason nodded; yes, perhaps that could be done. Then the village notary, with his steely eyes, spoke softly but authoritatively, stating that the sculpture would remain exactly where it was. Period. No need for further discussion.

Realizing that emotions had overwhelmed reason, Hancock had an idea. Perhaps a new solution might emerge if they continued the discussion in the church, where they could all see the Madonna. The small group walked the short distance to the front door of the mangled church. Hancock started to step through the shell hole, but hearing the sound of keys, he turned and followed the villagers using the main entrance. The motley crew gathered in a circle around the statue, waiting for someone to resume the discussion. Snow had started falling through the gaping hole in the roof, lightly dusting the Madonna. A gust of wind shifted one of the already loosened pieces of timber overhead, releasing a chunk of plaster that narrowly missed the Madonna—and the head of the village notary.

Mustering all the diplomacy he could, Hancock looked at the notary but asked the group if they still thought it a good idea to leave the Madonna inside the church. For a moment, all anyone could hear was the howl of the wind overhead, the squeak of a roof beam rocking back and forth, some loose papers and leaves rustling, and the almost imperceptible sound of snow gently landing. Just as Hancock had hoped, the notary spoke first. "I propose that the statue be moved to the cellar of the house of Monsieur George." Everyone nodded.

The mason had not exaggerated one bit. Separating the statue from the base was impossible. It took the collective effort of everyone, using two timber planks, to rock the pedestal loose. They then placed the Madonna and its stone base atop the boards and

Monuments Man Captain Walker Hancock (with helmet) leads the procession of townspeople as they relocate the Madonna of La Gleize.

used them like a battlefield litter. Moving it out the doorway of the church and down the icy path to Monsieur George's cellar required the balance of a ballet dancer and the brute strength of a wrestler. No one in the procession exerted more of himself than the village notary.

On the drive back to First Army headquarters, Hancock replayed the day's events over and over in his head. Working with local townspeople to protect the Madonna—their most revered cultural treasure—was a fundamental element of being a Monuments Officer. While salvaging a work of art was of course important, it was the act of demonstrating respect for the cultural treasures of others that filled him with a sense of mission accomplished. The whole experience provided encouragement for what he knew would be difficult days ahead.

Near Florence, Italy: February 1945

The bitter cold winter that gripped all of Europe validated the decision of Allied leaders in Italy to rest their troops and prepare for an offensive in the spring. Fifth and British Eighth Armies had tried in vain to blow through the Gothic Line and link up at Bologna, where they would then drive into the Po River Valley together to take northern Italy. The rainy autumn and a stubbornly entrenched Wehrmacht defense unraveled the plan. Now German troops continued work reinforcing their positions, well aware of the battle that was coming. In the interim, the two sides still skirmished from time to time where their lines met, adding to the casualties being moved back from the front.

Deane Keller and Fred Hartt spent their time supervising temporary repairs in some of the many damaged towns they had inspected. Their concern about the missing Florentine treasures continued, but with German forces in control of northern Italy, there wasn't anything they could do about it, even if they knew the precise location.

In mid-February, Keller had to figure out how to move a massive 350-year-old bronze statue of Cosimo I de' Medici, the great Florentine ruler, and his horse from a Tuscan villa fourteen miles back to its original location in Florence. The task seemed simple: Florentine art officials had moved the eight-ton sculpture to the countryside on an ox-drawn cart in August 1943. But passage was threatened by pending repairs to a railroad bridge damaged during combat, adding to the urgency of Keller's assignment.

After several days of planning and preparation, working in some of the muddiest conditions he had experienced, Keller arranged for a crane to hoist Cosimo onto the back of a truck. Moving the far larger and heavier horse, which was standing in a trotting position atop a wooden skid, with its front and rear legs astride a crisscrossed stack of logs for stability, proved far more difficult. It took three and a half hours to pull the skid into position on the tank trailer using a primitive moving technique Keller likened to "a Maine back countryman moving a house with pulleys and tackle and a horse for the power," but it worked.

Keller's driver and friend, Charley Bernholz, acted as traffic warden for the convoy, but Keller still needed a volunteer to ride atop the horse and lift the telephone and telegraph wires along the

Keller (center left with cap and overcoat) supervises the positioning of Cosimo's horse atop wooden skids.

route into the city. A boisterous GI named Smokey eagerly mounted Cosimo's horse and straddled the hole where the Florentine ruler and his saddle would normally be joined. As they approached the town, the driver of a horse-drawn carriage pulled even with the truck, raised his hat, and beaming ear to ear, shouted to Smokey and Keller, "Cosimo, welcome back!" Soon they reached the Piazza della Signoria in the center of Florence, where Fred Hartt, in Lucky 13, Superintendent of Florentine Galleries Giovanni Poggi, and a few hundred curious citizens braving the rain greeted them.

Keller knew that returning the statue to the city wasn't going to shorten the war even one second, but it was a victory for the people of Florence to see something they had cherished for more than three centuries restored to its prewar position. It demonstrated a respect for their culture and heritage that German troops had destroyed. But the joy of the achievement proved short-lived. One week later, Keller learned that Smokey had been killed in action.

Monuments Man Lieutenant Fred Hartt (standing left of Lucky 13) greets Keller and the return of Cosimo's horse to Florence.

CHAPTER 12

TREASURE MAPS

Paris, France: March 1945

Riding a bicycle through the streets of Paris, even on a frigid mid-March evening, was one of the joyful consequences of his assignment. Some of the city was still without electricity, but from Jim Rorimer's point of view, nothing could detract from the beauty of Paris, especially at such a hopeful moment. Just days earlier, he had received his new assignment as Monuments Man for Seventh Army. A phone call from Rose Valland inviting him to her apartment for dinner could mean only one thing: The courageous curator was finally ready to share her secrets. At the Warehouse for Enemy Property, where Rorimer had pressed Valland for the locations of the stolen art, she had walked away, telling him, "I'll tell you where, when the time is right." With orders in hand that would soon have him on the road to Germany, Rorimer hoped that moment had finally come.

A gust of wind passing through the Pont de la Concorde almost knocked Rorimer off his bicycle. After crossing the River Seine, he veered left at the National Assembly onto Boulevard Saint-Germain. The ride to Valland's apartment in the 5th arrondissement would take about twenty minutes more, just enough time to run through his checklist of questions.

The sting of the abrupt parting with Valland following their December inspection of the Warehouse for Enemy Property had long since faded. Rorimer knew he had pushed too hard, too fast, all but demanding that Valland turn over information she had risked her life to gather. Of course, his approach had offended her. But in the days that followed, he learned that Valland had experienced her own regrets about being so dismissive of a man who had done much to help Paris get back on its feet in the early days of liberation.

Sending a bottle of champagne to his apartment days later changed the dynamic of their relationship. Rorimer had returned the gesture by inviting Valland to his apartment for a Christmas dinner. It didn't take long for him to realize that she had come that evening to deliver a very important message. Valland, Jaujard, and Henraux wanted him reassigned. They believed he had surpassed his usefulness stationed in Paris. Having demonstrated his commitment to the preservation of the culture of France, they needed him in Germany at the very earliest moment to help find and return the tens of thousands of works of art stolen from their country.

The events that followed unfolded rapidly. His request for a transfer had been well received. In fact, as his superior officer noted, someone in the French mission had suggested the idea already. Rorimer remembered smiling upon hearing that. Clearly, Jaujard and Valland had been hard at work behind the scenes, and just in time.

The Allied victory at the Battle of the Bulge on January 17, and the Soviet crossing of the Oder River on January 31, which put the

Red Army just fifty miles east of Berlin, had the enemy in a vise. The fall of the German city Cologne to U.S. 3rd Armored Division just one week earlier left no doubt that Nazi Germany's days were numbered. Allied forces knew that soon they would find dozens of hiding places, if not more, containing thousands of stolen works of art—if the Nazis didn't first destroy them.

Valland's greeting alone confirmed Rorimer's hopes. The two were already on a first-name basis, but the warmth of her reception told him this visit was going to be different. Rorimer hardly felt surprise when Valland congratulated him on his new assignment with Seventh Army. She, too, had a checklist to discuss with him and wasted no time getting to it.

Rorimer had barely taken a seat before Valland reached into a small box, pulled out a stack of photographs, and placed them on the table. He felt a chill run down his spine at the sight of the first image: Nazi Reichsmarschall Hermann Göring. Valland painted the number two man in the Nazi Party as a person consumed with greed who used the Jeu de Paume Museum as a private hunting ground to add to his collection. A photograph of Alfred Rosenberg, the anti-Semite and namesake of the Nazi looting organization, the ERR, followed.

The men in the next three images at first appeared unfamiliar until Valland matched their faces with names that Rorimer knew well. Colonel Kurt von Behr, commandant of the Jeu de Paume and local leader of the ERR, whose officer's cap cast a shadow that covered his glass eye, was a social climber who thrived on his position of power. Bruno Lohse, one of Göring's chief art buyers, loved money and everything it could purchase. Young, tall, athletic, and with considerable power, he was popular with the ladies of Paris. Finally, there was Hermann Bunjes, a thirty-three-year-old art historian. As a consultant and middleman to the Göring theft ring and the Paris art scene, Bunjes had traded his career as a minor art scholar for rapid advancement as a corrupt official in the Kunstschutz, the German art protection unit.

Valland had group photographs as well: Göring, wearing a hat, overcoat, and scarf on one of his shopping expeditions with Lohse

Göring departs the Jeu de Paume Museum.
Art buyer Bruno Lohse is standing in the doorway, on the left; Kurt von Behr, leader of the ERR in Paris, is in the right foreground.

and Walter Andreas Hofer, his art curator, in tow; von Behr inspecting stolen property in one photo, and in his office surrounded by his staff in another; and Rosenberg parading through the Jeu de Paume in civilian clothes, personally inspecting the looting operation.

On the handful of occasions Rorimer and Valland had seen each other during January and February, Valland's stories about the activities at the Jeu de Paume were always sprinkled with the names of Göring, Rosenberg, von Behr, Lohse, and Bunjes. These photos were confirmation of all she had told him, and more—it struck Rorimer that these images were actually mug shots of the people he hoped to find, arrest, and bring to justice once he got to Germany. Valland was counting on it.

ERR namesake, Alfred Rosenberg, arrives at the
Jeu de Paume Museum for an inspection.

While Rorimer studied each photograph, Valland disappeared into the bedroom and quickly returned carrying another larger box. Having started with photos of the thieves, Valland now wanted him to see images of what they had stolen. Most were world-famous works of art that Rorimer recognized instantly, like *The Astronomer*, by Johannes Vermeer, one of only thirty-four works painted by the seventeenth-century Dutch master. Valland explained how the Nazis had stolen the painting off the wall of the famed Parisian banker and renowned art collector Édouard de Rothschild.

Rorimer saw photographs of more paintings, by Rembrandt, Rubens, Cranach, and other Old Master painters, but there were also images of Renaissance jewelry, Flemish tapestries, and rare furniture. These objects alone would have constituted one of the most important and comprehensive museums in the world. The breadth and quality of what the Nazis had stolen was staggering.

Valland then reached into the box to retrieve documents that she had transcribed or found in wastepaper baskets, including train manifests, shipping receipts, and the prize Rorimer most wanted to see: a list of where the stolen objects had been hidden—a treasure map. Valland had it all. Names, photos, and objects taken. It all added up to years' worth of work. Up to that moment, the Monuments Men had only dreamed of such an intelligence coup. Now, he was holding everything he needed.

Having the information was all that really mattered, but Rorimer couldn't help but wonder how Valland had gathered so many details and lived to tell about it. He recalled Jaujard's comments in late November about her unobtrusiveness, and how she'd used her knowledge of German without her captors being aware that she could understand all they were saying. But that alone couldn't possibly account for the information that filled the boxes on her dining room table.

After a long pause, Valland explained how circumstances demanded that she transform her shy personality into one that engaged others in small talk to earn their confidence and trust. Important details soon followed, in particular from Alexandre, the head packer, who monitored the movement of what the Nazis had confiscated. One of the chauffeurs used by the ERR to transport stolen works provided Valland with information about the loading of trains. Rorimer could only imagine the sense of relief she was feeling from sharing all of this after keeping it secret for five years.

Every few days, Valland walked the short distance to the Louvre for regular meetings with Jaujard or his secretary. Those visits provided her with a place where she could always count on receiving sound advice and encouragement from the few people, in fact the *only* people, she could trust. But those visits also ratcheted up the pressure by reminding her that mistakes would prove deadly to her, Jaujard, his secretary, and others.

There had been several close calls, but only once, in February 1944, did the Nazi lackeys catch her red-handed trying to read addresses on shipping documents. Bruno Lohse, Göring's art buyer, confronted Valland, warning that she could be shot for such indiscretions. But she sloughed it off, telling him, "No one here is stupid enough to ignore the risk," before walking away. Luck had favored her that day, but with the Allied landings at Normandy, threats became more frequent and menacing. Lohse and von Behr both considered her an embarrassing witness to be eliminated before the end of hostilities. She expected that they would send her to Germany with some of the stolen works of art and then shoot her once the train crossed the border.

None of that mattered now, she told Rorimer. All the risks taken, all the years of worry, would amount to nothing if Hitler, in a fit of rage, ordered his henchmen to destroy the works of art, the furniture, the tapestries—everything! Valland moved some of the documents aside to find the list that had so excited Rorimer, the treasure map of where the stolen objects had been taken. Some of the names on the list he had heard mentioned in their prior conversations, including Heilbronn, Buxheim, Hohenschwangau, and the one Valland urged him to get to first—Neuschwanstein Castle. There, she told him, you will find the works of art stolen from France and the ERR documents that evidence the work of the thieves.

The urgency in her voice revealed a genuine fear that Hitler or other Nazis might destroy the works stolen from France. Hitler hadn't hesitated to order the destruction of all but one of the bridges in Florence. Had General von Choltitz, his military commander in Paris, followed orders, the Allies would have entered the French capital to find only smoldering ruins. Then, as if to underscore the urgency and validate her concern, Valland told Rorimer another story.

On July 23, 1944, a German military truck delivered to the interior garden of the Jeu de Paume Museum five to six hundred paintings by Picasso, Dali, Léger, Miró, Klee, and others that the Nazis considered "degenerate" and unsuitable even for sale or trade. German soldiers then tossed them, one by one, onto a flaming bonfire. With a mixed look of anger and sorrow, she added, "Nothing could be saved."

The lightness of being that Rorimer had experienced riding his bicycle to Valland's apartment had changed in a matter of hours. His ride home felt completely different. Valland, no doubt with Jaujard's encouragement, hadn't just entrusted her information to Rorimer—she handed it over to him. He now had the weight of the world on his shoulders. The Nazi hiding places on Valland's list were all located in what would become Seventh Army territory—his army, his territory, and now his responsibility.

Fighting a war against an enemy was one thing; fighting a war against a madman was something entirely different. Would Hitler, a man who had professed his love of art and desire to be recognized as an artist, really order the destruction of the very thing he so revered? Valland had no doubt that he would; Rorimer agreed. And that added even more urgency to the mission of the Monuments Men. Now, it was a race against time.

Cleve, Germany: March 10, 1945

After two months in a hospital, British Monuments Man Ronald Balfour felt as though he could survive anything. At any other time in his life he would have praised the heavens to have so much uninterrupted time for reading. Being stuck on the sidelines at a time when an epic fight to the death was taking place at the Battle of the Bulge pained him more than the truck accident that broke his ankle did. The Allied armies already had a shortage of Monuments Officers. His unavailability just made things worse.

Balfour eagerly returned to action in February, making inquiries about the missing Bruges *Madonna* in the southwestern town of Vlissingen, Netherlands. Rumors continued to circulate that the thieves had loaded the Madonna onto a Red Cross ship that passed through the historic port before sailing the North Sea to Germany, but Balfour concluded that they were just rumors. Five months had passed since the theft with no sightings or substantiated leads. In all likelihood, Michelangelo's masterpiece had already been stashed somewhere in Germany. That suited Balfour, because First Canadian Army was now *in* Germany, which put him one step closer to finding it.

By early March, many German towns along the Lower Rhine River were in Allied hands, the result of Operations Veritable and Blockbuster, but the immensity of destruction from Allied bombing was astonishing. Estimates of damage to the town of Cleve, birthplace of Henry VIII's fourth wife, Anne, approached 90 percent. A dozen Monuments Men would have had a difficult time keeping up with all the work—First Canadian Army had just one.

Less than one mile from the front, under constant shelling, Balfour spent his days inspecting historic buildings, city archives, and churches, salvaging documents and objects, even fragments, of value. On March 3, during a lull in the fighting, he found time to write his friend Lieutenant Colonel Geoffrey Webb, the senior ranking Monuments Officer. Webb looked forward to Balfour's field reports more than those of any other Monuments Officer. Balfour's sense of humor and keen insights made them a good read. "It was a splendid week for my job—certainly the best since I came over," Balfour wrote. "On the one hand there is the tragedy of real destruction, much of it completely unnecessary; on the other the comforting feeling of having done something solid myself."

Looting by Allied troops was an unending problem. When OFF LIMITS signs proved ineffective, Balfour improvised and began confiscating objects himself as a measure of last resort. That created a new problem: Where to put them? Always up for a challenge, Balfour created a makeshift repository in the attic of a building in Cleve. Although occupied by troops and refugees, with no proper protection, the building had what most other buildings in town did not: a roof, doors, and windows. Inside the attic's locked doors, Balfour stored medieval town records, statues, and church vestments salvaged from various ruins. He even befriended a local monk who watched over the place when he was away on inspections.

On March 10, at 9:30 a.m. sharp, Balfour arrived at Allied Military Government headquarters in Cleve for a meeting with the sexton of Christus König Kirche, Christ the King Church, and four German workers who were going to assist with the removal of its treasures. Lack of transportation, bomb-cratered streets, and a relatively short distance made a handcart suitable for the job, which the four workers had positioned in front of the building. All present, Balfour signaled them to start. With any luck, they should cover the two-mile distance to the church in well under an hour.

They set out in a southwesterly direction, toward the train station, which lay about half the distance to their destination. Balfour walked on the left side of the road; the four German workers with the cart walked on the right, followed by the sexton. With the train station in view, Balfour started to cross the street, when the deafening swoosh of an artillery round, moving at the rate of twenty-seven hundred feet per second, slammed into the street. The violent, disorienting impact shook the ground, creating a plume of dust between Balfour and the group of five on the right side of the street. When it cleared, the sexton could see the cart up ahead, but the four German workers had fled the scene. Splayed by the blast against the sidewalk railing was the blood-covered body of Monuments Officer Major Ronald Balfour.

A death in their ranks stunned the other Monuments Men. Each of them had experienced their own close calls from booby traps, aircraft strafing, firefights, and artillery strikes. They all considered it something of a miracle that, up to this point, no one on their small team had been severely wounded or killed. Now that dreaded threshold had been crossed.

The sorrowful task of notifying Balfour's family fell on his superior officer and friend, Lieutenant Colonel Webb. With Balfour's March 3 letter nearby, Webb gathered his thoughts and began writing:

> I want very much to tell you how much Ronald was
> appreciated by all the officers who knew him in their
> work. He had a quality of clear headedness and practical
> common sense and a knowledge of the army combined
> with the obvious distinction of his mind that gave him a
> special position among the monuments officers. Both
> British and Americans felt that if they talked things over
> with him they would get help in their problems, and were
> always going to him for advice. I was in the same case as
> others, only more so, for Ronald was not only a friend of

long standing, but a stand by in difficulties, for I could
go to him and know that I would get something that for
fairness and a real understanding of a situation I could
get nowhere else. There are never very many men who
have got the combination of really penetrating
intelligence combined with fairmindedness and real
humourous appreciation of their fellow men that
Ronald had.

Trier, Germany: March 1945

The odd couple, Captain Robert Posey and Private First Class
Lincoln Kirstein, didn't prove to be very odd at all. Far from pushing them apart, the demands of war had threaded their differences
into a tightly woven team. The pace at which General Patton's
Third Army was liberating cities created plenty of work for the two
Monuments Men, but they still made time to identify people they
believed might know something—anything—about the whereabouts of the Ghent Altarpiece.

In the French town of Metz, they had spoken with a civilian
who had worked with the Kunstschutz. The man had only heard
rumors, but word had it that the Ghent Altarpiece could be found
in an underground bunker at the nearby fortress of Ehrenbreitstein.
Or possibly inside one of Göring's homes. Or even the Führer's
home in Berchtesgaden, the Berghof. It might even have been
taken to Switzerland, or some other neutral country. It was difficult to say. That sobering conversation provided just a sampling of
the challenges the two Monuments Men faced in trying to find a
single object in such a vast amount of space during war.

Passing through Luxembourg, they sought out and asked local museum directors if they knew the location of the Ghent Altarpiece. One of the directors indicated that, indeed, he did know. "It's in a salt mine somewhere, possibly in the South. Or perhaps in a subterranean vault in the Berlin Reichsbank." In other words, he, too, had no idea where it was hidden.

The same could be said for the people and places Posey and Kirstein saw during the rest of March. When they reached Third Army base in the German town of Trier, perhaps the oldest city in Europe and one of the largest in the Roman Empire, they couldn't believe the level of destruction. Kirstein, with a great appreciation for the city's storied history and its early Christian, Romanesque, and Baroque architecture, recorded the scene in a letter back home:

> *The desolation is frozen, as if the moment of combustion was suddenly arrested, and the air had lost its power to hold atoms together and various centers of gravity had a dogfight for matter, and matter lost.*

Only two thousand of the ninety thousand inhabitants remained in Trier, and most of them lived a bare existence, seeking shelter in a series of wine cellars. "Certainly St. Lô was worse, but it didn't have anything of importance," Kirstein added. "Here everything was early Christian, or roman or Romanesque or marvelous baroque."

By March 29, after overseeing protection programs in Trier, Posey had to address a toothache that he had been ignoring for several weeks. With very limited German-speaking skills, Kirstein sought help from a young blond boy they passed in the street, using three sticks of Pep-O-Mint gum and a few humorous moments pantomiming a sore tooth—and it worked. Hand in hand, the boy and Kirstein led Posey to a dentist's office just a few blocks away.

Their luck continued inside as the friendly, old dentist spoke English. Question followed question, even while treating Posey's impacted wisdom tooth. The dentist wanted to know where Posey and Kirstein were from, what they did in civilian life, and all about their mission as Monuments Men. Kirstein had to turn away at the sight of what followed, but Posey's scream told all. A few moments later, without missing a beat, the dentist insisted they speak with his son-in-law, an art scholar who had been in Paris during the occupation. The dentist didn't have a car, and his son-in-law lived in a remote valley, but he offered to accompany the Monuments Men and serve as their guide.

The trip took twice the time it should have due to stops the dentist insisted on making along the way. When he returned to the jeep with vegetables and bottles of wine instead of information, Kirstein and Posey, whose head felt like it was going to explode, began to suspect it was a trap. More than twelve miles from Trier, with fewer and fewer white pillowcases and sheets indicating surrender flying from homes, the two Monuments Men considered turning around. Suddenly the old dentist tapped Posey on the shoulder and pointed to a small weekend cottage sitting on a low hill. The smile on his face told them they had arrived.

A man in his midthirties greeted them speaking French and introduced his mother, wife, and their two children. His name was Hermann Bunjes. They entered the modest home to find bookshelves filled with scholarly tomes, walls lined with photographs of many of Paris's most famous sites, and small vases filled with flowers from the early blossoms of spring. For a moment, all thoughts of war vanished.

After exchanging pleasantries, the four men took a seat around the family table. Before Posey or Kirstein could ask their first question, Bunjes started recounting his experience in Paris working for Reichsmarschall Hermann Göring. Without revealing their surprise, the two Monuments Men sat in stunned silence and listened. Yes, it was true he had joined the Nazi Party in 1938, but he resigned the following year when he entered service in the Wehrmacht. As to his service to Göring, Alfred Rosenberg, and the Nazi looting organization, the ERR, it had but one purpose: the protection of art. Posey and Kirstein quickly realized that this was a man eager to tell a story, one that sounded rehearsed, as if Bunjes had prepared it for the day of reckoning he surely knew would come.

Without breaking stride, Bunjes continued. When he advised the Reichsmarschall on February 5, 1941, that the confiscation of Jewish property violated the Hague Convention's rules of land warfare, Göring simply raised his hand and said, "First, it is *my* orders that you have to follow. You will act directly according to my orders." Bunjes didn't let it go, pointing out that the German military commanders in France probably wouldn't agree with the Reichsmarschall. "Dear Bunjes," Göring replied, "let me worry about that; I am the highest Jurist in the State."

Possessing considerable knowledge of the looting operation and those involved, Bunjes now wanted to offer his services to the

Allies. He promised to share his information, including what was taken and where it could be found, in return for the chance to resume his life as an art scholar and live in peace. Posey and Kirstein looked at each other, both wanting to blurt out, "Where is the Ghent Altarpiece?" Posey chose to push back a little to gauge the reaction by informing Bunjes that he did not have the authority to offer any deals or assurances.

After a long pause, Bunjes slid his chair away from the table, stood up, and walked out of the room. Posey, despite his stone face, worried that he'd gone too far. What felt like minutes of awkward silence followed. When Bunjes reappeared, he had a large bound album in his hands that he placed on top of the table in front of the Monuments Men. As he opened the album, Posey and Kirstein looked on in disbelief. Catalogued on each page were works of art stolen from France. Beside each object was the name of the artist, title of the work, its size, the price paid and the exchange rate, and the name of the victim from whom it had been stolen, page after page after page.

Far from done, Bunjes asked the two men to spread their maps on the table. He then started pointing to the places where the stolen works of art could be found—if they hadn't since been moved. The SS art scholar knew that Göring's immense collection had been moved from Carinhall, outside Berlin, to another of his homes, called Veldenstein, in the southern state of Bavaria, but he added that it might have been relocated again. Names of art dealers in Berlin who were actively dealing in looted works followed.

"What about the Ghent Altarpiece?" Posey asked in such a manner as if to suggest that *he* knew the answer but wanted to see what Bunjes might say. Bunjes adjusted the map, placed his fore-finger on it, and began moving it around, searching for a particular spot. "It is here, in the salt mine in Altaussee, Austria, with the other works in Hitler's collection."

After more than seven months of dead ends, the Monuments Men had, by persistence and luck, hit the jackpot. But getting to Altaussee, 450 miles away, seemed like a pipe dream. Any route to the mountainous mining town passed through Bavaria, where U.S. Army intelligence officials believed Hitler's most die-hard fol-lowers would certainly fight to the death. By that time, the works of art might have been moved again. At this stage of the war, no one knew if Third Army and its two Monuments Men would be assigned that area, not even General Patton himself and certainly not Posey and Kirstein. But they had the information they needed, and much more—a veritable treasure map.

CHAPTER 13

GAINS AND LOSSES

Siegen, Germany: first week of April 1945

Walker Hancock and George Stout, accompanied by two American GIs and their guide, Father Stephany—the guardian angel of the six boys in the Aachen Cathedral fire brigade—entered Siegen's ghostlike ruins late on the afternoon of April 2 to the sound of sporadic gunfire. The helmet of a GI caught Hancock's eye, as did the pool of blood nearby, another horrible reminder that many men, like their friend and colleague Ronald Balfour, would never return home. Debris littered the streets, forcing them to continue by foot.

Almost five months had passed since Hancock discovered a key clue when digging through dust-laden documents: a museum catalogue with the name "Siegen" written inside. Only now, with the Allied advance more than one hundred miles inside Nazi Germany, were he and Stout able to reach Siegen. The long, frustrating wait to locate their first art repository neared an end.

First Army had taken Bonn and Cologne one month earlier, then swung north and west to link up with Ninth Army, capturing three hundred thousand prisoners and trapping the last effective enemy fighting force in northwestern Germany. Being in those German cities had provided Hancock with an opportunity to gather more information to determine the precise location of the Siegen repository. A well-placed German source informed him that the Suermondt Museum treasures could be found in a copper mine inside a hill beneath the city's medieval quarter. But another piece of information proved even more surprising. Contrary to what he had been told by Father Stephany months earlier, the Aachen Cathedral treasures and those of the cathedral in Cologne were also inside the mine.

Father Stephany, still embarrassed that he had been unwilling to trust Hancock with the truth, soon found one of the two entrances to the Siegen repository teeming with people. Stout was convinced that he had seen just about everything possible since setting foot on Utah Beach nine months earlier, but even he had a difficult time processing all that his senses were experiencing:

Around a hole in the steep hill stood some twenty people. They fell back and we went in. The tunnel—an old mineshaft—was about six feet wide and eight high, arched and rough. Once away from the light of the entrance, the passage was thick with vapor and our flashlights made only faint spots in the gloom. There were people inside. I thought we must soon pass them and that they were a few stragglers sheltered there for safety. But we did not pass them. It was a hard place to judge distance. We walked more than a quarter mile, probably less than a half a mile through that passage. Other shafts branched from it. In places it had been cut out to a width of about twenty feet.

Throughout we walked in a path not more than a
foot and a half. The rest was compressed humanity. They
stood, they sat on branches and on stones. They lay on cots
or stretchers. This was the population of the city, all that
could not get away. At one time the priest had to stop and
speak to a woman who was ill. Many must have been ill.
There was a stench in the humid air. Babies cried
fretfully.

We were the first Americans they had seen. They had
no doubt been told that we were savages. The pale grimy
faces caught in our flashlights were full of fear and hate.
Children were snatched out of our path. And ahead of us
went the fearful word, halfway between sound and
whisper—'Amerikaner.' That was the strange part of the
occurrence, the impact of hate and fear in hundreds of
hearts close about us and we the targets of it all.

Hancock felt it, too. He heard awed whispers as they walked deeper
into the mine. In front of them, mothers called for their children in
fear. The vicar, sensing the two men's discomfort, said, "They are
afraid that you will kill the children." To think that was one thing,
but to hear someone confirm it out loud saddened both men, especially Stout, father of two boys. Seeking to put his statement in
context, the vicar added, "The radio threatened that recently.
Anything to keep them fighting."

There was some indifference, though. Stout noticed a boy
about ten years old blowing on a cup, trying to cool its contents.
There was something else in that fetid air, something Stout could

only sense—until he felt a touch on his hand. Shining his flashlight, he saw a boy about seven years old. The boy looked up and smiled, took Stout's hand, and began walking. I shouldn't let him do this, Stout thought. Yet he didn't pull his hand away. He didn't feel any sense of regret.

The experience stuck with Stout. Later, he wondered why the boy was so trusting. With the horror of war that the seven-year-old had experienced in his town, and the propaganda that he had undoubtedly heard, Stout would always wonder how the boy sensed that he was not a monster.

After walking more than a quarter of a mile into the hill, Father Stephany reached a locked door and knocked. A short but muscular man, Herr Etzkorn, the guardian, opened the door and greeted the vicar by name. The guardian's demeanor changed quickly at the sight of four American soldiers standing behind him. After passing through several more doors, the group reached a hollowed-out chamber more than thirty feet long, containing wooden racks filled with paintings and sculpture rising to the ceiling.

It didn't require a detailed inspection for Stout and Hancock to realize that they had found what they were looking for—and more. Paintings by Rembrandt, Fragonard, van Gogh, Gauguin, Cézanne, and Cranach filled the chamber. Even works painted by Siegen's favorite son, the prolific Flemish artist Peter Paul Rubens, were there. In all, over four hundred paintings were jammed into fourteen wooden bays constructed inside the old mineshaft. The two Monuments Men quickly determined that the Siegen repository didn't house just the Aachen museum collection, but also those of Bonn, Cologne, Essen, and several other Rhineland cities.

A GI looks at racks of paintings and sculpture hidden inside the Siegen art repository.

A painting by Peter Paul Rubens, one of hundreds found in the Siegen art repository.

Of greatest interest to Father Stephany were the Aachen Cathedral treasures, safe inside their heavy cases, wax seals untouched.

As Hancock and Stout turned to leave, Herr Etzkorn pointed to a stack of crates, forty in all, and said they belonged to the Beethoven house in Bonn, birthplace of the genius composer and pianist. One of the crates contained the manuscript of his famous Sixth Symphony. Nearby were two ornately carved eleventh-century oak doors removed from Cologne's Saint Maria im Kapitol, a Romanesque church that had suffered gravely from the continual bombing of the city. The artist in Hancock admired the craftsmanship of the unknown sculptor who used his carving chisels and knives to make scenes from the life and death of Christ come alive.

A section of the eleventh-century carved oak doors from a church in Cologne that Walker Hancock so greatly admired.

Stout lamented the storage conditions. The heating system was not operational and, as a consequence, the air was filled with moisture, made worse by dripping water from the ceiling. Some canvas paintings had mold damage; wood panels had flaking paint. But all in all, Stout believed that the Siegen repository was the safest place for the objects until arrangements could be made to move them to a better storage facility.

The number of German cities falling to Allied forces increased each day. In the north, the British were bearing down on Hanover. Patton and his Third Army were leading the charge into the heart of Nazi Germany at an ever-increasing pace. To the east, the Soviets had amassed 2.5 million troops outside Berlin, poised for the final showdown. With more conquered territory, though, came more requests for inspections by the Monuments Men. Stout and Hancock were needed elsewhere. For now, all they could do was post guards at the Siegen copper mine until they could return. No one had any idea when that might be.

In transit to Recklinghausen, Germany: April 4, 1945

While Hancock and Stout were in Siegen inspecting the repository, Captain Walter "Hutch" Huchthausen and his new assistant and driver, Monuments Man T/5 Sheldon Keck, were investigating reports of a looted altarpiece.

After stopping at Ninth Army forward headquarters to check the situation map, Hutch and Keck headed to the town of Recklinghausen, about eighty miles northwest of Siegen.

Hutch thrived in his assignment to Ninth Army. His work at the Aachen Cathedral, overseeing repairs to the roof, shoring up

Monuments Men T/5 Sheldon Keck (kneeling) and Lieutenant Lamont Moore.

the choir buttresses, and covering empty window frames had drawn the attention of a reporter who was curious about the motivation of an American soldier determined to preserve a German landmark. Hutch, welcoming the question, smiled and said:

It may seem strange to some people that while we are still fighting the Germans we should be restoring their monuments. But Pilgrims from all over the world came to Aachen cathedral in the Middle Ages. Thirty kings were crowned there. It has survived every European war

since the seventh century and has an historical
significance which transcends political and economic
difference. It is architecturally unique and it is our duty
to preserve it for generations to come.

Then he thought about his answer for a couple of seconds and realized that there was an even simpler response. Looking the reporter in the eye, he added: "Aachen Cathedral belongs to the world and if we can prevent it from falling in ruins among the rest of Aachen's rubble then we are doing a service to the world."

The February arrival of Keck, an accomplished art restorer who had studied under George Stout at Harvard's Fogg Museum, and the availability—finally—of a jeep, enabled Hutch to make dozens of inspections in Dutch towns and villages along the border as well as inside western Germany, even while Allied forces continued their advance. Gradually, the character of his work shifted. Rather than initiating inspections, Hutch found himself more frequently responding to requests for assistance, like the one he and Keck were on their way to investigate.

Reaching Recklinghausen around 3:00 p.m., Hutch and Keck were unable to locate a passable road north. While stubbornly backpedaling, Wehrmacht troops had been executing the Führer's scorched-earth policy, destroying German bridges, roads, and all other infrastructure that might slow the Allied advance. Seeking an alternative route north, the two Monuments Men headed south out of town until they reached the autobahn, the world's first freeway network. There they turned left, hoping to use the high-speed road to find a northbound route not blocked by rubble or debris.

The sudden absence of U.S. Army markers on the highway indicated they were in an area where combat operations had recently ended, or might still be underway.

On the smooth road, the jeep's engine roared as the duo passed under three overhead bridges, hoping to find one that might lead them north to XIX Corps territory. Farther ahead, although difficult to make out, something appeared to be blocking their path. As they got closer, Keck slowed to a crawl. Wehrmacht troops had detonated the bridge, making the highway impassable. Keck started to make a U-turn left when he noticed the helmets of U.S. troops, who were peering at them over the northern embankment.

Seeking directions, Keck stopped. At that moment, machine-gun fire from enemy troops hiding near the bridge sprayed the right side of the jeep, perforating the hood. "They are firing at us!" Keck screamed. Out of the corner of his eye, as he instinctively jumped from the vehicle, Keck saw Hutch shift in his seat, as if he, too, were preparing to jump. Two infantrymen in a nearby foxhole pulled Keck into their defensive position while simultaneously firing in the direction of the overpass rubble. "Captain!" he yelled, "Captain!" but there was no reply.

All Keck could see from the foxhole was a column of black smoke rising above the jeep. However, an infantryman in the fox-hole farther east could see what Keck could not: the right side of the burning vehicle, with Captain Huchthausen still in his seat, motionless, bleeding from the ear. Amid the danger and chaos of bullets flying back and forth, acrid smoke belching out of the jeep, and incoming enemy artillery fire now that their position had been spotted, the infantryman crawled the distance to Keck. "Your captain is dead, corporal," the soldier shouted over the sound of the German buzz saw. "Head wound. He's white as snow."

Incoming artillery fire and the location of the jeep rendered medical assistance impossible, even if medics had been standing by. After about forty-five minutes, the artillery fire diminished enough for Keck to make his way to the company command post, where he requested medical assistance for Huchthausen and filed his report, but by that time medics had arrived and removed the body. Thirty-six excruciating hours passed before Keck received confirmation that his captain—and friend—was indeed dead, plenty of time to replay the dramatic and tragic events in his head over and over again. It had all happened in an instant, with such fury and confusion, but this much Keck knew for certain: By inadvertently shielding him from enemy fire, Walter Huchthausen had saved his life.

The news of a second death among the Monuments Men serving in northern Europe—two out of an initial nine—spread slowly to the other men in the field, to Keller and Hartt preparing for the start of the spring offensive in Italy, to Mason Hammond and the other senior officers at SHAEF headquarters in London, and finally, to Paul Sachs and the members of the Roberts Commission, who had approved Huchthausen's selection. Some nights later, Walker Hancock took out pen and paper to share the news with his wife, Saima:

> *The buildings that Huchthausen hoped, as a young architect, to build will never exist . . . but the few people who saw him at his job—friend and enemy—must think more of the human race because of him.*

CHAPTER 14

SURPRISES

Frankfurt, Germany: first half of April 1945

After crossing the Rhine River, U.S. 4th Armored Division sprinted across Germany, capturing Mainz, Frankfurt, and then . . . they just disappeared. Posey and Kirstein made a point of checking the wall-sized map at headquarters each evening, where spotters posted the day's advance onto transparent acetate overlays using a red crayon. The 4th Armored was General Patton's lead unit, so wherever it was, the other four divisions in Third Army would be heading next, including the two Monuments Men.

The map did indicate that the 90th Infantry Division had established a command post in the town of Kieselbach. That meant Third Army was moving away from, not closer to, Altaussee, Austria, and the repository containing Hitler's art collection and the Ghent Altarpiece. Some dumb luck, the two Monuments Men thought. All those months had passed without a clue on the whereabouts of the Ghent Altarpiece or Hitler's art hoard. Now, because of something as fluky as Posey's dental needs, they knew exactly where both were hidden—and their army was headed elsewhere.

Posey and Kirstein checked the wall map once again on the evening of April 4. The 4th Armored Division had reappeared and, along with soldiers of the 89th Infantry, neared the town of

Gotha, just two hundred miles southwest of Berlin. Rumors about some big discovery had been circulating since late afternoon. The following day brought firsthand accounts that left Posey and Kirstein, and every other soldier, seething.

Early that cold and rainy morning, April 4, Private Ralph G. Rush, part of an intelligence and reconnaissance platoon of the 89th Infantry, sighted a double-fenced barbed-wire enclosure. Seeing empty guard towers, he and his scout squad cautiously approached the front gate. A dozen dead bodies littered the ground in front of them, including three GIs, shot in the back of the neck

U.S. Third Army soldiers discovered this ghastly scene of death at Ohrdruf, where Nazi guards had executed prisoners before fleeing.

while kneeling, hands bound behind their backs. Their bodies were still warm to the touch. Emaciated prisoners, little more than skeletons tightly wrapped in skin with what remained of their ragged striped uniforms draped over them, sat in bed or on the ground, with barely the energy to die.

These Third Army advance units had by chance found Ohrdruf, a forced labor camp that once held thousands of prisoners from Russia, Poland, Hungary, and other European countries. It was the first Nazi camp liberated by American forces. Private Rush, and most every other soldier on or near the front lines, had seen the horror of death far too frequently, but the gruesome scenes he and the other scouts witnessed defined inhumanity:

> It seemed that dead bodies were everywhere—a large shed contained 50 or more naked bodies with parchment like skin, stacked like cordwood, with lye sprinkled on them to keep down the smell. We passed what appeared to be a torture apparatus—we later learned it was a whipping table . . . We also saw a gallows that we were told was used for prisoners who had attempted to escape . . . Further on we came upon a crude crematorium or burning pit—a long pit had been dug with a mound at each end and railroad rails laid about 3 feet apart from mound to mound. A fire was still smoldering in the pit and partially destroyed bodies remained on the rails and burnt parts were in the pit. The stench was overwhelming.

Two days later, Posey received a telegram ordering him and Kirstein to report immediately to the town of Merkers, forty miles west of Ohrdruf. Third Army had made another major discovery. Word had come down from the man himself, General Patton: TOP SECRET. NO PRESS.

The two Monuments Men reached the Merkers salt mine on the afternoon of April 8. Security was unlike anything Posey had ever seen. Tank battalions, infantry regiments, and military police—more than a thousand soldiers in all, with more reporting for duty each hour—surrounded the mine and its five primary entrances. Getting past the numerous sentry posts and maze of tanks, machine gun–mounted jeeps, and other military vehicles took time, but eventually the two Monuments Men reached the mine entrance, where they were quickly briefed.

Posey and Kirstein heard an impossible story. Two days earlier, MPs stopped two women, one of whom was pregnant, walking along a dusty road past curfew. Their explanation seemed simple enough: Both were French displaced persons on their way to visit a midwife. After confirming their story, MPs provided the women with a ride. Passing the Merkers mine, the MPs asked about the facility. One of the women said that the mine contained gold and valuable works of art, which local civilians and displaced persons had been forced to help unload. Within hours, Lieutenant Colonel William Russell of the 90th Infantry Division corroborated the woman's statement and ordered the first of multiple security detachments to guard the mine entrances.

The lieutenant colonel and his team had already descended

into the mine the day before, the two Monuments Men learned. At the bottom of the elevator shaft, just outside the cage, they found 550 bags of Reichsmarks stacked against the wall. They also found the room that reportedly contained the gold, but multiple attempts to open the steel door failed.

It wasn't until engineers used half a stick of dynamite to blow a hole in the wall that the gold was revealed—tons of it. Posey and Kirstein couldn't wait to see it for themselves. Their assignment was clear: They were to make a quick inspection of the gold and currency, assess the importance and quantity of the art, then report back with their findings.

Before stepping onto an elevator large enough to transport a jeep with room to spare, someone tossed the two Monuments Men a few rags to wipe the highly corrosive salt from their leather boots. The elevator then began its descent into total darkness. Kirstein hoped that the German operator wasn't one of the "stay-behind SS men" they'd been hearing about, intent on causing destruction behind the lines. It took several minutes for the elevator to reach the base of the mine, twenty-one hundred feet beneath the surface.

They stepped out of the elevator into a subterranean beehive of activity, with heavily armed soldiers, MPs, and army photographers all running about. Finely pulverized salt blanketed the mine floor, irritating both sinus and throat. A large but still shut bank-type steel door, with combination lock and a hole in the brick wall next to it, made finding Room No. 8—and the gold—easy. Kirstein stepped through the opening, one leg at a time, just as an officer was playfully having his photograph taken staring at a helmet filled with gold coins.

Even 2,100 feet below ground, security was tight inside the Merkers mine.

Posey and Kirstein could see that Room No. 8 was nothing more than a walled-up cavern with large storage areas on either side of a mine cart track running down the center. The space measured about 75 feet wide, 150 feet long, and 12 feet high, illuminated by a string of floodlights that hung above the track. Thousands of canvas bags in knee-high piles lined the right side of the cavern, from the vault door to as far as they could see. Each bag had been stenciled with the word "Reichsbank." Nearby, bales of currency stacked in chest-high rows stretched to the back of the cavern.

The seal had already been broken on one of the bags, exposing a gold bar stamped with the weight of the ingot, the purity of the gold, and an eagle atop a swastika, the emblem of the Nazi Party.

The discovery at Merkers included bags of gold bars and coins worth $250 million (about $8.5 billion at today's gold price).

Now all the security aboveground made sense, Posey thought. Third Army had just discovered the entirety of Nazi Germany's gold reserves.

While others continued their analysis of the discovery in Room No. 8, Posey and Kirstein made their way to the art, which was no simple task. The mine complex had thirty-five miles of tunnels. The gold rush had drawn all attention away from the art. But upon seeing thousands of crates containing many of the riches of Berlin's world-class museums, the duo knew that the value of the art was no less stunning. Gold could be appraised at face value; one-of-a-kind works of art like the Bust of Nefertiti, which was more than thirty-two hundred years old, were truly priceless.

For a brief while, Kirstein felt transported to another world, one he knew intimately well, far from the horror and destruction of war. Walking among so many beautiful treasures, studying photographs that curators had clipped from museum catalogues and then pasted onto the crates to identify contents, provided a joyful escape. Almost every period of civilization was represented: Egyptian, ancient Greek and Roman, Gothic, Renaissance, Baroque, and the nineteenth and twentieth centuries. The crates contained paintings, drawings, sculpture, tapestries, rugs, prints, and rare books—even eight lead boxes filled with Egyptian papyri. In their haste to evacuate bomb-ravaged Berlin, curators had also

Monuments Man Sergeant Kenneth C. Lindsay poses with the Bust of Nefertiti, one of many museum treasures found inside the Merkers mine.

brought four hundred additional loose paintings, some master-pieces, which were standing in racks, back-to-back.

Posey reached two conclusions quickly: The art in the Merkers mine belonged to German museums. None of it appeared stolen. The second conclusion took but an instant. For the art to safely be moved out of the mine, they needed George Stout.

After returning to the surface and sharing their findings with Lieutenant Colonel Russell, the two Monuments Men and a Civil Affairs officer drove back to Third Army headquarters in Frankfurt to deliver their reports. The Civil Affairs officer's report on the gold stole the show. The preliminary tally of Reichsbank assets inside Room No. 8 included 8,189 gold bars, 711 bags of American twenty-dollar gold pieces, and more than 1,300 bags of other gold coins, in all worth more than 250 million dollars. That figure did not include hundreds of millions of dollars in assorted foreign currencies, and bundles of Reichsmarks totaling about 2.76 billion dollars at face value.

Posey called Stout the following morning and told him that he was urgently needed in Merkers. Having just learned of Huchthausen's death, Stout was busy lining up a Monuments Officer to fill the vacancy at Ninth Army. By the time Stout arrived on the afternoon of April 11, he heard that General Eisenhower had made the decision to relocate the contents of Merkers to a safer location. He wanted the now almost two thousand soldiers guarding the mine, and all their equipment, released from guard duty and returned to the front as quickly as possible. Eisenhower hoped that with the enemy's primary source of war funding now in the hands of the Western Allies, the war might be one step closer to ending.

At 10:30 on the morning of April 12, Generals Patton, Bradley, and Eisenhower visited the Merkers mine, their first stop on a day-long inspection tour. As the generals descended into the darkness on the rickety single-cable elevator, with a German operator at the controls, Patton quipped, "If that clothesline should part, promotions in the United States Army would be greatly stimulated."

"Okay, George, that's enough." Even in complete darkness, all those on the elevator instantly recognized Eisenhower's voice. "No more cracks until we are above ground again."

The generals entered Room No. 8 in awe. Slowly they walked alongside the mine cart track the entire distance of the cavern, past the bags of gold bars and coins and the bundled currency. In the farthest reach of the mine, almost two hundred common suitcases containing gold and silver household items—forks and knives,

General Eisenhower examining one of the two hundred suitcases overflowing with gold and silver objects stolen by the Nazis from Jews and other victims of the Holocaust.

watch bands, cigarette cases, and cups—had been lined up, side by side. Sacks containing gold tooth fillings and rings taken from concentration camp victims were nearby. Unable to smelt their loot into gold and silver bars, the SS had simply delivered the objects, including the gold fillings, to the German Reichsbank for safekeeping. With the other generals looking on, Eisenhower reached down to one of the open suitcases and brushed his hand across the top of all that remained of thousands of people, as if to confirm the whole experience wasn't some horrific nightmare.

April 12, 1945, Generals Bradley, Patton, and Eisenhower (left to right) inspecting paintings in the Merkers min[e]

GIs placed this painting by French artist Édouard Manet atop one of the mine carts.

Before departing, the group passed through the chamber containing some of the crated art objects and racks of loose paintings from Berlin, which included a masterpiece by the French painter Édouard Manet. The mine had been cleared of nonessential personnel for the duration of the generals' visit, but Monuments Man George Stout, deemed absolutely essential, continued his evacuation planning nearby.

Weimar, Germany: mid-April 1945

Several days later, at First Army headquarters in Weimar, Walker Hancock had a rare moment of calm to catch up on developments outside his small part of the war. Leafing through an edition of *Stars and Stripes* newspaper, he read updates about all that had happened on April 12: the generals' inspection of the Merkers mine, their trip later in the day to see firsthand the horrors at Ohrdruf, the forced labor camp that Third Army forces had liberated eight days earlier, and the sudden death of the thirty-second president of the United States, Franklin D. Roosevelt. Any one of those events would have dominated the news, Hancock thought, but for all three of them to happen on the same day?

Stout's evacuation of the Merkers mine had, like everything else involving the leader of the Monuments Men, come off exactly as planned. The art convoy, code name Task Force Hansen, departed the mine for Frankfurt on the morning of April 17, escorted by hundreds of infantry soldiers, military police, machine-gun platoons, an antiaircraft platoon with mobile antiaircraft guns, wreckers, an ambulance, and air cover from a P-51 Mustang fighter. Hancock marveled at Stout's organizational ability. No one else could have pulled off a move of that magnitude in such a short period of time.

Ohrdruf, where the generals had just been, was thirty miles west of the town of Weimar. Hancock stared out the window of his office, trying to imagine what it must have felt like to see an underground complex filled with Nazi treasure and, only hours later, witness something that went far beyond the savagery of war. The scene of dead and emaciated bodies at Ohrdruf had clearly gut-punched the generals. Even battle-hardened General Patton refused to enter a room containing the stacked bodies of twenty to thirty

General Eisenhower and his commanders visited Ohrdruf on the afternoon of April 12, 1945, and were sickened to see the partially charred remains of inmates murdered by the Nazi guards.

naked men, killed by starvation, fearful it would make him sick. General Eisenhower, disgusted that anyone, even an enemy, could systematically behave so cruelly, had ordered every nearby unit not on the fighting lines to tour Ohrdruf. He was incensed. "We are told that the American soldier does not know what he is fighting for. Now, at least, he will know what he is fighting against."

But the discovery of the Buchenwald concentration camp, on a hill just five miles from where First Army and Hancock were headquartered at Weimar, dwarfed what Eisenhower had seen at

Ohrdruf, or at least Hancock heard that it did. Fellow officers who had traveled the short distance returned with stories of murdered men and boys, some lying where they had fallen and died, the charred remains of others found inside industrial-sized ovens.

Hancock knew that his job as a Monuments Man depended on maintaining goodwill with German civilians. Would seeing such atrocities destroy his ability to remain committed to his mission, or sear into his mind sights of such ugliness that he might never create anything beautiful again? Possibly, he thought, and for that reason he decided against going. Besides, as an artist who had made a living studying the human form, Hancock needed to do no more than look into the hollow faces of the emaciated men, survivors of Buchenwald, wandering the streets of Weimar, barefoot, wearing their soiled striped garments, to have a sense of the inhumanity they had somehow survived.

For all the barbarity that had taken place on that hill and at Ohrdruf, an opportunity for a moment of grace appeared one day, and Hancock seized it. His friend, a Jewish chaplain, visited him after conducting the first religious service for Buchenwald survivors since its liberation. Emotionally drained, the chaplain described the experience. If only he had had a Torah, he lamented. Alas, where in Nazi Germany would someone find the most important Jewish religious object?

Hancock broke into a wide smile and said, "I have one here." Just hours earlier, Hancock had come into his office to discover a Torah sitting on his desk, which had been found at the local SS headquarters. Soldiers regularly stopped by his office when they found works of art or other cultural objects and didn't know what else to do with them. None had ever been so well-timed or more greatly appreciated. The chaplain returned to Buchenwald carrying the Torah, an experience he described days later to his friend: "The people weeping, reaching for it, kissing it, overcome with joy at the sight of the symbol of their faith."

Army Chaplain Samuel Blinder examines one of hundreds of Torah scrolls stolen by the ERR.

CHAPTER 15

ON THE MOVE

Near Worms, Germany: last half of April 1945

By the third week in April, word had come down from the top concerning the final push to end the war in Europe. General Eisenhower intended for his armies to cut off and destroy the enemy's fighting forces. The Soviet Red Army, not the Western Allies, would get the prize of encircling and crushing Berlin. And Private Harry Ettlinger would continue his walks in the countryside outside Worms, Germany, reading *Stars and Stripes*, chatting with other soldiers about news from the front, and playing an occasional game of craps—or at least, that's how it looked to him.

Three months had passed since Harry's nineteenth birthday, when he was pulled out of the convoy of replacement troops headed into battle. When he jumped off the tailgate of that truck with his gear and waved goodbye to the eight buddies in his squad, Harry figured some new assignment awaited him. But the only new assignment that came his way was to repack his gear and move to a new location—and then do it all over again, and again. Then came the news that three of his eight friends had been killed in action, and four seriously wounded. A cloud of guilt had hovered over him ever since.

Between the scuttlebutt floating around and what Harry could find in the newspapers, he learned that First Army had reached the Elbe River, just eighty-five miles from Berlin. Rather than push on farther east, or north toward Berlin, Eisenhower sent his armies, lumbering formations of one hundred thousand to one hundred fifty thousand soldiers each, to the remaining borders of Germany: the British 21st Army to the north, the French First Army to the southwest, and the U.S. Sixth and Twelfth Armies to the southeast. First, Third, and Seventh Armies marched south to form a backward L, blocking German forces from retreating southeast into neighboring Czechoslovakia, or south to Austria or Switzerland. With the spring offensive in Italy underway, and Fifth and British Eighth Armies on the move north of Florence, German troops had to choose: fight and die, or surrender. They had nowhere to run.

Now assigned to Seventh Army, all Harry could do was hope that these new orders south, toward Munich, would provide him with an assignment that might in some way make sense for having been spared the fate of his friends.

Outside Worms, Germany: last half of April 1945

Rorimer reported for duty near Worms, Germany, in mid-April as Monuments Officer for Seventh Army. Before Rorimer departed Paris for his new assignment, Valland had warned him: Get to the castle of Neuschwanstein quickly or run the risk of Bruno Lohse, or one of the other Nazi ERR gangsters, destroying the evidence of their looting operation. Even worse, they might destroy the works of art.

Eisenhower's orders removed one obstacle. The hiding places that Valland had identified, including Neuschwanstein, now fell squarely into his area of operations. But with each passing day in his new job, overwhelmed with work, Rorimer worried about getting there in time. Flooding inside a salt mine in Heilbronn, the first repository on Valland's list, threatened to destroy thousands of museum treasures from German cities, along with stained-glass windows, some dating from the twelfth century, stolen from Strasbourg Cathedral in France. Getting the pumps restarted would take days he could not afford with Seventh Army on the move.

The Heilbronn mine.

Stained-glass windows from the cathedral in Strasbourg, France, found among thousands of cultural objects inside Heilbronn mine.

Dozens of known repositories, and hundreds of leads on others, all needed to be checked by Seventh Army's lone Monuments Man. War crimes investigators wanted information and captured documents. Rorimer had plenty of both, but no spare time to assess any of it. Accusations of looting by American soldiers were on the rise and had to be followed up and reported on. Rorimer had cringed when the owner of Castle Warsberg described how an army sergeant had forced her, at rifle point, to turn over the keys to the safe before taking her jewelry and two paintings.

Jim Rorimer intended on fulfilling his duty as a Monuments Officer. He would go to his grave before disappointing Rose Valland for trusting him with her secrets. But in less than two weeks on the job, he grew increasingly concerned that a shortage of manpower placed both commitments in jeopardy.

Paris, France: last half of April 1945

The speed of the Western Allied advance into Germany, and behind-the-scenes prodding by French museum leaders Jacques Jaujard and Albert Henraux, had prompted French First Army to issue an urgent request for volunteers—men or women—to serve as Monuments Officers. Valland applied immediately. Each morning since, with a cigarette in one hand and a cup of espresso in the other, she scanned the pages of *Le Figaro*, tracking the progress of the various armies, especially U.S. Seventh and her friend Jim Rorimer. Soon she hoped to be in uniform and in Germany, engaged in the hunt for tens of thousands of treasures stolen from France, and the Nazi thieves who had threatened to kill her.

Hungen, Germany: last half of April 1945

Since learning about Altaussee, Austria, and its possible treasures from Hermann Bunjes, the corrupt Kunstschutz official, Posey and Kirstein expected that the prized target would fall outside their area of operations. Instead, General Eisenhower's order for Third Army to head southeast, deep into Austria, actually charted a direct path in that direction. Because the remote mountaintop village had no particular military value, Posey had to request Third Army tactical commanders to make the area a priority for occupation.

While Third Army troops plunged deeper into the heart of Nazi Germany, Posey and Kirstein continued their inspections. Entering the town of Hungen, they found eight large buildings filled with Jewish archives, religious items, and nearly 1.5 million books. Why torture and murder Jews at places like Ohrdruf and Buchenwald while at the same time preserving sacred objects that defined their history and faith? Initially, Posey couldn't figure it out; neither could the polymath Kirstein, himself a Jew. Both men listened in disbelief as a custodian explained that the materials had in fact been gathered for the Institut zur Erforschung der Judenfrage—Institute for the Research of the Jewish Question—a pet project of Nazi Party ideologue Alfred Rosenberg.

Acting on a hunch, the two Monuments Men decided to return to Trier and question Hermann Bunjes a second time. Now desperate for any sort of assurance of safe passage for him and his family, Bunjes eagerly revealed more. At Schloss Ellmann, owned by Nazi Reichsmarschall Göring, Posey and Kirstein would find masterpieces from the Naples museums that the Hermann Göring Tank Division had stolen from the Abbey of Monte Cassino to give to their leader on his birthday.

Bunjes also named names. A sketch of the looting operation, along with the names of Nazi officials and art dealers, like Karl Haberstock and Hildebrand Gurlitt, would certainly be helpful to war crimes investigators. With the size of Nazi Germany continuing to shrink, chances were good that the Monuments Men would be the ones to find, arrest, and interrogate some of Hitler and Göring's art henchmen. For a second time, Posey and Kirstein left Bunjes with nothing more than a goodbye, adding Schloss Ellmann and other repositories he had mentioned to their list of stops on the way to Altaussee.

Weimar, Germany: last half of April 1945

Walker Hancock pinpointed the last of the repositories on his list and circled it on the map. After a few hours of work stooped over his desk, he paused to admire his handiwork. The map looked like an utter mess, as if it had developed the measles, with hundreds of little circles around small towns, castles, churches, and mines throughout central Germany. The list of known repositories in First Army's area of operation alone now numbered 230, with more being reported daily.

During his first six months as a Monuments Man, Hancock had struggled to identify even one hiding place containing Nazi loot. Now, in a matter of weeks, the speed of the Allied advance into Germany was yielding repositories faster than they could be inspected and protected. One Monuments Man in all of First Army responsible for checking 230 locations? Impossible. Hancock knew that Posey and Kirstein in Third Army and Rorimer in Seventh Army faced similar challenges, but that in no way diminished his frustration. Nothing about the Monuments operation was more upsetting than knowing that the shortage of manpower made it a certainty that preventable damage would occur.

In the initial months of his job, Hancock, like Posey, Rorimer, Balfour, and Huchthausen, found creative solutions to overcome the chronic lack of transportation. But a soldier hitchhiking with a duffel bag was one thing; trying to move thousands of works of art on a moment's notice was something entirely different. No amount of creativity or resourcefulness could change the fact that getting to the repositories required wheels. Relocating the contents required fleets. The Monuments Men had neither.

Lack of transportation wasn't the only problem. Tens of thousands of displaced persons were wandering all over Germany, seeking any kind of shelter possible, looking for anything of value that might help them survive another day. Hiding places containing valuable works of art were, for some, a prayer twice answered. The Monuments Men needed security teams to guard the repositories, at least until they could get there and inspect them. But during combat operations, spare troops simply weren't available.

Sometimes the storage conditions inside a repository were adequate. Hancock remembered how, despite mold growing on some of the paintings in the copper mine at Siegen, George Stout had judged the overall conditions tolerable until the objects could be relocated. But relocated where? As Hancock took another look at his map, he realized that no one, not even Stout, had anticipated discovering such vast quantities of priceless treasure in so many bizarre and oftentimes remote locations.

One other thing had changed, and it sickened Hancock's artistic roots just as much as it did his sense of mission protecting cultural treasures from the destruction of war. Following the discoveries of Ohrdruf and Buchenwald, compassion for the enemy was in short supply. In the minds of some soldiers, German-owned works of art were looked at no differently than the men and women who had constructed and operated the concentration camps. As their thinking went, these cultural objects belonged to German citizens, so many of whom had stood by watching it snow during the warmth of summer, pretending they didn't know that the grayish ashes were all that remained of Jews and others judged unworthy of life by the Nazis. Or perhaps the works of art had once belonged to the family of a Wehrmacht soldier who had killed a buddy or wounded a comrade. Anything considered German was fair game for retribution.

For the time being, all Hancock could do—all any of the Monuments Men could do—was triage each reported repository, continue pleading for transportation and security, and be on the lookout for temporary shelters to relocate the priceless objects they were finding.

Frankfurt, Germany: last half of April 1945

George Stout understood the immense stress on his fellow officers. The demands on each Monuments Man serving on or near the front were increasing, but their numbers were not. The job had become even more dangerous, as the deaths of Balfour and Huchthausen confirmed. Stout shared his colleagues' frustrations about the lack of army resources and support. He remembered the loneliness of the job from his early months setting up the operation in France. Those days seemed easy compared to the enormity of what they now faced. A trickle of hidden works of art had become a flood, with no place to move them, and oftentimes no one to guard them.

On April 20, while visiting Third Army headquarters, Stout received a call from Hancock, who was "desperate for need of help." Having worked with Hancock so closely in Aachen and at the discovery in Siegen, Stout knew his friend was in trouble.

When Hancock called back three days later and reported "repos out of hand," Stout was sure of it. Posey at least had Kirstein's help. Rorimer had just received temporary support from Monuments Man Charles Kuhn, a superior officer who recognized that the need in the field was greater than in his office. But Hancock was entirely on his own.

Florence, Italy: last half of April 1945

The start of the spring offensive in Italy—Operation Grapeshot—put a very restless Deane Keller and Fred Hartt back in the hunt for the priceless treasures, 735 objects in all, belonging to the Florence museums and churches. Keller accompanied Fifth Army troops north, who were racing to beat German forces to the Po River before they could escape across the border into Nazi Austria. Hartt remained in Florence, removing the protective coverings on various monuments while scrounging for information about the missing masterpieces.

Eight months had passed since the theft by Wehrmacht troops of paintings and sculpture from a handful of Tuscan repositories. During that time, all efforts to identify the location of the missing masterpieces, including Hartt's overture to the Vatican through Cardinal Elia Dalla Costa, the archbishop of Florence, had met with dead ends. Ernest DeWald, director of the MFAA in Italy, thought the Germans might move the trove of paintings and sculpture across the border into Switzerland "when the stampede begins." But Hartt, filled with anxiety, envisioned a far worse scenario: In a last desperate act, some German commander might order the works of art destroyed. With the U.S. Fifth Army and British Eighth Army now fighting their way north toward Nazi Germany, the Monuments Men were running out of time.

Hartt had squeezed every one of his contacts in Florence hoping for a fresh lead. Major Alessandro Cagiati, an American intelligence officer whom Hartt had befriended one month earlier, had provided a break of sorts. The Florentine treasures, thought to be in a "good state," could be found in the Alto Adige region. Cagiati's operatives didn't know the actual location. Hartt grabbed his map of Italy, quickly unfolded it on the table, and followed his finger up the map, stopping at the regional capital, Bolzano. The Alto Adige, located more than 250 miles north of Florence, shared a long border with Austria, which meant the works of art were already in Nazi territory, as far as Hartt was concerned. Another message from Cagiati soon followed. Hartt read it, shaking his head in horror: "It is feared by the Germans themselves (those who are friends of the arts) that these works of art will be at the last minute removed or ruined in the haste of removing them by the SS . . ."

Bologna, Italy: last half of April 1945

Deane Keller, Charley Bernholz, and British Monuments Man Teddy Croft-Murray entered Bologna on the evening of its liberation, April 21. The sixty-seven-mile drive from Florence took eight hours as traffic crawled along blacked-out roads jammed with vehicles. Keller had seen his share of how war visited small Italian towns. "Coming into town late at night," he wrote to his parents, he saw "houses on fire, mines exploded by engineers." All around was the "smell of death, dead animals, a couple of German soldiers, one in two pieces, another headless." It all left him wondering if the destruction—and the war—would ever end.

The rapid advance meant Fifth Army needed its Monuments Officer, so Keller departed, leaving the task of locating and questioning the art superintendents of Bologna and other nearby towns to someone else. Finding anyone amid such destruction involved a fair bit of luck, but soon enough the British Monuments Officer located Dr. Pietro Zampetti, Director of Galleries in Modena. Wasting no time, with notebook in hand, Croft-Murray asked Zampetti what he knew about the Florentine treasures. The museum director answered in a very matter-of-fact manner: The works of art taken by German forces could be found in two small villages in the Alto Adige, San Leonardo in Passiria and Campo Tures.

CHAPTER 16

THE BEGINNING OF THE END

Verdun, France: end of April through the first week of May 1945

George Stout walked into his office at Twelfth Army headquarters in Verdun, France, on April 29 to find another message from Walker Hancock, his third in nine days. This one was different. "Very urgent matter . . . request inspection . . . earliest possible opportunity." Stout knew that Hancock didn't panic, and he didn't use words like "urgent" carelessly. If he said something was "urgent," that meant *urgent!* Efforts to find out more by telephone proved fruitless.

Bitter winds combined with a lingering winter chill made the daylong, three-hundred-mile drive miserable. Stout wondered what would end sooner, the cold weather or the war. But the following morning, May 1, a hot cup of coffee at First Army headquarters in Weimar and a warm welcome from Hancock worked wonders. After several brief meetings, the two Monuments Officers and an army photographer made their way ninety miles north to Bernterode, a salt mine in the Thuringian Forest, and the reason for Hancock's urgent call.

With Stout at the wheel, Hancock filled in the details of how this latest bizarre episode had begun. Two days earlier, an army captain had walked into the chief of staff's office and laid on his desk a jeweled scepter and orb, both made of gold, which he'd removed from the mine. This made quite an impression on the boss, General Hodges, who promptly ordered Hancock to substantiate the young captain's fantastic story and report back. Having been inside the copper mine in Siegen, surrounded by priceless works of art and the Aachen Cathedral treasures, Hancock believed anything was possible in this war. Still, he drove to Bernterode with a certain degree of skepticism.

Bernterode wasn't a town as much as it was a camp for two thousand displaced men and women, Italian, French, and Russian slave laborers, who for nine years had worked in the munitions plant and storage depot deep inside the mine. A squad of GIs searching for stockpiles of ammunition reached Bernterode, made the eighteen-hundred-foot descent, and discovered the mother lode: more than four hundred thousand tons of explosives, a staggering quantity equal to the weight of about twelve thousand Sherman tanks.

As the squad searched the mine's fourteen miles of tunnels, they came upon a freshly plastered wall. Curiosity got the better of them. Six feet of rubble later, they discovered a padlocked door, which they promptly dispensed with, and entered the subterranean chamber. The room, a long rectangle measuring seventeen feet wide by forty-five feet long, had been partitioned, using salt blocks and mortar, into a series of bays, each containing paintings, military banners, tapestries, crates—and four caskets. Draped across the top of one of the three wooden boxes was a wreath and broad red silk ribbons bearing a swastika and the name "Adolf Hitler."

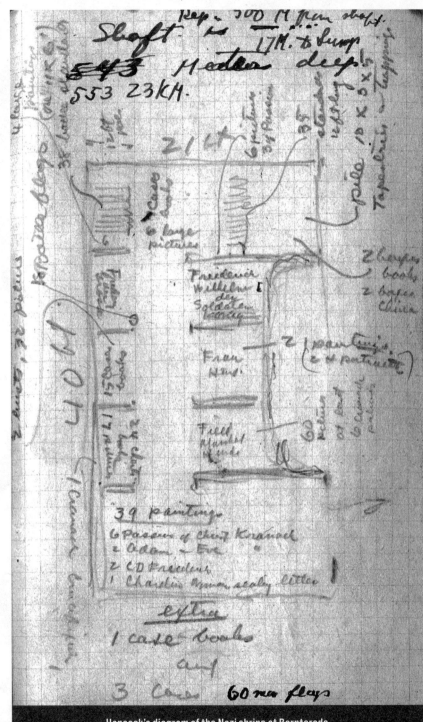

Hancock's diagram of the Nazi shrine at Bernterode.
The four caskets are indicated in the center of his sketch.

Thinking they had found the body of the leader of Nazi Germany, the sergeant posted guards, then hightailed it back to his command post to report the stunning news to his commanding officer, Captain Greenspan. The following day, the captain returned to conduct his own inspection, astonished to see exactly what the squad sergeant had described. Knowing his credibility would be on the line, and not wanting to submit such an outlandish report without some proof, the young captain departed for First Army headquarters, taking the scepter and orb with him.

Stout, Hancock, and an army Signal Corps photographer soon reached the mine and made the descent into darkness. Bernterode wasn't quite as deep as the Merkers mine, nor was its tunnel

U.S. soldiers initially believed this coffin contained Hitler's remains.

complex as vast, but Stout knew that the danger of entering a powder keg primed to explode made this, his third major repository in as many weeks, by far the most dangerous.

After crawling through the opening, it took just seconds for Stout, as it had for Hancock, to realize that Bernterode was far more than just another art repository. The two Monuments Men had entered a shrine to German military tradition to be preserved for future generations. Regimental banners, 225 in all, hung in rows over caskets containing the remains of 3 of the most important German leaders of the previous 250 years: Frederick William I, known as the "soldier-king"; his son, Frederick the Great, a champion of the arts; and Field Marshal Paul von Hindenburg. A fourth casket contained the remains of the field marshal's wife.

Stout looked at the casket that bore Hitler's name, then looked quizzically at Hancock. It's not him, Hancock said with a shake of his head. The ordnance men had thought that it was Hitler, but it's not. Someone had hastily written each of the names in reddish crayon on small strips of paper and fastened them to the respective caskets using tape, but two had become detached, causing much confusion. The wreath and red silk ribbons bearing Hitler's name rested atop the wooden casket of Frederick William I.

More than 270 priceless paintings, mounds of tapestries, and chests of books filled other spaces inside the chamber. Stout and Hancock also found three cases containing treasures from the Hohenzollern Museum in Berlin, including swords, crowns, and other coronation items—minus the jeweled scepter and orb, which Captain Greenspan had presented to General Hodges two days earlier. Taking no chances, the two Monuments Officers decided to immediately evacuate the gold and silver objects. That night they developed their plan: Hancock would deliver the three cases of coronation treasures to General Hodges at First Army headquarters while Stout scoured the mine buildings at Bernterode for packing materials. Hancock would then return and assist Stout with the removal of the remaining objects.

The following morning brought long-awaited yet shocking news. Overnight, German radio had announced that the leader of Nazi Germany, "fighting till his last breath against Bolshevism,"

had fallen. Adolf Hitler was dead, but the fighting—and the dying—continued. For how long, neither Stout nor Hancock knew. But this much was certain: The dangers to cultural treasures in the hands of a desperate enemy added even greater urgency to finding the remaining hidden repositories before Nazi fanatics and other opportunists could loot or destroy them.

On the road to Modena, Italy: first week of May 1945

On May 2, after eleven exhausting days of inspections, Deane Keller and Charley Bernholz finally headed back to Fifth Army base camp in Modena. Since departing Bologna on April 21, they had driven through bitter cold, rain showers, and mud as thick as pudding, assessing damage to monuments and other cultural treasures in dozens of towns and villages in northern Italy. Now they just wanted to get home, as much as base camp could ever be called "home," and regroup before heading out again.

Seeing another military checkpoint up ahead, Bernholz slowed the jeep to a crawl and then stopped. Passing their documents to the MP, he noticed that the mood of the soldiers seemed jovial. Never one to miss out on a good joke, Bernholz asked what was up. "Haven't you heard, corporal? The war in Italy is over!" The two Monuments Men had heard that partisans had killed the Italian dictator, Benito Mussolini, and other leaders of the Fascist regime, just a few days earlier. That news, like the radio announcement of Hitler's death, had spread like wildfire. But word that all German forces in Italy had surrendered caught them by surprise.

By the time Bernholz pulled the jeep into base camp, the place was abuzz with rumors. Keller wanted facts. After speaking with a military intelligence officer, a much clearer picture emerged. Earlier in the day, representatives of Nazi SS General Karl Wolff had signed an agreement involving the surrender of one million German soldiers stationed in Italy. The war in Italy was officially over. At that moment, the Allied armies extended from the Po Valley north to the Alps, and from the port cities of Genoa on the Ligurian Sea east to Venice on the Adriatic. Troops of Fifth Army were racing north to link up with lead elements of Seventh Army pushing south, through Germany and Austria, to seal the Brenner Pass and trap enemy forces, especially high-ranking Nazis suspected of war crimes.

The sudden collapse of German forces had taken everyone by surprise. Keller walked to his tent feeling numb. Like many other officers, what excitement he felt was muted out of respect for the men still fighting to end the war in Europe. At least more of the boys in Italy would be spared and could go home to their families, he thought. But the danger of booby traps continued, and so did his work.

Before lights out, Keller started a letter to Kathy and sketched a drawing for Dino. Thoughts of home prompted him to reach for his field journal. From Fort Myer, Virginia, to Tizi Ouzou, Algeria, to Naples, Italy, and all the way up the peninsula, Keller had been away from his family 584 days. He'd missed one of his son's birthdays, and with the amount of work remaining, he was certain to miss another. Soon the combat troops would begin returning home to their families, but the work of the Monuments Men was increasing. Going home still seemed a long way off.

On May 4, while loading gear into the jeep for an inspection trip to Milan, a private came running up to Keller with an urgent telegram. The message, from Monuments Man Major Norman Newton with British Eighth Army, was short and to the point: The missing treasures from Florence were missing no longer. They could be found in the Alto Adige region, in the villages of San Leonardo in Passiria and Campo Tures. Newton's message lacked any details about the condition of the repositories or the works of art, but Keller knew that time was of the essence.

As much as he wanted to hop in the jeep with Bernholz and drive those 150 miles north, Keller had to be in Milan to hand over responsibility for the Lombardy region to Monuments Officer Lieutenant Perry Cott. For the time being, all he could do was notify Monuments Officer Lieutenant Colonel Ward-Perkins of the discovery and ask him to head north as soon as possible. Keller also sent a message to Fred Hartt ordering him to depart Florence for the Alto Adige region. Hartt had more knowledge than anyone about what had been stolen. He also had the all-important inventory lists, which they would need to check the contents and determine if anything was missing. With any luck, Keller hoped he could wrap up his work in Milan and still get to the two repositories in time to greet Ward-Perkins and Hartt.

Near Darmstadt, Germany: first week of May 1945

When Rorimer first heard the news, he immediately cabled SHAEF headquarters, but what he wanted to do was call Rose Valland. Colonel Kurt von Behr, the Nazi commandant of the Jeu de Paume who, along with Bruno Lohse, had threatened to kill her, had been found dead. In full dress uniform, the once-powerful head of the ERR in Paris had opened a 1918 vintage bottle of champagne, pouring one glass for his wife and one for himself, added a touch of cyanide to both, and cheated the hangman's noose.

The chain of events that followed were as sudden as they were dramatic. Mussolini's capture and grisly death at the hands of partisans, the news of Hitler's death in Berlin, and the German surrender in Italy all occurred in a matter of just four days. Something else happened during that period that made Rorimer's heart race: Lead elements of Seventh Army had captured Neuschwanstein Castle, apparently intact, and were awaiting his arrival.

Valland's pleas that he get to the castle with all due haste never left his thoughts. Taking no chances, Rorimer had forwarded that information to his commanders weeks earlier, making certain they knew the importance of the repository. Finally, the obstacles to getting to the castle were out of the way. Primed and full of excitement, Rorimer raced to the transport depot only to be informed that no vehicles were available.

After nine months of work as a Monuments Officer, crossing seven hundred war-torn miles, from Utah Beach in France to small towns deep in the heart of Nazi Germany, Rorimer wasn't about to let a lack of transportation stop him. Soon the war would be over; he was sure of it. Finding the remaining repositories was now more urgent than ever. Rorimer quickly cornered a Red Cross worker in a nearby office and, after explaining his predicament, talked him into lending one of their jeeps.

One of the other repositories on Valland's list happened to be on the way to Neuschwanstein Castle, so Rorimer decided to stop and inspect it. According to her notes, the Nazis were using a Carthusian monastery in the town of Buxheim, near Memmingen, just fifty miles north of the castle, to store overflow items and as a studio for the restoration of damaged works of art. A detachment of Seventh Army soldiers had already arrived and was busy securing the monastery from looting by displaced persons.

Rorimer quickly found what Valland had assured him was there. Looted Renaissance and eighteenth-century furniture filled the corridors. Some rooms were in shambles, with pottery and paintings lying about; others contained shelving with sculpture and art objects neatly stacked. Every space had something that belonged to someone else.

Wooden crates in an adjacent room, each bearing black stencil marks on the side, caught his eye. As he got closer, the lettering came into focus: D.W., the Nazi ERR inventory code for objects stolen from Pierre David-Weill, one of the world's most prominent collectors of art. Rorimer counted seventy-two crates in that one room alone. Upon entering the chapel, Rorimer stopped dead in his tracks. The Nazis had converted this place of worship into a storage facility for rugs and tapestries, all ERR loot stolen from the Rothschild family and other Jewish collectors. Every piece he had seen up to this point had passed through the Jeu de Paume Museum under the watchful eye of Rose Valland.

Rorimer barely had time to catch his breath when he found the ERR restoration studio and more than 150 paintings by some of the most admired artists in the world, including Goya, Watteau, Fragonard, Murillo, and Renoir. Few museum collections in the world could rival what filled just this one room. Valland had tried to prepare him for sights such as this; Jacques Jaujard had, too. But hearing about it couldn't compare with finally seeing it. "Works of art could no longer be thought of in ordinary terms—a roomful, a carload, a castle full, were the quantities we had to reckon with." If this was just the ERR overflow, what awaited him at Neuschwanstein Castle?

The sudden death of Walter Huchthausen one month earlier served as a constant reminder of the dangers of driving on the roads in Nazi Germany, even with vastly superior forces. After a restless night filled with anticipation of what he might find, Rorimer completed the journey to Füssen, a small town at the foot of the mountaintop castle, the following morning. Troops of the 20th Armored Division, which just days earlier had participated in the liberation of Dachau, the first concentration camp constructed by the Nazis, had acted on Rorimer's tip and secured the castle.

Local guidebooks described the castle of Neuschwanstein, built on a rugged cliff against a picturesque mountain backdrop, as the fairy-tale castle of King Ludwig II of Bavaria. But from Rorimer's point of view, it was nothing more than a "romantic and

Rorimer found stolen paintings inside the Nazi restoration studio at the Buxheim monastery.

Neuschwanstein Castle.

remote setting for a gangster crowd to carry on its art looting activities." Driving up the forested winding road in the crisp mountain air brought Rorimer and Major Duncan, of the 20th Armored Division, to the castle entrance. The cannon-mounted armored cars parked on either side of its great iron doors made quite an impression, even on Rorimer.

Christoph Wiesend, custodian of the castle for fourteen years, served as their guide and led them through the lower court entry and up the first of many steep flights of steps. At each door Wiesend stopped, reached for a large ring with dozens of skeleton keys, unlocked the door for all to enter, then turned and locked it behind him. The first room they entered contained crates stacked to the ceiling, each stenciled with an ERR inventory code that identified the Jewish collector from whom it had been stolen.

The small group continued ascending a spiral stairwell, stopping for the custodian to perform his door unlocking and locking ritual, only to find another room filled with more crates of art objects stolen from France, many with the shipping labels still intact. They also came across thirteen hundred paintings that belonged to German museums in Bavaria, including those in Munich. Some rooms contained rare furniture belonging to Paris collectors, while others had sculpture and art objects. Rorimer felt like he was in a trance seeing so many important art objects stored in such a place. Delving further would have to wait for another day.

The next room required two keys to open a concealed steel door. Valland's voice echoed in Rorimer's mind: "Get to the castle of Neuschwanstein quickly or run the risk of Bruno Lohse, or one of the other Nazi ERR gangsters, destroying the evidence of their looting operation." Had he made it in time? The room—more like a vault—didn't contain the ERR records as Rorimer had hoped, but instead was filled with thousands of pieces of silver from the David-Weill and other collections, along with two large chests of priceless medieval jewelry belonging to the Rothschild family.

Their mind-boggling tour moved on to the *Kemenate*, a room in the castle containing two coal stoves and proof that the Nazis had at least started if not completed the destruction of evidence. Rorimer grabbed a poker and pulled out what remained of a Nazi uniform. The sight of charred documents, including one with the signature of Adolf Hitler, made his heart sink.

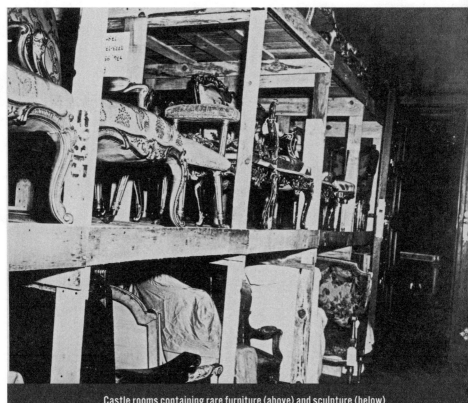

Castle rooms containing rare furniture (above) and sculpture (below) stolen from private collectors in Paris.

Rorimer holds a priceless piece of jewelry stolen from the Rothschild family in Paris.

Moments later, the custodian ushered them into yet another room. In an instant, Rorimer knew his search for the documents had come to an end. It was all there: file cabinets containing more than eight thousand photo negatives of stolen objects, individual catalogue cards of what had been taken and from whom, and thirty-nine brown leather albums containing photographs of the most important and valuable stolen works, a gift for the Führer from the head of the ERR, Alfred Rosenberg. This one room contained documents that not only proved the guilt of those involved but provided a road map of the ERR looting operation, which would enable the Monuments Men to run the theft in reverse and get the stolen items back to their rightful owners.

Rorimer discovered these file cabinets containing records documenting the Nazi looting operation in Paris.

While making plans to return to the castle the following day, Rorimer casually flipped through the security logbook until the sight of a familiar name caught his eye: Dr. Bruno Lohse. The custodian confirmed that Lohse had indeed been at the castle just one week earlier. To bag all the ERR records *and* possibly one of the most notorious thieves, all in a day? The very idea seemed too good to be true. After a few more questions, Rorimer learned that Lohse was hiding in a nearby village. Before departing, he ordered the sentry to deny admission to anyone who tried to enter—no exceptions.

Several hours later, with very little daylight left, Rorimer, accompanied by an army counterintelligence officer, pulled up to a Methodist nursing home. A short conversation with the mother

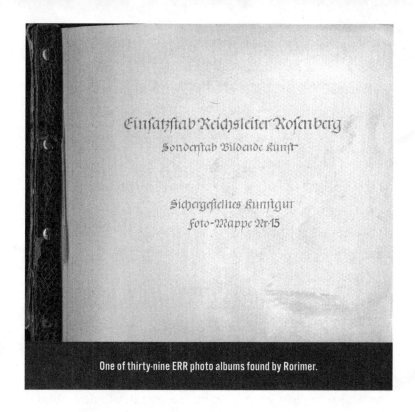

Einsatzstab Reichsleiter Rosenberg

Sonderstab Bildende Kunst

Sichergestelltes Kunstgut
Foto-Mappe Nr 15

One of thirty-nine ERR photo albums found by Rorimer.

superior confirmed that Lohse and Dr. Günther Schiedlausky, another ERR figure, were in residence. She hadn't wanted to admit them, but as they insisted, she figured that taking in "dogs and fiends" was a reasonable price to pay for liberation.

By 7:00 p.m., Dr. Bruno Lohse, successor to Colonel Kurt von Behr as chief of staff of the western division of the ERR, had a new temporary residence: the local jail. Thousands of paintings, drawings, sculpture, and pieces of furniture and jewelry belonging to private collectors in France had been found safe. Evidence of the Nazi looting operation in France had been secured. And the remaining living figure who had threatened to kill Rose Valland was under arrest. Rorimer considered it a pretty good day.

Near Munich, Germany: first week of May 1945

Three days later, a disconsolate Private Harry Ettlinger found himself sitting in a German military barracks on the outskirts of Munich. The war would end soon—everyone knew it—and he had yet to make a single meaningful contribution. Lost in thought, the sound of a nearby voice startled him.

"I hear you speak German," the voice said.

"Yes, sir," Private Ettlinger replied, almost saluting before noticing that the soldier speaking to him was also a private.

"I've been translating for the last two days. It's interesting work, but it's not for me. Perhaps you'd be interested in taking the job?"

Ettlinger jumped at the chance to do something, anything, while there was still something to be done. Following the directions the private had given him, he crossed the parade ground in front of the barracks and went to the second floor of the building that housed Seventh Army headquarters. Inside a small office he found two men working at their desks. A third man standing in the middle was asking questions rapid-fire.

"Are you the new translator?" asked the standing man, a lieutenant.

"Yes, sir. Private Harry Ettlinger, sir."

"You sound German, Ettlinger."

"American, sir. But born a German Jew. From Karlsruhe."

"Are you assigned to a unit, Ettlinger?"

"Not that I know of, sir."

The lieutenant reached for a stack of papers and handed them to Ettlinger. "Read these documents and tell us what's in them.

Just the gist, and anything specific: names, locations, works of art." And just that quickly, the lieutenant turned and hurried out the door.

"What a wheeler-dealer," Harry said to one of the men sitting at his desk.

"You don't know the half of it," the man replied. "He's trying to secure the two most sought-after buildings in Munich, Hitler's office and the former Nazi Party headquarters. Patton wants them for his regional headquarters, but knowing our lieutenant they'll soon be the MFAA collecting points for all the stolen art that's been found."

Seeing that Ettlinger looked a bit confused, the man laughed and introduced himself. "Welcome to Monuments work. I'm Lieutenant Charles Parkhurst, from Princeton University."

"Harry Ettlinger, from Newark. And who was *that*?"

"That was Lieutenant James Rorimer. Your new boss."

CHAPTER 17

SALT MINES AND JAIL CELLS

Bernterode, Germany: first week of May 1945

After delivering the three cases of jewel-encrusted gold and silver coronation items removed from Bernterode to the Reichsbank vault in Frankfurt, Walker Hancock hurried back to the mine to assist George Stout. Packing the rare books, paintings, tapestries, and military banners and preparing them for removal to the surface started on May 4. Over the next three days, wet conditions inside the mine, along with power outages that made it seem like

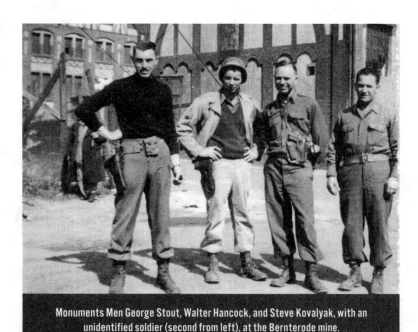

Monuments Men George Stout, Walter Hancock, and Steve Kovalyak, with an unidentified soldier (second from left), at the Bernterode mine.

the darkness had swallowed them up, complicated an already exhausting process.

With Hitler dead and the war near an end, Hancock's mind periodically drifted to thoughts of seeing his wife, Saima, again. Another power outage threw the mine into total darkness, which brought work to a halt. Until the generators could be restarted, Hancock took advantage of the moment and reached for his flashlight—and a four-hundred-year-old painting by German master Lucas Cranach. Using the back of the wood-panel masterpiece as a writing desk, Hancock aimed the flashlight beam and began writing:

> *Dear Saima, You could never imagine what strange circumstances this is being written under. I can't tell you now, but I do want you to have a line actually written in one of the most unbelievable places . . . Geo. Stout is here to give me an urgently needed boost. He really is a friend in need.*

By the time the two packing crews finished work on the night of May 6, everything but the four caskets had been wrapped, waterproofed, transported to the surface, and placed in a shed at ground level. The following morning, Hancock directed the men, fifteen in all, as they strained to lift the casket containing Frau von Hindenburg, to carry it through the narrow chamber passageway, around a tight corner, and down the dimly lit corridor to the mineshaft elevator fifteen hundred feet away. Maneuvering the lightest of the four caskets into the limited space of the elevator took some time, but soon it was on its way. The mortal remains of Frederick William I, the "soldier-king," followed hours later.

With more than half the day gone, Hancock decided to end his subterranean existence and rode to the surface atop the third casket, containing Field Marshal von Hindenburg. Only the massive steel chest with Frederick the Great remained. It took the underground evacuation team an hour to load the twelve-hundred-pound casket into the elevator. After four days of constant use, everyone hoped that the groaning elevator would survive the journey and make it to the surface.

A radio installed in the mine office next to the elevator landing was blaring in the background, but Stout and Hancock focused all their attention on the elevator and its cargo. The trip up normally took about six minutes, but rising at the slowest possible pace would more than double that time. Around 11:00 p.m., the sound of the elevator engines signaled that the eighteen-hundred-foot journey had started. At that moment, the unmistakable melody of "The Star-Spangled Banner" blared out from the radio. Upward Frederick the Great's remains rose toward the surface. His casket emerged when yet another well-known song began playing: "God Save the King." The war in Europe was over.

Altaussee, Austria: second week of May 1945

The German surrender brought an end to the fighting, but with hundreds of repositories to check and the big prize of Hitler's collection still missing, Posey and Kirstein hardly felt like celebrating. That changed quickly on May 12, however, when they learned that

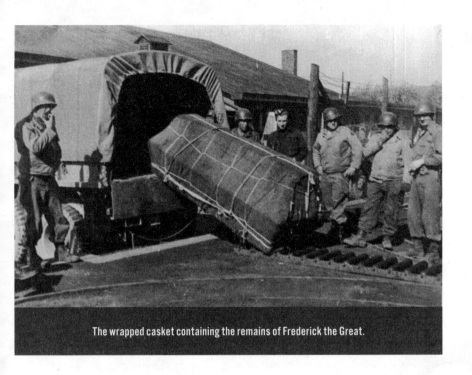

The wrapped casket containing the remains of Frederick the Great.

troops of the 80th Infantry Division had reached Altaussee. They set out immediately.

With Kirstein at the wheel and Posey serving as navigator, they headed south. In towns, it seemed like every piece of white cloth available was hanging out of windows. On the highways, they passed columns of surrendered German forces, still armed, which made a far greater and more ominous impression. Constantly outnumbered, Posey and Kirstein at times felt as if *they* were the prisoners. By the time they reached the border and crossed into Austria, the steady stream of defeated troops and displaced persons, including women and the wounded, had become a flood.

The sight of snowcapped mountains in the distance confirmed that they had entered the Salzkammergut, a mountainous region of Austria containing vast reserves of salt, which locals had mined for thousands of years. Winding hairpin roads took them up forested hills that opened into a series of valleys dotted with Alpine lakes and villages, each seemingly untouched by war. Soon they reached the tiny and picturesque hamlet of Altaussee, where an SS unit had just surrendered to U.S. forces. After a brief stop, they returned to their jeep to drive the short distance to the mine entrance, nervous and excited about what they would find.

On the last stretch of gravel-covered road, the two Monuments Men spotted a two-story rectangular building that housed the mine administration offices. Several days earlier, commanding officer Major Ralph Pearson and a truckload of GIs had captured the building and mine without a fight. Dozens of soldiers and miners were now milling about in the cleared area in front of the mine offices, awaiting orders.

After brief introductions, Major Pearson summarized the situation. The mine had been blown. Hearing the words they had feared most, Posey stared straight ahead, wanting more information. Kirstein, shoulders slumped, shook his head in disgust. Seeing their reactions, Pearson quickly clarified: It was the miners, not the Nazis, who had set off the detonations in the hopes of blocking the salt mine passageways. After entering the administration office building, which housed the Steinberg mine entrance to Altaussee, Pearson continued recounting what he knew.

Weeks earlier, August Eigruber, a Nazi fanatic loyal to the Führer, delivered to the mine for storage eight wooden cases marked *"Vorsicht—Marmor—nicht stürtzen"*: "Attention—Marble—Do Not Drop." The miners assumed the contents were more statues

Monuments Man Captain Robert Posey (center) outside the Steinberg mine at Altaussee.

being shipped to the mine for storage. But the cases didn't contain statues. Inside each crate was a fifteen-hundred-pound high-explosive bomb, essential components of Eigruber's plan to destroy the mine and all its priceless contents.

Soon the miners discovered the contents of the crates. Fearful of seeing their livelihood destroyed along with the works of art, mining executives prevailed upon a high-ranking SS officer hiding nearby to order Eigruber to remove the bombs. The mining executives then immediately enacted their own plan to prevent Eigruber's men from entering the mine: They detonated 6 tons of explosives, sealing 137 tunnels.

Passageways providing access to the mine chambers were now blocked by rubble. The extent of damage to the works of art was

Gauleiter August Eigruber (far left) meeting with Hitler, years before his hastily arranged plan to destroy the works of art stored at Altaussee.

unknown. Standing in front of a pair of wooden doors on either side of a mine cart track, like the one they had seen at Merkers, Pearson handed Posey and Kirstein small acetylene lamps and encouraged them to have a look.

Unlike Merkers, the Altaussee mine contained a maze of horizontal shafts that ran for miles inside the Sandling Mountain, each branching off to some hollowed-out cavern. Timber lined the narrow upside-down-U-shaped passageways to protect against the immense pressure of the mountain. Holding the lamp in front of him, Posey bent his head slightly and stepped into the cold darkness. After months of searching for clues, the time had come to find out what remained of the Ghent Altarpiece and the rest of Hitler's hoard.

Slowly the two men proceeded in single file, rhythmically swinging their lamps side to side, unable to see more than a few feet in front of them. The mine was deathly silent but for the crunching of gravel beneath combat boots, an occasional trickle of water, and then a *yelp!* Kirstein inadvertently bumped his hand against the stone wall, scraping an exposed live electrical wire. The surprise of it startled him more than hurt him. The frigid air helped by partially numbing his hand. A few feet ahead they had to stop again, this time to crawl over debris, and that's when they noticed it: Someone had drilled a hole in a block of stone and inserted a stick of dynamite, which, for whatever reason, had not detonated. More exposed electrical wires, and now sticks of dynamite—Posey wondered what was next.

Taking a few more steps forward, Posey stopped so suddenly that Kirstein almost bumped into him. Standing shoulder to shoulder, they suspended their lamps to see a wall of rubble. Not even two thousand feet into the mine, they had reached a dead end. Posey wondered if the rubble from the explosions had damaged or destroyed whatever was hidden beyond the debris. Did the force of the explosions blast a path for water to flood the chambers and their contents? Until they could get on the other side, there was no way for Posey and Kirstein to know.

After exiting the mine, Posey hastily arranged a meeting with Major Pearson, an army combat engineer, and several of the miners. "How long will it take the workmen to clear the blocked passageways so we can get in?" he asked. The Austrian mine workers estimated seven to fifteen days at best. Posey, convinced the work could be done with the help of the army engineer within a week, perhaps even in just a couple of days, ordered the miners to start immediately and work around the clock. Each day of work meant a sleepless night for the two Monuments Men, wondering what they would find.

Milan, Italy: second week of May 1945

On May 11, with Fred Hartt in transit to the German art repositories at San Leonardo in Passiria and Campo Tures, Deane Keller was still in Milan, and none too happy about it. An army clerical error had prevented Lieutenant Perry Cott, the new Monuments Officer for the Lombardy region, from reporting for duty on time, so Keller had no choice but to extend his stay. At best, he hoped to meet Hartt the following evening in San Leonardo in Passiria.

Most of the cultural landmarks in Milan had sustained some degree of damage from Allied bombing, but the one that worried Keller the most was the church of Santa Maria delle Grazie and its refectory, housing Leonardo da Vinci's greatest artistic achievement, *The Last Supper*. The scene of devastation took his breath away:

> *Bomb hit of August 1943 in the cloister destroyed the right [east] wall of the refectory facing Leonardo's Last Supper. The roof was hit and collapsed when the wall fell. The painting had been sandbagged for protection, plus wood planks and iron scaffolding . . . The roof is nearing completion and the [east] wall has been reconstructed. Until there is no danger from the elements, or danger from what is left of the vaults, which is little, the painting will not be uncovered . . . Its fate is not known.*

For a fleeting moment, standing inside the long rectangular room, with the sound of workmen overhead hammering away, Keller thought about the Camposanto in Pisa and how close its frescoes had come to being lost forever. Had an incendiary instead of high-explosive bomb landed in the courtyard of Santa Maria delle Grazie, the wooden scaffolding would have ignited. The resulting fire would have baked Leonardo's masterpiece to the wall. After his experience in Pisa, Keller knew all too well how that would have turned out. But for the protective bracing installed by local art officials, the high-explosive detonation that destroyed the east wall and roof would have taken the north wall and the painting with it.

Inside the Santa Maria delle Grazie refectory, with its newly constructed east wall and roof, just weeks before the removal of the scaffolding covering *The Last Supper*.

A miracle had taken place inside this space on August 15, 1943; of that Keller was sure. All he could do now—all anyone could do—was hope that Leonardo's *The Last Supper* would emerge intact from behind the scaffolding. In his judgment, for that to happen, they needed a second miracle.

On the road to the Alto Adige region, Italy: second week of May 1945

With orders in hand, and an inventory of what had been stolen from the Florentine art repositories, a very excited Fred Hartt departed for San Leonardo and Campo Tures on May 10. He was accompanied by his driver, Franco Ruggenini, and Professor Filippo Rossi, Director of the Galleries of Florence. They drove two full days, covering 240 miles, through the vast countryside. Everywhere they looked, they saw

> *shell holes, and mountainsides showing more shell holes than grass. The trees were shaved into spikes by the passing shells, the farmhouses reduced to sand heaps, the roads torn by artillery and mines, the villages smashed and tottering, reeking sharply of death in the warm air of a spring morning . . . Mass raids of Flying Fortresses had altered the very landscape, plowing it into craters twenty feet deep, leaving freight and passenger trains dangling into the muddy stream like bunches of grapes.*

Lucky 13 and its passengers stopped in Bolzano on May 11. Hartt desperately wanted to continue, but darkness argued against it. Just thirty-five miles and a few lousy hours of sleep separated him from the Florentine treasures. Finding a hotel in Bolzano proved nearly impossible. Armed and arrogant, lingering German officers occupied all the best lodging in the city. SS generals drove through town in cars loaded with women. Drivers of German staff cars and armored personnel carriers took delight in running U.S. Army vehicles off the road. The sudden end to the war resulted in Allied forces being greatly outnumbered, perhaps ten-to-one or more, by German military personnel in the Alto Adige region. Until reinforcements arrived, Hartt had orders: Avoid incidents and keep a low profile.

The following morning, arriving to the sound of honking geese and screaming children, Franco pulled Lucky 13 up to a three-story building that had once served as the town jail, and stopped. Only iron bars on the ground-floor windows provided a

The jail in San Leonardo in Passiria, Italy.

hint of the building's previous use. After identifying himself to the security detachment from the 88th Infantry Division—known as the "Blue Devils"—that had arrived several days earlier, Hartt waited while a GI fumbled through a massive ring of keys. Impatience quickly changed to excitement as Hartt entered the dark and damp ground floor hallway. Then another delay: The individual jail cells had to be unlocked.

With the jingling of forty skeleton keys, it took what for Hartt felt like an eternity for the nervous GI to find the right one. When he finally opened the door, Hartt nearly fainted. Inside the damp, narrow cell, leaning one against the other, painted sides exposed, were some of the masterpieces stolen from the repository in Montagnana the previous summer.

The first cell alone left him speechless. He immediately recognized Caravaggio's painting *Bacchus*, and other paintings by Rubens, Titian, and Dosso Dossi, propped against the wall like prisoners from the pages of his art history books. Moments later, Hartt jumped when Rossi let out a shriek of joy. There before them were the two fifteenth-century paintings by German master Lucas Cranach, *Adam* and *Eve*, stolen by SS Colonel Langsdorff nine months earlier.

Hartt found other paintings by Botticelli, Andrea del Sarto, Signorelli, and Lorenzo Monaco stacked every which way on the wood plank floors of another cell. The overcrowding of paintings inside such small spaces prevented him from seeing everything that the Germans had stashed inside the jail. Conducting an inventory would have to wait for another day.

He tried to take it all in, but his mind was racing. Cell after

Professor Filippo Rossi standing next to a painting of *Eve*, by German master Lucas Cranach.

This painting by Italian artist Filippino Lippi, was one of more than three hundred found inside the San Leonardo jail by Fred Hartt.

cell, floor upon floor, three hundred paintings—more than half of them among the most important in the world—had survived being transported hundreds of miles over bombed-out roads, stacked side by side on open trucks, many with no more protection than a few blankets and strands of straw. Miraculously, aside from one painting that suffered a split down the entire length of the panel, most of the damage consisted of relatively minor scratches to the paintings and frames from handling and transportation.

It was late, so the three men returned to Bolzano hoping to find Deane Keller and to prepare for the next day's trip to the second art repository, in Campo Tures. Hartt knew that they had been extremely lucky their first day out. With hundreds of works of art still unaccounted for, including all the sculpture, plenty could still go wrong.

CHAPTER 18

CLOSURE

Campo Tures, Italy: May 13, 1945

Early in the morning on May 13, Hartt and Rossi departed Bolzano for the two-hour drive to Campo Tures. The engine of Lucky 13 moaned as it made the gradual climb through the mountainous valley. Snowmelt-filled streams and verdant meadows sprinkled with gingerbread cottages provided a beautiful distraction from war, but Hartt thought only of the hundreds of Florentine treasures that he hadn't found the day before inside the San Leonardo jail.

Months of investigative work during the winter lull had paid dividends. More than just arriving to the Alto Adige region with the inventory of stolen objects, Hartt had also gathered extensive details about the German art looting operation. Florentine superintendent Giovanni Poggi recounted how SS Colonel Alexander Langsdorff, head of the Kunstschutz in Italy, had personally assured him that not a single work of art would be removed from any of the thirty-eight Florentine repositories unless they were in immediate danger. What he didn't tell Poggi was at that very moment, German troops were already loading paintings and sculpture onto trucks for the trip north. And now, just a few miles up the road, Hartt hoped to confront the man whom he believed was responsible for executing the "greatest single art-looting operation in recorded history."

At the end of the V-shaped valley, Hartt could see two prominent castles set against snow-covered Alpine peaks. The larger of the two, Taufers Castle, was nestled on a hill behind the small town of Campo Tures. Neumelans Castle, which reportedly housed the Florentine treasures, marked the beginning of the town and was constructed on the valley floor. A curious mix of GIs from the 85th—the "Custer" Division—Italian partisans, and German soldiers had been guarding Neumelans, a sixteenth-century Tyrolean castle, for about one week while waiting on the Monuments Men to arrive.

As Franco slowed Lucky 13 to a stop in front of the stone wall perimeter, Hartt peered through the metal gate and noticed a very irritated-looking German officer standing in front of the castle door. Rossi recognized him immediately as the man who had promised to protect the cultural treasures of Florence when, in fact, he had facilitated their theft, SS Colonel Langsdorff. The introductions were strained. When the SS colonel criticized Hartt for the delay in getting to the two repositories—after all, he explained,

British Monuments Officer John Bryan Ward-Perkins (far right) supervises SS Colonel Alexander Langsdorff (second from right) and others at the Campo Tures art repository.

he had been on location since April 30 on direct orders from SS General Wolff—and sought credit for his role in protecting the works from Florence, Hartt snapped. After giving Langsdorff a brief tongue-lashing, Hartt entered the castle hoping to find the remaining stolen masterpieces.

In contrast to the damp jail cells at San Leonardo, the dry, airy, high-ceilinged rooms here made Neumelans Castle an ideal storage facility, to Hartt and Rossi's initial relief. They quickly found some of the less important paintings from the Florence museums and works belonging to private collectors. Another room contained small bronzes, ceramics, and tapestries, but still no sculpture. "Where are the works by Michelangelo and Donatello?" Hartt

SS General Karl Wolff.

demanded to know. When someone mentioned the nearby carriage house, Hartt bolted out the front door.

The Gothic stone carriage house had long since been converted into a garage with two large wooden double doors. Hartt wanted them unlocked and opened immediately. A couple of GIs peeled back the creaky doors while everyone watched in rapt anticipation. The darkness of the interior made it difficult for Hartt and Rossi to make out the contents, but once their eyes adjusted, they smiled with glee. The carriage house was packed, wall-to-wall, with crates containing the Florentine treasures. Hartt squeezed in between the tight spaces and found Donatello's sculpture *Saint George* and Michelangelo's *Bacchus*, signature pieces he once feared might be lost forever.

Until Hartt, Rossi, and Keller could inventory the contents of both repositories and check the results against the list that Hartt had brought from Florence, there was no way to know for certain that they had found everything. Transporting a group of the most important works of art in the world nearly three hundred war-torn miles back to Florence presented another obstacle. But those would be challenges for another day. For now, with the cultural and artistic treasures of Florence safe, and Langsdorff and several other members of the Kunstschutz under detention, Hartt felt elation—and relief.

Altaussee, Austria: May 13, 1945

Less than 140 miles away, Posey and Kirstein entered the Steinberg mine at Altaussee for a second time, accompanied by two Austrian miners. Laboring through the night, mine workers had cleared enough rubble for one man at a time to squeeze through the opening. They followed the two miners down the main passageway they had walked the previous day until a pile of sledgehammers and shovels leaning up against the walls told them that this was the spot. At the top of a fifteen-foot-high rubble pile Posey could see a narrow crawl space illuminated by the glow of one of the miner's lamps.

Feeling a mixture of fear and excitement about what he might find, Posey climbed the forty-five-degree slope of debris using his hands and feet, grabbed an acetylene lamp from the lead miner, and disappeared through the opening. Kirstein did the same and followed. From the other side, Posey could see that the miners had done their job well. The detonation had blocked a single short passageway but caused no other apparent damage. Most important, Posey didn't see any sign of flooding.

The two Monuments Men and one of the miners soon reached an iron door with two padlocks, which they ordered removed. The narrow path opened into a small hollowed-out chamber. Ducking down, they entered and saw resting on four empty cardboard boxes eight of the twelve panels of the Ghent Altarpiece.

Eight months had passed since Posey received his first briefing package photo of the van Eyck brothers' masterpiece, and three years since its theft, and now the "odd couple," Captain Robert Posey and Private First Class Lincoln Kirstein, had found it. For a fleeting moment, its beauty seemed to wash away all the ugliness they had seen since setting foot on the beaches of Normandy.

Posey and Kirstein slid over this rubble pile to access the Steinberg mine chambers.

"By our flickering acetylene lamps," Kirstein wrote, "the miraculous jewels of the Crowned Virgin seemed to attract this light. Calm and beautiful, the altarpiece was, quite simply, there."

With their hearts racing, Posey and Kirstein maneuvered around another blocked passageway that took them deeper into the dark, frigid mine. Soon the narrow path opened into a much larger cavern that vaulted nearly three stories high. The floor of the mine had been covered with wooden boards. Heavy beams supported racks filled with hundreds of paintings. Off to the side, almost as a castaway, lying on her shoulder with her son firmly embraced between her legs, was Michelangelo's Bruges *Madonna*, still wrapped in the mattress mentioned in the reports of British Monuments Man Ronald Balfour.

The Monuments Men found these disassembled panels from the Ghent Altarpiece inside the Steinberg mine.

Overwhelmed by what they had seen and unable to reach other chambers, Posey and Kirstein called it a day and followed the lead miner back to the surface. Realizing that much, if not all, of what Hermann Bunjes had told them was true—that somewhere in the Altaussee mine they would find thousands of objects destined for Hitler's Führermuseum—Posey stepped up security.

One major problem emerged after another. The mountain had many access points besides the main mine tunnel entrance Posey and Kirstein had been using. By entering through one of the abandoned mine chambers that had not flooded from use, a person could gain access to the caverns that Posey was desperately trying to secure. Then Posey learned that an ex–mine foreman had a duplicate set of keys to all the security doors. When two gunmen

George Stout hoists the Bruges *Madonna*, still wrapped in the mattress German soldiers used when stealing it

sent by someone in one of the offices of Nazi ERR leader Alfred Rosenberg arrived at the mine in an empty truck, no doubt unaware that U.S. forces had taken control, Posey had them arrested.

Within three days, the Austrian miners had cleared enough debris that Posey and Kirstein were able to reenter the mine to inspect several other chambers. The two Monuments Men entered a cavern known as a *Mineralienkammer*, which contained various crystal samples found in the mine—and the remaining panels of the Ghent Altarpiece. They also found many other valuable paintings, including "R-1," Vermeer's *The Astronomer*, the first object stolen by the Nazis from the Paris branch of the Rothschild family. Keeping track of all the riches they had seen was becoming increasingly difficult.

Another cavern used as a memorial chamber contained rare gold coins and medals as well as valuable collections of military guns, swords, and other weapons. In the *Springerwerke* chamber, they found all eleven paintings that Balfour had reported stolen from the church in Bruges the night the sailors came for the Michelangelo, and hundreds of paintings looted from thirty Jewish Viennese private collectors.

The extensive network of tunnels that connected different levels of the mine complicated the inspection process. Then there was the temperature. Working inside a mountain that functioned like

Monuments Men holding Vermeer's *The Astronomer,*
perhaps the single work of art that Hitler coveted most.

a giant refrigerator set at forty-six degrees chilled one to the bone, especially for newcomers like Posey and Kirstein. Soon enough they reached the *Kammergrafe*, a huge cavern that housed rack after rack of paintings and other art objects that made it a museum unto itself. Kirstein, who had lived a life surrounded by the arts, felt overwhelmed with the variety of what each bin contained, including drawings, prints, etchings, rare books, a theatrical collection, armor, sculpture, tapestries, and furniture.

While Posey added to his inspection notes, Kirstein began flipping through some of the paintings stacked in a different area of the cavern. These were masterpieces of the very highest quality, including Pieter Bruegel the Elder's *The Blind Leading the Blind*, Titian's painting *Danaë*, and other stellar works by Botticelli, El Greco, and Raphael. After a little more digging, Kirstein discovered bronze sculpture from the ancient site of Pompeii. When he saw the words "Monte Cassino" written in crayon on the

The Monuments Men found thousands of stolen paintings stored inside this hollowed-out mine chamber.

temporary frame of one of the paintings, he realized that these were the treasures from the National Museum in Naples that had been stored at the Abbey of Monte Cassino and later stolen by the Hermann Göring Tank Division.

Posey knew right away that conducting any kind of inventory was a job for George Stout and a team of people that he and Kirstein didn't presently have. To prepare for Stout's arrival, Posey ordered the miners to work around-the-clock shifts clearing rubble from the passageways of the Steinberg mine at Altaussee, the closest anyone would ever come to finding Aladdin's magic treasure cave.

A painting by Italian master Bernardino Luini, one of the treasures stolen by the Hermann Göring Tank Division from the Abbey of Monte Cassino.

CHAPTER 19
GOING HOME

Altaussee, Austria: late May to mid-July 1945

By the time word of the discovery at Altaussee reached George Stout, he and Walker Hancock had already relocated the treasures—and four coffins—from the Bernterode mine to a temporary collecting point in Marburg and were in the process of evacuating the contents of the Siegen discovery. Leaving Hancock behind to supervise the remaining work, Stout departed on May 21 for Altaussee.

With the miners still at work clearing the passageways, Stout used the time to develop a preliminary removal and transfer plan. Having worked with him at the Merkers mine, Posey knew that Stout would need to see summary reports of the mine contents to make those calculations. He had them ready.

Sitting inside the mine administration office, beneath an annoyingly dim bulb, Stout strained his eyes as he scanned the mine logbook. After studying just a few pages, he realized that emptying Altaussee of its contents wasn't going to take days or weeks, but months. The quantity of what Hitler had accumulated inside this one mine was staggering. According to the logbook, the various chambers of the Steinberg mine at Altaussee contained:

6,577 paintings

230 drawings or watercolors

954 prints

137 pieces of sculpture

129 pieces of arms and armor

79 baskets of objects

484 cases of objects thought to be archives

78 pieces of furniture

122 tapestries

181 cases of books

1,200–1,700 cases of books or similar

283 cases of contents completely unknown

Clearing the mine passageways was agonizingly slow work, but in mid-June, Stout commenced the first shipment of Hitler's hoard to a central collecting point that Jim Rorimer had established in Munich. A shortage of food, sleeping quarters, and power had everyone in a cranky mood. Incessant rain added to the complications, but still the work continued. Day after day, Stout and his small team loaded trucks with works of art stolen by Hitler's lackeys and watched as they descended the hazardous mountain road bound for Munich.

On the morning of July 10, Stout gathered his team for a short announcement. "This looks like a good day for the gold-seal products," he said. His understated manner caught no one by surprise. The team had spent days crating each separate panel of the Ghent Altarpiece and wrapping the Bruges *Madonna* expecting that they would soon be on their way. That day had now come.

George Stout (center, wearing helmet) crating the central panel of the Ghent Altarpiece.

Using a specially designed rope and pulley system, Stout carefully elevated Michelangelo's marble sculpture about four feet off the ground, then gently lowered it a few inches onto one of the mine carts that had been positioned beneath it. "I think we could bounce her from Alp to Alp, all the way to Munich, without doing her any harm," Stout confidently told one of his coworkers.

Slowly Stout walked alongside the mine cart, his hand gently resting on the Madonna that his friend Ronald Balfour had so desperately hoped to find. Down the dark and narrow passageway, the miners pushed the cart past several chambers that Stout and his team had already emptied. After a bend in the track, it was a straight shot to the mine entrance doors. They offloaded the Bruges *Madonna* and returned for the crates containing the panels of the Ghent Altarpiece.

The following morning, after double-checking that the precious cargo in each truck was firmly secured in place, Stout boarded the lead vehicle and gave the signal to head out. The time had come for the Ghent Altarpiece and Bruges *Madonna*, two of the most important and beautiful works of art in Western civilization, to begin their journey home.

Campo Tures, Italy: late May to late July 1945

Deane Keller finally connected with Fred Hartt for his first visit to the Alto Adige art repositories on May 14. They began at Campo Tures, then drove to San Leonardo the following day. While Hartt rejoiced about finding the masterpieces intact, Keller was already focused on logistics: hundreds of paintings lying about uncrated, persistent shortages of packing materials, roads to Florence that were pulverized, and a railway system that didn't function because Allied aircraft had destroyed it.

Keller initially hoped to transport the works to Florence in a truck convoy that would conclude with a prominent ceremony, allowing Florentines to bear witness to the return of their art. For his plan to succeed, he needed fifty trucks. The only person he knew with that kind of authority was the man who had come to the rescue of the Camposanto, General Hume. "Remember how crowded the Piazza della Signoria was when they put up Michelangelo's David?" he quipped in his request to the general. "You don't, and neither do I, but that's the idea." Alas, the trucks were not available; the army had a duty to feed the starving populations of Milan and other northern Italian cities. He would have to find another solution.

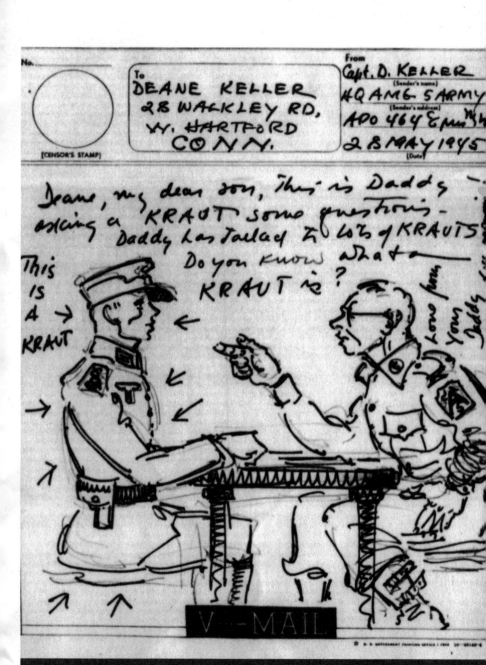

Keller's drawing of one of his interrogations of a German officer.

Dusting off old plans, Keller realized that it might be possible to return the Florentine treasures by rail now that the bridge crossing the Po River neared completion. With Keller at Campo Tures and Hartt at San Leonardo, the two Monuments Men set to work inventorying and packing the art. Hartt soon discovered that ten paintings from the Florence repository at Montagnana, including several of immense value and importance, never made it to the Alto Adige. German soldiers had stolen them en route.

On July 20, Keller watched as 109 crates of paintings from San Leonardo and 46 crates of mostly sculpture from Campo Tures were loaded onto the art train at Bolzano. In filling out a freight

Keller (center, back turned) supervises the removal of sculpture from the carriage house in Campo Tures, Italy.

waybill for the shipment, Keller noted the contents as "art treasures." Under remarks, he wrote simply, "Extreme care necessary." The form also had a space to declare the value of the shipment. After conferring with Professor Rossi, Keller adjusted his glasses, took a deep breath, and wrote in the blank, "$500,000,000."

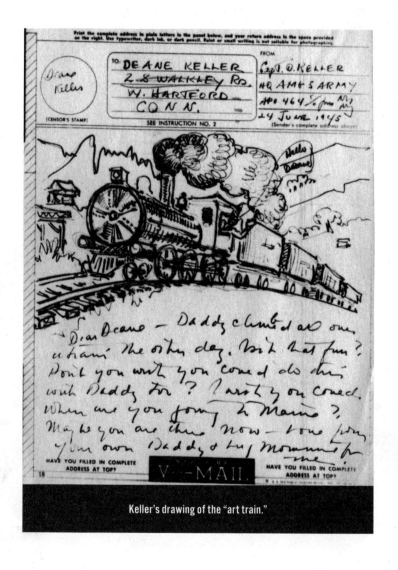

Keller's drawing of the "art train."

The art train arrived in Florence in just under twenty-four hours without incident. The following day, a small convoy, headed by a jeep loaded with MPs, then followed by Hartt in Lucky 13, Keller and Bernholz in their jeep, and six Fifth Army trucks containing some of the art treasures, rolled into the Piazza della Signoria, where thousands of cheering Florentines had gathered. The trucks parked within a few feet of where Nazi leader Adolf Hitler and Italian dictator Benito Mussolini had shared their twisted vision of a new world order seven years earlier. A banner attached to the side of one of the Fifth Army trucks had an inscription in Italian, which, translated, read plainly, "The Florentine works of art return from the Alto Adige to their home."

The triumphant return of the Tuscan treasures to Florence.

Bavaria, Germany: last half of May 1945

After four years of watching Nazi Reichsmarschall Hermann Göring and his SS henchmen use her country like a piggy bank, Rose Valland finally had a chance to do something about it. Being commissioned into the French First Army provided her with a uniform and transportation. Captain Rose Valland headed straight for the Neuschwanstein Castle.

Valland reached the castle in mid-May, just ten days after Rorimer's astonishing discovery. Driving up the same winding road, she got as far as the great iron doors of the castle before a

French First Army Captain Rose Valland.

young GI on guard duty, having no idea who she was, denied her entry. Even through her disappointment, Valland felt a measure of satisfaction. By going to such lengths to protect the stolen works inside the castle, Rorimer had proven to be the ally and friend that France needed.

Hoping to connect with Rorimer and let him know about her new position, Valland turned the jeep around and headed for the MFAA office in Munich. This was just the beginning of her mission in Germany hunting for stolen objects. A visit inside the castle would have to wait for another day.

Rorimer and his new translator, nineteen-year-old Private Harry Ettlinger, moved from place to place at a breakneck pace, rarely setting foot inside his Munich office. After four months of sitting around doing nothing, that suited Harry just fine. Working alongside such a "wheeler-dealer" was exciting. One day he found himself translating for Rorimer as he interrogated a high-level Nazi; the next they were on their way to investigate the discovery of some new art repository.

Toward the end of May, Harry accompanied Rorimer to Neuschwanstein Castle, a place he had grown up hearing about but had never seen. Walking through the iron gates was like stepping into a fairy tale from his childhood, but the fairy tale became a nightmare when he entered the first of dozens of rooms bulging with objects stolen from Jewish collectors in France. Harry couldn't help but wonder how many of the Jewish owners were still alive to claim their belongings.

Because the objects inside the castle had come from France, Rorimer saw no reason to send them to one of the Allied collecting points for processing. Better to ship them back directly. Organizing the trains and emptying the castle might take several months, but until then, everything inside was safe.

The arrest of Nazi Reichsmarschall Hermann Göring on May 9 created quite a stir. His wife was found carrying stolen paintings in her handbag. His trains, which had been abandoned, were overflowing with loot. Then troops of the 101st Airborne found a freshly plastered cave containing hundreds of gold and silver objects, paintings, and sculpture. While Rorimer investigated, Harry hitched a ride to Hitler's mountain chalet, the Berghof. British bombing had damaged portions of the home. Retreating SS troops had tried but failed to burn down what remained. And now

Part of the Göring loot found in a hidden bunker by troops of the 101st Airborne.

Monuments Man Harry Ettlinger, an American, and the last Jewish boy in his hometown of Karlsruhe to celebrate a bar mitzvah before the Nazis unleashed their reign of terror, stood in the expansive windowsill of the home of Adolf Hitler, overlooking a free Germany.

The grand window inside the fire-damaged remains of Adolf Hitler's mountain home, the Berghof.

EPILOGUE

World War II was the most destructive conflict in history, claiming sixty-five million lives, including six million Jews systematically persecuted and murdered by the Nazi regime. The study of this war often focuses on the motivations and actions of the dictators who set these cataclysmic events into motion. The story of the Monuments Men instead highlights the actions of a few good men who, with established careers and families and no reason to volunteer for military service, risked their lives to preserve our shared cultural heritage. In a break with civilizations past—and a victory for the rule of law—it was the policy of the Western Allies to return stolen objects to the countries from which they had been taken for ultimate restitution to the rightful owner. The last Monuments Man didn't depart Europe for home until 1951. By that time, the Monuments Men had overseen the return of nearly four million stolen objects. Good had triumphed over evil.

While this book focuses on the wartime experiences of ten Monuments Men and Rose Valland, there were in fact about 350 or so Monuments Men and Women from 14 nations who served from 1943 to 1951. Initially, the operation comprised Americans and citizens of the British Commonwealth, but the liberation of Western European nations expanded the participation as

Monuments Officers from France, Holland, Belgium, and other European nations volunteered.

Rose Valland remained in Germany for several years after the war, tracking down thousands of stolen works of art. Finding household belongings and personal items taken from the homes of Paris's Jews, which filled 29,436 German railroad cars—in most cases all that remained of the more than 70,000 French Jews who perished in Nazi concentration camps—proved exceedingly difficult. Far from being a shy and timid curator, Valland was bold, strong-minded, intelligent, and courageous. She was a tireless and vocal advocate for the restitution of stolen art until her death in 1980. For her efforts, Rose Valland received the French Legion of Honor and the Medal of Resistance and was made a Commander of the Order of Arts and Letters, making her the most decorated French woman of her time.

Ronald Balfour is buried in the British cemetery outside Cleve, Germany, not too far from where he was killed in action. In 1954, his photograph was placed in the Cleve archive building beside a plaque that reads, in part, "This gentleman saved as a British Monuments Officer precious medieval archives and items of lower Rhine towns. Honor to his memory."

Walter Huchthausen is buried in the Netherlands American Cemetery in Margraten, Holland, among more than eighty-three hundred fallen comrades. His death was a devastating blow to the van Schaïk family, who had befriended Hutch when he was stationed near their home in Maastricht, Holland, several months before he departed on his fateful mission. Frieda van Schaïk was

The author and Monuments Man Harry Ettlinger at the Netherlands American Cemetery, visiting the grave of Monuments Man Captain Walter Huchthausen.

among the first to care for his grave, a tradition that continues through the Foundation for Adopting Graves program and its adopters. Huub, Marlie, and Peter Schouteten care for Walter's grave today. They are the most recent, living proof of the eternal commitment of the people of Holland to honor those who made the ultimate sacrifice for their freedom.

Walker Hancock returned home to his wife, Saima, at the end of 1945. Soon they became parents to a daughter, Deanie. Hancock continued to be a sought-after sculptor and teacher. His most enduring work is the Pennsylvania Railroad War Memorial, located in the 30th Street train station in Philadelphia, a tribute to the thirteen

Walker Hancock's towering sculpture *Angel of the Resurrection*, at the 30th Street train station in Philadelphia.

hundred railroad employees who died during World War II. He received the National Medal of Arts and the Presidential Medal of Freedom from President George H. W. Bush. Walker Hancock died in 1998, beloved to his last day by all who knew him.

Robert Posey accompanied the Ghent Altarpiece to Belgium in August 1945, the very first work of stolen art restituted after the end of the war in Europe. He returned home to Alice, "Woogie," and the Zoo in September 1945 and resumed his career as an architect, working on such notable projects as Sears Tower in Chicago and the Lever House skyscraper in New York. He received the

President George H. W. Bush enjoys the unveiling of his bust alongside sculptor Walker Hancock.

Order of Leopold, one of the highest honors in Belgium, and the French Legion of Honor. Robert Posey died in 1977.

Lincoln Kirstein also returned home in September 1945. The following year, he and his business partner, choreographer George Balanchine, established a new dance troupe, the Ballet Society (renamed the New York City Ballet in 1948), one of the most influential dance companies of the twentieth century. By the end of his life, Kirstein was widely considered one of the major cultural figures of his generation. He received the National Medal of Arts and the Presidential Medal of Freedom from President Ronald Reagan. Lincoln Kirstein died in 1996.

Fred Hartt returned home in 1946 to begin a lifelong teaching career as one of the foremost experts on art of the Renaissance, but only after being made an honorary citizen by the city of Florence for his service during the war. In 1966, he traveled back to Florence to help combat raging floodwaters that threatened much of the city. During his prolific career, he published eighteen books, including *The History of Italian Renaissance Art*, still a widely used textbook on the subject. Fred Hartt died in 1993. He is buried in Florence, Italy, adjacent to the eleventh-century San Miniato al Monte Church, overlooking the only city he ever considered home.

Jim Rorimer was the first of several Monuments Men to receive the French Legion of Honor. He continued work as a Monuments Officer until 1946, when he returned to New York City to become the director of The Cloisters, home of The Metropolitan Museum's medieval art collection. In 1955, he became the sixth director of The Metropolitan Museum of Art. Extremely proud of his military service, Rorimer wore his army combat boots to work almost every day. His sudden death in 1966 cut short a brilliant career. When asked his formula for success, Rorimer offered, "A good start, a willingness—even eagerness—to work beyond the call of duty, a sense of fair play, and a recognition of opportunities before and when they arrive. In other words, it is important to find a course and steer it." He might as well have been describing the MFAA and his role within it.

George Stout, the father of the MFAA operation, returned to the United States in late July 1945, but not for long. By October, he was in Japan setting up the Arts and Monuments Division in the Pacific Theater. After his deployment to Japan, Stout accepted a position as the director of the Worcester Art Museum, and later the Isabella Stewart Gardner Museum in Boston. Like the other Monuments Men, and World War II veterans in general, he seldom discussed his military service. George Stout died in 1978. Monuments Officer Craig Hugh Smyth, who worked with Stout near the end of his tour of duty in Europe, described Stout as "a leader—quiet, unselfish, modest, yet very strong, very thoughtful and remarkably innovative . . . One believed what he said; one wanted to do what he proposed." Perhaps Lincoln Kirstein put it best: "George Stout was the greatest war hero of all time—he actually saved all the art that everybody else talked about."

Deane Keller didn't return home until May 1946, after two and a half years of military service overseas. In addition to the Order of the Crown of Italy and the U.S. Legion of Merit, Keller was made a member of the Order of Saint John Lateran by the Vatican and awarded the British Empire Medal. He resumed his teaching career at Yale, where his uniform hung proudly in a corner of his classroom. One of his students, also a World War II veteran, noted that "Keller tried to hide his humanity and soul with gruffness, but those of us who had served in uniform could see he was a pussycat underneath." During the 1950s he became the unofficial portrait painter at Yale. One of his most prized subjects was a portrait of his friend and driver, Charley Bernholz. Deane Keller died in 1992. Portions of his ashes are interred on the north side of the Camposanto in Pisa, Italy, the only non-Italian to be so honored.

Harry Ettlinger was discharged in August 1946 and returned to New Jersey to attend college on the GI Bill. With a degree in mechanical engineering, Harry worked for Singer, overseeing the manufacture of sewing machine motors. He later changed careers and accepted a position in the defense industry. In his last position,

Keller's portrait of his friend and driver, Charley Bernholz.

DEANE KELLER
PITTORE
14 XII 1901 12 IV 1992

UFFICIALE DELLA V ARMATA STATUNITENSE
NEL SETTEMBRE · OTTOBRE 1944
INCOMBENTE ANCORA LA MINACCIA NEMICA
PROCURO MATERIALI E MEZZI
PERCHE QUESTO CAMPOSANTO
QUASI DISTRUTTO DALLA GUERRA
FOSSE PRESERVATO DALL'ESTREMA ROVINA

AMICISSIMUS AD AMICOS

MAGGIO 2000

The tombstone honoring the resting place of Monuments Man
Deane Keller at the Camposanto in Pisa.

he served as deputy program director in the development and production of the guidance system for the submarine-launched Trident missile. Harry has remained active in veterans' groups and Jewish causes and is a lifelong supporter of the Raoul Wallenberg Foundation. In October 2015, speaking in the halls of Congress, he accepted on behalf of the Monuments Men and Women of all fourteen nations the Congressional Gold Medal, the highest civilian honor bestowed by the United States.

And what of the murderers and thieves? Nazi leader Adolf Hitler did not die "fighting till his last breath against Bolshevism," as the May 1 radio announcement proclaimed. The father of the Holocaust committed suicide in an underground bunker, but only after leading his nation and its people to utter ruin.

Harry Ettlinger accepting the Congressional Gold Medal on behalf of the Monuments Men and Women of all fourteen nations.

U.S. forces arrested Nazi Reichsmarschall Hermann Göring on May 9, 1945. At first, he denied his role in the Holocaust, proclaiming, "I revere women and I think it unsportsmanlike to kill children . . . For myself I feel quite free of responsibility for the mass murders." In a private interview during the Nuremberg trials, Göring noted, "They tried to paint a picture of me as a looter of art treasures . . . However, none of my so-called looting was illegal . . . I always paid for them or they were delivered through the Hermann Göring Division, which, together with the Rosenberg Commission [ERR] supplied me with my art collection." On October 15, 1946, the night before his scheduled hanging, Göring, like Hitler, cheated the hangman's noose and committed suicide.

Alfred Rosenberg, leader of the ERR and Hitler's chief racial theorist, denied complicity in any wrongdoing. He was tried, found guilty of war crimes, and hanged on October 16, 1946.

August Eigruber, the Nazi fanatic who ordered bombs placed inside the Altaussee mine, was arrested in May 1945. He was tried and found guilty of war crimes committed at Mauthausen concentration camp. Unrepentant to the bitter end, his last words before the trapdoor of the gallows opened were "Heil Hitler!"

Hermann Bunjes, the art scholar who sold his soul in Paris to Göring and the ERR, and later tried to buy it back by telling what he knew to Monuments Men Robert Posey and Lincoln Kirstein, hanged himself from the window of his prison cell on July 25, 1945. He left his family penniless and starving in a broken Germany.

Bruno Lohse, who as Göring's representative to the ERR in Paris threatened to kill Rose Valland, later admitted that he had been involved with the looting operation in Paris, but he insisted that he had done nothing wrong. In exchange for leniency, Lohse testified against some fellow looters and helped French authorities locate several caches of stolen art. He was released from prison in 1950 and resumed his art dealing activities, insisting he was a legitimate art dealer who had been a victim of the Nazis. Lohse died in March 2007 at the age of ninety-five. Within two months of his death, a safety deposit box he controlled was discovered in a Zurich, Switzerland, bank. Inside were tens of millions of dollars in paintings stolen during the war.

Alexander Langsdorff, whom Monuments Man Fred Hartt believed was responsible for the theft of the Florentine treasures, was arrested and interrogated by Monuments Man Deane Keller, but the will to prosecute such crimes in Italy quickly faded at war's end. Langsdorff returned to Germany, where he died of ill health in 1946.

SS General Karl Wolff, who authorized Langsdorff to take the Florentine treasures and ordered that they be brought to the Alto Adige region of Italy, was, incredibly, not tried for war crimes, at least not initially. Wolff was later found guilty as a "minor offender" and released. In 1964, the German government tried Wolff a second time and found him guilty of complicity in genocide. He was sentenced to fifteen years in prison, but released after serving less than five due to ill health. Maintaining his innocence to the end, Wolff lived another fifteen years before his death in 1984.

"Who owns art?" Nazi leader Adolf Hitler, like many conquerors before him, believed that to the victor belong the spoils of war.

Hitler went one step further, defining what, in his view, constituted "good" art, while destroying those objects that he judged inferior. The Monuments Men had a simple answer to this question that explained why they believed so strongly in their mission. Their answer: "Everyone." Works of art are part of our shared cultural heritage, no matter where in the world the art is located. Consequently, the Monuments Men believed that it was incumbent on everyone to protect it.

"Is art worth a life?" This question was also central to the mission of the Monuments Men. The image of a person running into a burning building to save a work of art is certainly dramatic. But would it be worth risking or even sacrificing a human life for an object, no matter its importance?

Monuments Man—and artist—Deane Keller answered this question by making an important distinction: dying to save an object versus dying to defend a cause. Neither Ronald Balfour nor Walter Huchthausen wanted to lose their lives, but both men accepted the risks because they believed in the cause.

During World War II, the United States and Britain, under the leadership of President Franklin D. Roosevelt and British Prime Minister Winston Churchill, fought to preserve democracy, freedom of speech, freedom of religion—in fact, our very way of life. The Monuments Men believed that fighting to preserve our cultural heritage was no less important. They could not imagine living in a dark and ugly world without these things of importance and beauty that have for centuries defined who we are as a civilization.

★

No one person spent more of his life thinking about the importance of protecting cultural treasures during times of conflict and then doing something about it than Monuments Man George Stout. His words serve not only as a reminder but as a call to action for world leaders, military commanders, and each one of us.

In areas torn by bombardment and fire are monuments cherished by the people of those countrysides or towns: churches, shrines, statues, pictures, many kinds of works. Some may be destroyed; some damaged. All risk further injury, looting or destruction . . .

To safeguard these things will not effect [sic] *the course of battles, but it will affect the relations of invading armies with those peoples and their governments . . .*

To safeguard these things will show respect for the beliefs and customs of all men and will bear witness that these things belong not only to a particular people but also to the heritage of mankind. To safeguard these things is part of the responsibility that lies on the governments of the United Nations. These monuments are not merely pretty things, not merely valued signs of man's creative power. They are expressions of faith, and they stand for man's struggle to relate himself to his past and to his God.

GLOSSARY

ALLIED NATIONS
A coalition led by the United States, Great Britain, France, and the Soviet Union formed in opposition to the Axis Powers.

AMG
Allied Military Government, the governing body put in place to ensure public order and safety during the Allied occupation of Germany.

ANTI-SEMITE
A person who is hostile to, prejudiced, or discriminatory against Jews.

AXIS POWERS
A coalition led by Germany, Italy, and Japan formed in opposition to the Allied Nations.

BBC
British Broadcasting Corporation.

CARABINIERI
The military police for the Italian armed forces that also functions as the state police.

ERR
Abbreviation for Einsatzstab Reichsleiter Rosenberg, a special task force that Nazi Germany established to plunder cultural valuables in occupied countries.

FATHERLAND

German term for homeland, used primarily in the Nazi era to refer to the state, often in a nationalist sense.

FLYING FORTRESS

Name for the Boeing B-17, a four-engine heavy bomber the U.S. Army Air Forces flew during World War II.

GESTAPO

Abbreviation of Geheime Staatspolizei, Nazi Germany's secret police.

GI

A nickname given to U.S. Army soldiers during World War II.

GOTHIC LINE

A series of fortifications two hundred miles long that the Germans built into the northern range of Italy's Apennine Mountains as a last line of defense against the Allied armies.

GUSTAV LINE

Also called the Winter Line, it was the first formidable German tripwire for the Allies in Italy, located at the skinniest part of the peninsula, south of Rome.

HAGUE CONVENTION

A series of international treaties that dictate the laws of war. These treaties were negotiated during two international peace conferences in 1899 and 1907.

HITLER YOUTH

State organization established in 1926 to educate young boys in the Nazi worldview and train them for eventual service in the armed forces.

HOLY SEE
Originating from *Sancta Sedes*, Latin for "Holy Chair," it is the authority of the pope in Rome to serve as the sovereign head of the Catholic Church.

KUNSTSCHUTZ
A German term for the policy of preserving cultural objects during armed conflict. Those in opposition to Nazi Germany saw the policy as veiled looting.

MFAA
Monuments, Fine Arts, and Archives Sections of the Civil Affairs Division of the U.S. Army. Tasked with safeguarding works of art and other cultural objects in war zones, the members of this special program were more commonly known as the Monuments Men.

MP
Military police.

NAZISM
Common term for the political ideology of the National Socialist German Workers' Party, which governed Germany from 1933 to 1945. Defined by extreme racism and authoritarian views.

OD
Olive drab, the color of the standard uniform for U.S. GIs and military vehicles during World War II.

RHINELAND
Region in western Germany along both banks of the Rhine River.

RHINO BARGE
A flat, rectangular deck with outboard engines used to ferry troops and equipment short distances.

ROBERTS COMMISSION

Established by President Franklin D. Roosevelt on June 23, 1943, the commission provided lists and reports on cultural treasures to military units and proposed the establishment of the MFAA.

ROTC

Reserve Officers' Training Corps, a leadership program that prepares college students to become officers in the U.S. military.

SCUTTLEBUTT

Slang term for gossip.

SHAEF

Supreme Headquarters Allied Expeditionary Force, led by General Dwight D. Eisenhower, exercised command over the armed forces of eleven nations that contributed men and materiel to operations against Nazi Germany.

STORMTROOPERS

Term used for members of the Sturmabteilung, the Nazi Party's semimilitarized force.

V-1

Guided missiles the Germans launched primarily at Britain from the French and Dutch coastlines.

BIBLIOGRAPHY

BOOKS

Aksenov, Vitali. *Favorite Museum of the Führer, Stolen Discoveries.* St. Petersburg: Publishing House Neva, 2003.

Atkinson, Rick. *The Guns at Last Light: The War in Western Europe, 1944–1945.* New York: Henry Holt and Company, 2013.

Blumenson, Martin. *U.S. Army in World War II, European Theater of Operations: Breakout and Pursuit.* Washington, DC: Center of Military History, 1961.

Caddick-Adams, Peter. *Monte Cassino: Ten Armies in Hell.* New York: Oxford University Press, 2013.

D'Este, Carlo. *Eisenhower: A Soldier's Life.* New York: Henry Holt and Company, 2002.

Downing, David. *The Nazi Death Camps.* New York: Gareth Stevens Publishing, 2006.

Duberman, Martin. *The Worlds of Lincoln Kirstein.* New York: Alfred A. Knopf, 2007.

Dulles, Allen W. *The Secret Surrender: The Classic Insider's Account of the Secret Plot to Surrender Northern Italy During WWII.* Guilford: Lyons Press, 2006.

Edsel, Robert M. *Saving Italy: The Race to Rescue a Nation's Treasures from the Nazis.* New York: Norton, 2013.

Edsel, Robert M., with Bret Witter. *The Monuments Men: Allied Heroes, Nazi Thieves, and the Greatest Treasure Hunt in History.* New York: Center Street, 2009.

Fasola, Cesare. *The Florence Galleries and the War: History and Records.* Florence: Casa Editrice Monsalvato, 1945.

Feliciano, Hector. *The Lost Museum: The Nazi Conspiracy to Steal the World's Greatest Works of Art.* New York: Basic Books, 1997.

Fowler, Michelle. "A Biography of Major Ronald Edmond Balfour." Included in Geoffrey Hayes, Mike Bechthold, and Matt Symes, eds.

Canada and the Second World War: Essays in Honour of Terry Copp. Waterloo: Wilfrid Laurier University Press, 2012.

Fröhlich, Elke, ed. *Die Tagebücher von Joseph Goebbels.* Vol. 3, part 1. Munich: K. G. Saur Verlag, 1987.

Gilbert, Martin. *Kristallnacht: Prelude to Destruction.* New York: Harper Collins, 2007.

Goldensohn, Leon. *The Nuremberg Interviews: An American Psychiatrist's Conversations with the Defendants and Witnesses.* New York: Alfred A. Knopf, 2004.

Hancock, Walker, with Edward Connery Lathem. *A Sculptor's Fortunes.* Gloucester: Cape Ann Historical Association, 1997.

Hartt, Frederick. *Florentine Art Under Fire.* Princeton: Princeton University Press, 1949.

Hoving, Thomas. *Making the Mummies Dance: Inside the Metropolitan Museum of Art.* New York: Simon & Schuster, 1994.

Howe, Jr., Thomas Carr. *Salt Mines and Castles.* New York: Bobbs-Merrill, 1946.

Il Führer in Italia. S.1., Agenzia Stefani, Milano: Alfieri & Lacroix, 1938.

Kesselring, Albert. *The Memoirs of Field-Marshal Kesselring.* London: Greenhill Books, 2007.

Kirstein, Lincoln. *The Poems of Lincoln Kirstein.* New York: Antheneum, 1987.

Linklater, Eric. *The Art of Adventure.* London: Macmillan and Co., 1947.

MacDonald, Charles B. *United States Army in World War II, European Theater of Operations: The Last Offensive.* Washington, DC: Center of Military History, 1973.

———. *United States Army in World War II, European Theater of Operations: The Siegfried Line Campaign.* Washington, DC: Center of Military History, 1990.

Methuen, Lord. *Normandy Diary: Being a Record of Survivals and Losses of Historical Monuments in North-Western France, together with those in the Island of Walcheren and in that Part of Belgium traversed by 21st Army Group in 1944–45.* London: Robert Hale Limited, 1952.

Nazi Conspiracy and Aggression. Vol. 3. Washington, DC: U.S. Government Printing Office, 1946.

Nicholas, Lynn. *The Rape of Europa: The Fate of Europe's Treasures in the Third Reich and the Second World War.* New York: Vintage Books, 1995.

Petropolous, Jonathan. *Art as Politics in the Third Reich.* Chapel Hill: University of North Carolina Press, 1996.

Piña, Leslie A. *Louis Rorimer: A Man of Style.* Kent, OH: Kent State University Press, 1990.

Report of the American Commission for the Protection and Salvage of Artistic and Historic Monuments in War Areas. Washington, DC: U.S. Government Printing Office, 1946.

Rorimer, James J. *Survival: The Salvage and Protection of Art in War.* New York: Abelard Press, 1950.

Sigal-Klagsbald, Laurence and Isabelle le Masne de Chermont. "*À qui appartenaient ces tableaux?: La politique françaises de recherche de provenance, de garde et de restitution des oeuvres d'art pillées durant la Seconde Guerre mondiale.*" Exhibition catalogue. France, 2008.

Simon, Matila. *The Battle of the Louvre: The Struggle to Save French Art in World War II.* New York: Hawthorne Books, 1971.

Smyth, Craig Hugh. *Repatriation of Art from the Collecting Point in Munich after World War II.* Montclair, NJ: Abner Schram, 1988.

Trial of the Major War Criminals before the International Military Tribunal. Vol. 9. Nuremberg, 1947.

Valland, Rose. *Le Front de l'art: Défense des collections françaises, 1939–1945.* Paris: Réunion des Musées Nationaux–Grand Palais, 2014.

War Department Historical Division. *American Forces in Action Series: St-Lô (7 July–19 July 1944).* Washington, DC: Center of Military History, United States Army, 1946.

Wilson, George. *If You Survive: From Normandy to the Battle of the Bulge to the End of World War II—One American Officer's Riveting True Story.* New York: Ballantine Books, 1987.

Woolley, Sir Leonard. *The Protection of the Treasures of Art and History in War Areas.* London: His Majesty's Stationery Office, 1947.

Yeide, Nancy H., Konstantin Akinsha, and Amy L. Walsh. *The AAM Guide to Provenance Research.* Washington, DC: American Association of Museums, 2001.

Ziemke, Earl F. *The U.S. Army in the Occupation of Germany, 1944–1946*. Washington, DC: Center of Military History, United States Army, 2003.

UNPUBLISHED WORKS

Ettlinger, Harry. *Ein Amerikaner: Anecdotes from the Life of Harry Ettlinger* (New Jersey, 2002).

ARTICLES

Bigart, Homer. "12 Old Masters in Loot from Naples Museum: Nazis Will Be Billed for Two Titians, a Raphael and Other Paintings." *New York Herald Tribune*, 4A (July 12, 1944). ProQuest Historical Newspapers: *New York Tribune / Herald Tribune* (1282911536).

Bradsher, Greg. "Nazi Gold: The Merkers Mine Treasure." *Prologue: Quarterly of the National Archives and Records Administration* 31, no. 1 (Spring 1999): n.p. www.archives.gov/publications/prologue/1999/spring/nazi-gold-merkers-mine-treasure.html.

———. "Monuments Men and Nazi Treasures: U.S. Occupation Forces Faced a Myriad of Problems in Sorting Out Riches Hidden by the Third Reich." *Prologue: Quarterly of the National Archives and Records Administration* 45, no. 2 (Summer 2013): 13–21.

———. "The Monuments Men and the Recovery of the Art in the Merkers Salt Mine April 1945." *The Text Message Blog*, National Archives. January 27, 2014, https://text-message.blogs.archives.gov/2014/01/27/the-monuments-men-and-the-recovery-of-the-art-in-the-merkers-salt-mine-april-1945/.

Churchill, Rhona. "Elderly Germans Being Used to Restore Aachen." March 12, 1945, n.p. *The Journal News*. Newspapers.com (162391017).

Hancock, Walker. "Experiences of a Monuments Officer in Germany." *College Art Journal* 5, no. 4 (May 1946): 271–311.

Houghton, Jr., Arthur A. "James J. Rorimer." *The Metropolitan Museum of Art Bulletin* (Summer 1966, Part Two).

Kirstein, Lincoln. "The Quest for the Golden Lamb." *Town and Country* 100, no. 428 (Sept. 1945): 115, 182–86, 189, 198.

von Lingen, Kerstin. "Conspiracy of Silence." *Holocaust and Genocide Studies*, 22, no. 1 (Spring 2008): 74–109. http://hgs.oxfordjournals.org.

PUBLIC COLLECTIONS

Archives des Musées Nationaux, Paris, France

Rose Valland Papers

Archivio Catalogo Beni Storico-Artistici, Florence, Italy

Giovanni Poggi Archive

British School at Rome, Rome, Italy

John Bryan Ward-Perkins Papers

Dokumentationsarchiv des österreichischen Widerstandes, Vienna, Austria

Max Eder Papers, DÖW 10610

Harvard University Archives, Harvard University, Cambridge, Massachusetts

Imperial War Museum, London, United Kingdom

King's College Archive Centre, University of Cambridge, Cambridge, United Kingdom

Papers of Ronald Edmond Balfour

Monuments Men Foundation for the Preservation of Art, Dallas, Texas

Robert K. Posey Papers

National Archives and Records Administration (NARA), Washington, DC

OSS Art Looting Investigation Unit Reports, 1945–46, M1782

MFA&A: Personnel: Officers—U.S.: Personal Histories

Record Group 239

Record Group 260

Record Group 331

A3380: Microfilm Copies of Reports from the Mediterranean and European Theaters of Operations Received from the Allied Military Government, 1943–1946

DN1924: Records relating to the administration and operation of the Foreign Exchange Depository Group within the Office of the Finance Advisor, OMGUS, 1944–1950

M1941: Records Concerning the Central Collecting Points ("Ardelia Hall Collection"): OMGUS Headquarters Records, 1938–1951

M1944: Records of the American Commission for the Protection and Salvage of Artistic and Historic Monuments in War Areas (The Roberts Commission), 1943–1946

M1946: Records Concerning the Central Collection Points ("Ardelia Hall Collection"): Munich Central Collecting Point, 1945–1951

M1949: Records of the Monuments, Fine Arts, and Archives (MFAA) Section of the Reparations and Restitution Branch, OMGUS, 1945–1951

Gallery Archives, National Gallery of Art, Washington, DC

Frederick Hartt Papers

James J. Rorimer Papers

New York Public Library for the Performing Arts, Jerome Robbins Dance Division, Archives, New York, NY:

Lincoln Kirstein Papers, c. 1914–1991 MGZMD 97

[Writings by Lincoln Kirstein are © 2019 by the New York Public Library (Astor, Lenox and Tilden Foundations) and may not be reproduced without written permission.]

Princeton University Archives, Princeton University, Princeton, New Jersey

Ernest Theodore DeWald Papers

Smithsonian Archives of American Art, Washington, DC

W. G. Constable Papers

Walker Hancock Papers

George Leslie Stout Papers

Manuscripts and Archives, Yale University Library, Yale University, New Haven, Connecticut

Deane Keller Papers

PRIVATE COLLECTIONS

Charles Bernholz Papers

ONLINE SOURCES

"Death of Hitler in the Berlin Chancellery." May 2, 1945. *Guardian.* https://www.theguardian.com/world/1945/may/02/secondworldwar .germany.

Italian National Institute for Statistics

Opera della Primaziale Pisana

Rush, Ralph G. "Holocaust: Confirmation and Some Retribution."
www.89infdivww2.org/memories/pstory2.htm.

Stato della Città del Vaticano

AUTHOR INTERVIEWS AND CONVERSATIONS

Harry Ettlinger

Leonard Fisher

Thomas Gibbs

James Huchthausen

Robert M. Posey

Marlie Schouteten

Thomas Stout

Judy Thompson

INTERVIEWS COURTESY OF ACTUAL FILMS

Frédérique Hébrard

SOURCE NOTES

BACK COVER

"Works of art" "Preservation of Works of Art in Italy," May 8, 1944. NARA, RG 239, M1944: Records of the American Commission for the Protection and Salvage of Artistic and Historic Monuments in War Areas (The Roberts Commission), 1943–1946, Roll 63.

EPIGRAPH

Prior to this war Lord Methuen, *Normandy Diary: Being a Record of Survivals and Losses of Historical Monuments in North-Western France, together with those in the Island of Walcheren and in that Part of Belgium traversed by 21st Army Group in 1944–45* (London: Robert Hale Limited, 1952), xv–xvi.

Dear Dennis Posey to Dennis, November 29, 1944, Robert K. Posey Papers, Monuments Men Foundation for the Preservation of Art, Dallas, TX.

PRELUDE

sixteen thousand "degenerate" works Jonathan Petropolous, *Art as Politics in the Third Reich* (Chapel Hill: University of North Carolina Press, 1996), 52.

Almost five thousand were destroyed Lynn Nicholas, *The Rape of Europa: The Fate of Europe's Treasures in the Third Reich and the Second World War* (New York: Vintage Books, 1995), 25.

"In so doing" Elke Fröhlich, ed., *Die Tagebücher von Joseph Goebbels* (Munich: K. G. Saur Verlag, 1987), vol. 3, part 1, entry for July 29, 1938.

spent two hours *Il Führer in Italia* (Agenzia Stefani, Milano: Alfieri & Lacroix, 1938).

veil of legality Petropolous, *Art as Politics in the Third Reich*, 80.

The document on p. xxvi is reproduced from Vitali Aksenov, *Favorite Museum of the Führer, Stolen Discoveries*, photo p. 3; the caption is drawn from Art Looting Investigation Unit, "Consolidated Interrogation Report #4: Linz," Attachment 1, NARA.

The document on p. xxvii is drawn from *Nazi Conspiracy and Aggression*, vol. 3, 188–189.

SECTION I

CHAPTER 1: LETTERS HOME

lying face down in the road Deane Keller, "Letter to the Editor," April 1, 1948, *The Hamden Chronicle*, Deane Keller Papers, MS 1685, Manuscripts & Archives, Yale University Library, Yale University, New Haven, CT, Box 2, Folder 18.

"the boys" Keller to Kathy, March 18, 1944, Deane Keller Papers, Box 7, Folder 45.

As he knelt beside Keller, "Letter to the Editor," April 1, 1948, *The Hamden Chronicle*, Deane Keller Papers, Box 2, Folder 18.

"is a big sacrifice" . . . "but I am thankful" Mother to Keller, October 7, 1943, Deane Keller Papers, Box 5, Folder 30.

"Rejected: poor eyesight" Keller to Parents, n.d., Deane Keller Papers, Box 5, Folder 24.

"Don't be so damned MODEST" . . . "Put it on thick" Theodore Sizer to Keller, May 30, 1943, Deane Keller Papers, Box 12, Folder 99.

Keller reported to Fort Myer, Virginia "Status of Officer," January 4, 1945, Deane Keller Papers, Box 21, Folder 33.

among the first *Report of the American Commission for the Protection and Salvage of Artistic and Historic Monuments in War Areas* (Washington, DC: U.S. Government Printing Office, 1946), 51.

"Buona gente" Deane Keller, "American Impressions of Italians and Italian Customs," NARA, RG 331, 10000 / 145, 1.

Keller visited a hospital Keller to Kathy, December 18, 1944, Deane Keller Papers, Box 7, Folder 51.

impregnable mountain bastion Gen. Harold Alexander, Companion of the Order of the Bath citation speech, Polish Institute and Sikorski Museum, cited in Peter Caddick-Adams, *Monte Cassino: Ten Armies in Hell* (New York: Oxford University Press, 2013), n.p.

"If we have to choose" Sir Leonard Woolley, *The Protection of the Treasures of Art and History in War Areas* (London: His Majesty's Stationery Office, 1947), 22.

first Monuments Man to reach Norman Newton, "Inspection of Abbey of Montecassino," May 19, 1944, NARA, RG 331, 10000 / 145 / 45.

"Reconstruction of entire Abbey" Norman Newton, "Montecassino Abbey," May 18, 1944, NARA, RG 331, 10000 / 145 / 45.

fifty-five thousand Allied soldiers dead . . . twenty thousand dead Thomas Gibbs (Historian, The National World War II Museum), in discussion with the author via email correspondence, June 18, 2012.

which he had purchased Keller, handwritten account, Deane Keller Papers, Box 22, Folder 39, 4.

"I haven't worn my ribbon" . . . "I feel the boys" Keller to Kathy, March 18, 1944, Deane Keller Papers, Box 7, Folder 45.

"Toozy Woozy" Keller, "Dear Deane: This is Daddy's History," Deane Keller Papers, Box 6, Folder 33.

"The life of one American boy" Keller to Kathy, June 25, 1944, Deane Keller Papers, Box 7, Folder 47.

were the treasures "MFAA Inventory No. 31: Art Objects from Carpegna, Sassocorvaro, Urbino actually in the Vatican," John Bryan Ward-Perkins Papers, British School at Rome, Rome, Italy, Inventories of Art Deposits.

After presenting his credentials H. C. Newton, "Report on Status of Monuments, Fine Arts, and Archives in the Mediterranean Theater of Operations," August 20, 1944, NARA, RG 331, 10000 / 145 / 203, 17.

The media spectacle Robert M. Edsel, *Saving Italy: The Race to Rescue a Nation's Treasures from the Nazis* (New York: Norton, 2013), 89–90.

two trucks Ernest DeWald, "Works of Art Formerly Stored at Montecassino and Later Transferred to the Vatican," July 20, 1944, NARA, RG 331, 10000 / 145 / 400, 1.

Crate number 1 Ibid., 2.

"There can be no doubt" Homer Bigart, "12 Old Masters in Loot from Naples Museum: Nazis Will Be Billed for Two Titians, a Raphael and Other Paintings," *New York Herald Tribune*, July 12, 1944, 4A. ProQuest Historical Newspapers: *New York Tribune / Herald Tribune* (1282911536).

seventeen works of art DeWald, "Works of Art Formerly Stored at Montecassino and Later Transferred to the Vatican," July 20 1944, NARA, RG 331, 10000 / 145 / 400, 1–2.

were in Nazi Germany *Report of the American Commission for the Protection and Salvage of Artistic and Historic Monuments in War Areas*, 75.

CHAPTER 2: INDEPENDENCE DAY

the summer he spent Thomas Stout (George Stout's son), in an interview with the author, 2008.

aboard the Liberty ship SS *Joseph Story* George Stout daily journal, entry July 4, 1944, George Leslie Stout Papers, Smithsonian Archives of American Art, Washington, DC.

Almost 156,000 men . . . 7,000 ships crossing Rick Atkinson, *The Guns at Last Light: The War in Western Europe, 1944–1945* (New York: Henry Holt, 2013), 29, 84.

twelve thousand American, British, and Canadian soldiers Ibid., 85.

just seven miles inland George Wilson, *If You Survive: From Normandy to the Battle of the Bulge to the End of World War II—One American Officer's Riveting True Story* (New York: Ballantine Books, 1987), 7.

about five hours George Stout daily journal, entry July 4, 1944, George Leslie Stout Papers.

"brain child" . . . "because not only is this commission" Craig Hugh Smyth, *Repatriation of Art from the Collecting Point in Munich after World War II* (Montclair, NJ: Abner Schram, 1988), 77–78.

"You are kind" . . . "but you magnify it" Stout to Paul Sachs, September 13, 1943, NARA, RG 239, M1944, Roll 57.

In October 1936 Nicholas, *The Rape of Europa*, 50.

on his own for four weeks Mason Hammond to David Finley, NARA, RG 239, M1944, Roll 14.

His original plan Smyth, *Repatriation of Art from the Collecting Point in Munich after World War II*, 81–82.

his personal library finding aid, Papers of Ronald Edmond Balfour, King's College Archive Centre, University of Cambridge, Cambridge, United Kingdom, https://janus.lib.cam.ac.uk/db/node.xsp?id =EAD%2FGBR%2F0272%2FPP%2FREB.

Volunteers in the United States *Report of the American Commission for the Protection and Salvage of Artistic and Historic Monuments in War Areas*, 2.

overlaid this information Ibid.

"Shortly we will be fighting" Ibid., 102.

a makeshift fireworks display George Stout daily journal, entry July 4, 1944, George Leslie Stout Papers.

"I'm sure much of the horrific results" Wilson, *If You Survive*, 7–9.

"The ghastly stories we had heard" Ibid.

after laying out his bedroll George Stout daily journal, entry July 5, 1944, George Leslie Stout Papers.

CHAPTER 3: "LITTLE SAINTS, HELP US!"

"open city" Albert Kesselring, *The Memoirs of Field-Marshal Kesselring* (London: Greenhill Books, 2007), 309.

"artistically bypassed" "Fine Arts Section," Deane Keller Papers, Box 19, Folder 10, 27.

Officials in Rome Frederick Hartt, *Florentine Art Under Fire* (Princeton: Princeton University Press, 1949), 16.

Keller entered the palace . . . Keller walked over Field Report, June 11, 1944, Deane Keller Papers, Box 21, Folder 31.

Other smaller paintings Ibid.

he wrote Ernest DeWald Hartt to DeWald, April 6, 1942 [sic], Ernest Theodore DeWald Papers, Princeton University Archives, Princeton University, Princeton, NJ, Box 4.

On the night of August 15, 1943 Hartt, "Notes on Bomb Damage to Cultural Monuments in Enemy-Occupied Italy," NARA, RG 331, 10000 / 145 / 7.

battered army jeep Hartt, *Florentine Art Under Fire*, 9.

He'd first visited Italy Eddie DeMarco, "After 17 years as professor, Hartt reflects on art, life," Frederick Hartt Papers, RG 28, Gallery Archives, National Gallery of Art, Washington, DC, Box 23, Folder 1.

while eating breakfast Hartt, *Florentine Art Under Fire*, 16.

"armed and helmeted" Ibid.

Linklater, who had been commissioned Eric Linklater, *The Art of Adventure* (London: Macmillan and Co., 1947), 255–57.

"But they're very good!" Ibid., 257.

"The whole house" Ibid., 258.

Cesare Fasola, librarian of the Uffizi Cesare Fasola, *The Florence Galleries and the War: History and Records* (Florence: Casa Editrice Monsalvato, 1945), 57.

After leaving Florence . . . With nothing more . . . "The packing cases" Ibid., 57–59.

"Little Saints, help us!" Ibid., 60.

All 246 paintings Hartt, *Florentine Art Under Fire*, 19.

"Five deposits located." Hartt, telegram, July 31, 1944, NARA, RG 331, 10000 / 145 / 362.

He then prepared a memo . . . "The fate of" Hartt, memo, "Secret," Frederick Hartt Papers, Box 3, Folder 8.

CHAPTER 4: THE MEETING

twelve hundred of its twelve thousand inhabitants George Stout daily journal, entry August 12, 1944, George Leslie Stout Papers.

On the evening of the D-Day landings Martin Blumenson, *U.S. Army in World War II, European Theater of Operations: Breakout and Pursuit* (Washington, DC: Center of Military History, 1961), 146–48.

Twice the number War Department Historical Division, *American Forces in Action Series: St-Lô (7 July–19 July 1944)* (Washington, DC: Center of Military History, United States Army, 1946).

No one was to enter George Stout daily journal, entry August 4, 1944, George Leslie Stout Papers.

the Germans had mined James J. Rorimer, *Survival: The Salvage and Protection of Art in War* (New York: Abelard Press, 1950), 15.

The meeting took place George Stout daily journal, entry August 13, 1944, George Leslie Stout Papers.

What matters Stout to Sachs, September 13, 1943, NARA, RG 239, M1944, Roll 57.

"There's so much to do" Rorimer, *Survival*, 9.

"attempt to record" Ibid., 2.

American GIs sharing their rations Ibid., 11.

American general had ordered Ibid., 10.

commandeered a printing press Ralph Hammett, "Meeting of Monuments, Fine Arts and Archives Specialist Officers 13 August—Master Supply," August 14, 1944, James J. Rorimer Papers, Gallery Archives, National Gallery of Art, Washington, DC, Box 3, Folder 2.

the bombing of his encampment George Stout daily journal, entry July 11, 1944, George Leslie Stout Papers.

CHAPTER 5: PRICELESS DUST

A fortuitous meeting Hartt, *Florentine Art Under Fire*, 37.

Now it provided refuge Ibid., 38.

Toward the end of July . . . Several days passed . . . "The bridges, the bridges!" Ibid., 39–43.

"one gigantic trash pile" Ibid., 45.

The intense heat Ibid., 48.

Barefoot women . . . There were shortages *Il Martirio di Firenze*, archival film, Imperial War Museum, London, United Kingdom, CO153; Edsel, *Saving Italy*, 189.

in the nearly four months Keller to Kathy, October 3, 1944, Deane Keller Papers, Box 7, Folder 49.

Keller and a small team "Fine Arts Section," Deane Keller Papers, Box 19, Folders 10, 36-37; Edsel, *Saving Italy*, 179.

hang the Stars and Stripes and the Union Jack Ibid.; Field Report, September 7, 1944, Deane Keller Papers, Box 21, Folder 32.

prewar population of seventy-two thousand people This data comes from ISTAT, the Italian National Institute for Statistics. The census of the population in Pisa was taken in 1936 and registered precisely 72,468 people living in the city.

Entering the piazza Field Report, September 7, 1944, Deane Keller Papers, Box 21, Folder 32.

contained more painted surface The painted area of the Camposanto was 16,145 sq. feet, whereas the painted area of the Sistine Chapel is slightly more than 12,972 sq. feet. "Affreschi del Camposanto," in Opera della Primaziale Pisana, 2003–2007, http://www.opapisa.it/it/attivita/cantieri-e-restauri /affreschi-del-camposanto.html; "Cappella Sistina," Stato della Città del Vaticano, http://www .vaticanstate.va/content/vaticanstate/en/monumenti/musei-vaticani/cappella-sistina.paginate.1.html.

"On the floor next to the walls" "Fine Arts Section," Deane Keller Papers, Box 19, Folder 10, 42.

Five weeks earlier . . . Even from the ground . . . A small group of volunteers . . . A shell whistled in Bruno Farnesi, "Cronaca della distruzione dell'incomparabile gioiello d'arte che era il/celebre Camposanto Monumentale di Pisa, Avvenuta il 27 Luglio 44 a causa di una granata di artiglieria," July 28, 1944, Frederick Hartt Papers, Box 4, Folder 6.

"in the night, the Piazza dei Miracoli" Ibid.

of San Miniato Field Report, August 24, 1944, Deane Keller Papers, Box 21, Folder 32.

"My assignment is MFAA officer" . . . **"I am not supposed to"** Keller to Parents, July 24, 1944, Deane Keller Papers, Box 5, Folder 26.

his time in Sezze Romano Edsel, *Saving Italy*, 185.

his stop in Monte Oliveto Ibid.

instructed him to bar entry Field Report, September 7, 1944, Deane Keller Papers, Box 21, Folder 32.

CHAPTER 6: OBJECTIVES

German artillery pieces still warm Rorimer, *Survival*, 46–47.

After spending the night Rorimer to Rockefeller, September 25, 1944, James J. Rorimer Papers.

U.S. Army soldiers Rorimer, *Survival*, 50.

requiring thirty-seven convoys Matila Simon, *The Battle of the Louvre: The Struggle to Save French Art in World War II* (New York: Hawthorne Books, 1971), 23.

his team had evacuated Ibid., 26.

it found safety Frédérique Hébrard, interview courtesy of Actual Films, n.d.

Jaujard estimated Rorimer, *Survival*, 51.

The tankers gathered around Ibid., 49.

"We do not want to destroy" . . . **"These examples"** . . . **"If these things are lost"** "Draft Lecture," Papers of Ronald Edmond Balfour, Misc. 5, 9.

Sometime around midnight . . . **"We're taking the Michelangelo."** "Removal of Works of Art from the Church of Notre-Dame at Bruges," September 24, 1944, Papers of Ronald Edmond Balfour, Misc. 5.

The two German officers . . . **Four days earlier** . . . **The dean and sacristan** Ibid.

With a towel wrapped around his neck Posey to Alice, September 23, 1944, Robert K. Posey Papers.

"things that seem luxuries" Posey to Alice, September 5, 1944, Robert K. Posey Papers.

A Posey had fought Robert M. Posey (Robert K. Posey's son), in an interview with the author, February 29, 2008.

A detailed description Lincoln Kirstein, "The Quest for the Golden Lamb," *Town and Country* 100, no. 428 (Sept. 1945): 182.

three trucks carrying the Ghent Altarpiece Nicholas, *The Rape of Europa*, 85.

"the Zoo" Posey to Alice, November 1, 1944, Robert K. Posey Papers.

added a bunny rabbit Posey to Dennis, April 5, 1944, Ibid.

his first ride Posey to Dennis, August 9, 1944, Ibid.

being at his side Posey to Dennis, April 22, 1944, Ibid.

"Dear Dennis" Posey to Dennis, October 3, 1944, Ibid.

CHAPTER 7: RESURRECTION AND TREACHERY

he'd come himself "Fine Arts Section," Deane Keller Papers, Box 19, Folder 10, 42–43.

Overseeing a small army Ibid.

A midnight "requisition" Leonard Fisher (friend of Deane Keller), in an interview with the author, December 23, 2010.

"The job is done" Letter, October 12, 1944, Deane Keller Papers, Box 21, Folder 32.

"This is the biggest job" . . . **"It has been interesting"** Keller to Kathy, October 9, 1944, Deane Keller Papers, Box 7, Folder 49.

"The destruction" . . . **"but it paralyzed the city"** . . . **"houses, towers, palaces"** Hartt, *Florentine Art Under Fire*, 45-46.

"Santo Stefano" "Damage to Monuments in Florence," August 20, 1944, Frederick Hartt Papers, Box 3, Folder 8.

had received a bizarre telegram Hartt, *Florentine Art Under Fire*, 68.

greeted as liberators Ibid., 69.

the dates of the theft "Report on German Removals of Works of Art from Deposits in Tuscany," October 8, 1944, Frederick Hartt Papers, Box 3, Folder 10; Edsel, *Saving Italy*, 196.

"Dear Ernest" Hartt to DeWald, September 7, 1944, NARA, RG 331, 10000 / 145 / 71.

took place at gunpoint Hartt, *Florentine Art Under Fire*, 72.

"A grand total of 529 paintings" . . . **"had suffered a robbery"** Ibid., 76.

CHAPTER 8: SEARCHING FOR CLUES

he failed the physical examination Walker Hancock with Edward Connery Lathem, *A Sculptor's Fortunes* (Gloucester: Cape Ann Historical Association, 1997), 122.

Hancock crossed the English Channel handwritten note, Walker Hancock Papers, Smithsonian Archives of American Art, Washington, DC.

his first night in Paris Hancock with Lathem, *A Sculptor's Fortunes*, 135.

A forced evacuation Charles B. MacDonald, *United States Army in World War II, European Theater of Operations: The Siegfried Line Campaign* (Washington, DC: Center of Military History, 1990), 307.

they wheeled artillery into position MacDonald, Ibid., 311–12.

hitchhiked their way Walker Hancock, "Experiences of a Monuments Officer in Germany," *College Art Journal* 5, no. 4 (May 1946): 273.

twisted trolley lines Ibid., 272.

unleashed a barrage Ibid., 273.

Native American headdress Ibid., 272.

the double doors Ibid., 273.

stench of soiled mattresses Ibid.

"I am Father Erich Stephany" . . . **Shelling and confinement** Ibid., 274.

American GIs had detained Ibid.

he'd prevented the army from converting James Rorimer typescript journal, entry September 3, 1944, James J. Rorimer Papers, 28MFAA-J1 Wartime Journals and Reports, 1944–1945, Box 1-1.

he'd managed to get the army to remove Rorimer, *Survival*, 63–64.

"no matter what" Jacques Jaujard, Introduction, Rapports de Mademoiselle R. Valland, Rose Valland Papers, Archives des Musées Nationaux, Paris, France.

"Middle-age" handwritten note, James J. Rorimer Papers, 28MFAA-J2 Survival Research Files, 1940–1989, Box 2-12 Paris [1944–1945].

Le Figaro Robert M. Edsel with Bret Witter, *The Monuments Men: Allied Heroes, Nazi Thieves, and the Greatest Treasure Hunt in History* (New York: Center Street, 2009), 121.

That had made quite an impression Rose Valland, *Le Front de l'art: Défense des collectiones françaises, 1939–1945* (Paris: Réunion des Musées Nationaux–Grand Palais, 2014), 218.

CHAPTER 9: GETTING HELP

Nearly every building Hartt to Walter W. S. Cook, November 24, 1944, NARA, RG 239, M1944, Roll 23.

"the works of art" Poggi, "Memo," November 11, 1944, Giovanni Poggi Archive, Archivio Catalogo Beni Storico-Artistici, Florence, Italy, Serie VIII, n. 155, 5.

Hartt couldn't find Hartt, *Florentine Art Under Fire*, 96.

Hartt received new information Fasola to Hartt, November 20, 1944, NARA, RG 239, M1949: Records of the Monuments, Fine Arts, and Archives (MFAA) Section of the Reparations and Restitution Branch, OMGUS, 1945–1951, Roll 4.

Nazi-sympathetic Italian officials announced Fascist Radio, "Messaggio sull'ispezione fatta dal Direttore Generale delle Arti, prof. Carlo Anti," December 11, 1944, Giovanni Poggi Archive, Serie VIII, n. 155, 5.

disaster struck when his vehicle crashed Balfour, "Sixth Report—Dec 44 and Jan 45," February 1, 1945, NARA, RG 239, M1944, Roll 70.

British Captain George Willmot L. Bancel LaFarge, "Progress Report, MFA&A, for fortnight of 29th Dec 44 to 11th Jan 45," January 12, 1945, NARA, RG 239, A3380: Microfilm Copies of Reports from the Mediterranean and European Theaters of Operations Received from the Allied Military Government, 1943–1946, Roll 1, 114.

Walking door-to-door Hancock, "Experiences of a Monuments Officer in Germany," 275.

"Well, I'll be damned" . . . "Here they are" Ibid., 276.

request denied George Stout daily journal, entry October 29, 1944, George Leslie Stout Papers.

Stout would now be George Stout daily journal, entry November 6, 1944, George Leslie Stout Papers.

Shattered glass Hancock, "Experiences of a Monuments Officer in Germany," 279.

Hancock found Ibid., 279–80.

Huchthausen was seriously injured Judy Thompson and James Huchthausen, in discussion with the author, n.d.

Stout had instructed Kirstein Martin Duberman, *The Worlds of Lincoln Kirstein* (New York: Alfred A. Knopf, 2007), 393.

had been so poor Robert M. Posey (Robert K. Posey's son), in discussion with the author, n.d.

Some arcane army rule Duberman, *The Worlds of Lincoln Kirstein*, 389.

Snuggly taped between . . . After an agonizingly . . . "say anything you want" Posey to Alice, December 16, 1944, Robert K. Posey Papers.

CHAPTER 10: LONGINGS

was standing next to him Rorimer, *Survival*, 109–10.

"Too often" Valland, *Le Front de l'art*, 218.

visited six of the nine locations Rorimer, *Survival*, 114–16.

into a concentration camp Valland, *Le Front de l'art*, 96.

"The atmosphere around me" . . . "The rooms and offices" Valland, *Le Front de l'art*, 81–82.

"room of martyrs" Hector Feliciano, *The Lost Museum: The Nazi Conspiracy to Steal the World's Greatest Works of Art* (New York: Basic Books, 1997), 107–08.

"France and its art" Valland, *Le Front de l'art*, 122.

Twenty visits J. S. Plaut, "Consolidated Interrogation Report No. 1: the ERR," August 15, 1945, OSS Art Looting Investigation Unit Reports, 1946-46, M1782, NARA, 6.

sometimes jingling loose emeralds Valland, *Le Front de l'art*, 98.

"R-1" "2609/Aussee 1953/1," Ardelia Hall Collection: Munich Property Cards, NARA, RG 260, M1946: Records Concerning the Central Collecting Points ("Ardelia Hall Collection"): Munich Central Collecting Point, 1945–1951, Roll 170.

A final spasm Rorimer, *Survival*, 109.

Train number 40044 Laurence Sigal-Klagsbald and Isabelle le Masne de Chermont, *"À qui appartenaient ces tableaux?: La politique françaises de recherche de provenance, de garde et de restitution des oeuvres d'art pillées durant la Seconde Guerre mondiale,"* exhibition catalogue (France, 2008), 217.

As they walked through Rorimer, *Survival*, 110.

"Rorheimer" Leslie A. Piña, *Louis Rorimer: A Man of Style* (Kent, OH: Kent State University Press, 1990), 123.

"Keep firing" . . . And that's exactly what he did Robert M. Posey (Robert K. Posey's son), in an interview with the author, February 29, 2008.

Walker Hancock spent Christmas Day Hancock with Lathem, *A Sculptor's Fortunes*, 146.

"He's discouraged" . . . "but we are guaranteeing" Hancock to Saima, December 4, 1944, Walker Hancock Papers.

Bernholz had pulled Mark Clark, "Award of Bronze Star Medal," May 21, 1944, Charles Bernholz Papers, Private Collection.

to transport the poor children T. Parr to Keller, December 30, 1944, Deane Keller Papers, Box 21, Folder 32.

"Today is Christmas" Letter to Kathy, December 25, 1944, Deane Keller Papers, Box 7, Folder 51.

SECTION II
CHAPTER 11: SMALL VICTORIES

Almost twenty thousand American boys lay dead Charles MacDonald, *United States Army in World War II, European Theater of Operations: The Last Offensive* (Washington, DC: Center of Military History, 1973), 53.

Harry didn't see himself . . . In 1937 Harry Ettlinger, *Ein Amerikaner: Anecdotes from the Life of Harry Ettlinger* (unpublished, New Jersey, 2002), 9, 11–14, 17.

seven thousand Jewish-owned businesses Martin Gilbert, *Kristallnacht: Prelude to Destruction* (New York: Harper Collins, 2007), n.p.

the last bar mitzvah Monuments Man Harry Ettlinger, in an interview with the author, 2008.

Harry's father spent . . . Once America entered World War II . . . In mid-October . . . Harry found himself Ettlinger, *Ein Amerikaner*, 26–28, 43.

the eight buddies Ibid., 44.

"The following three men" Ibid.

Being pulled off that truck Ibid.

Hancock entered the church Hancock with Lathem, *A Sculptor's Fortunes*, 149.

Hancock couldn't find the curé . . . In an effort to appease . . . Realizing that emotions . . . Mustering all the diplomacy . . . "I propose" . . . The mason Ibid., 149–50.

Florentine art officials Poggi, "Relazione sui Monumenti e le Opere d'Arte di Firenze durante la Guerra 1940–1945," June 5, 1945, Giovanni Poggi Archive, Serie VIII, n. 157, 12; Field Report, February 17, 1945, Deane Keller Papers, Box 21, Folder 33; "Bronze Statue of Cosimo I," February 21, 1945, Frederick Hartt Papers, Box 3, Folder 14.

After several days of planning . . . "a Maine back countryman" Field Report, February 17, 1945, Deane Keller Papers, Box 21, Folder 33.

"Cosimo, welcome back!" Ibid.

Smokey had been killed photo, Deane Keller Papers, Box 36, Folder 222.

CHAPTER 12: TREASURE MAPS

A phone call Rorimer, *Survival*, 111.

Sending a bottle of champagne Ibid., 110.

wanted him reassigned Valland, *Le Front de l'art*, 222.

pulled out a stack of photographs Rorimer, *Survival*, 113.

another larger box Ibid., 113–14.

in particular from Alexandre Valland, *Le Front de l'art*, 104–105.

One of the chauffeurs Ibid., 105.

the Nazi lackeys . . . "no one here is stupid enough" Valland note, February 1944, R 32-1, Rose Valland Papers.

She expected Valland, *Le Front de l'art*, 105.

you will find Rorimer, *Survival*, 114.

delivered . . . five to six hundred paintings Valland, *Le Front de l'art*, 187. The date of the burning of these artworks is drawn from notes by Rose Valland of her eyewitness account, July 23, 1943, Rose Valland Papers.

"Nothing could be saved" Rapports de Mademoiselle R. Valland, entry July 23, 1943, Rose Valland Papers.

the thieves had loaded Michelle Fowler, "A Biography of Major Ronald Edmond Balfour," included in Geoffrey Hayes, Mike Bechthold, and Matt Symes, eds., *Canada and the Second World War: Essays in Honour of Terry Copp* (Waterloo, Canada: Wilfrid Laurier University Press, 2012), n.p.

"It was a splendid week" . . . "On the one hand" Translation of article in *Rheinpost*, September 12, 1985, Hachmann, "The Sexton, Eyewitness of Major Balfour's Death," Papers of Ronald Edmond Balfour, Misc. 5.

created a makeshift repository Fowler, "A Biography of Major Ronald Edmond Balfour," included in Hayes, Bechthold, and Symes, eds., *Canada and the Second World War: Essays in Honour of Terry Copp*, n.p.

On March 10, at 9:30 a.m. sharp . . . They set out Translation of article in *Rheinpost*, September 12, 1985, Hachmann, "The Sexton, Eyewitness of Major Balfour's Death," Papers of Ronald Edmond Balfour, Misc. 5.

"I want very much to" handwritten letter excerpt, Webb to Balfour's Mother, Papers of Ronald Edmond Balfour, Misc. 5.

but word had it Kirstein, "The Quest for the Golden Lamb," 182.

"It's in a salt mine" Ibid.

"The desolation is frozen" Kirstein to Groozle, March 24, 1945, Lincoln Kirstein Papers MGZMD 97, New York Public Library for the Performing Arts, Jerome Robbins Dance Division, Archives, New York City, NY, Box 2–25.

Only two thousand Ibid.

"Certainly St. Lô was worse" . . . "Here everything" Ibid.

Kirstein sought help Lincoln Kirstein, *The Poems of Lincoln Kirstein* (New York: Antheneum, 1987), 264.

the dentist insisted . . . The trip took twice the time . . . A man in his midthirties . . . After exchanging pleasantries Kirstein, "The Quest for the Golden Lamb," 182–83.

he had joined the Nazi Party in 1938 . . . RG 260, M1941: Records Concerning the Central Collecting Points ("Ardelia Hall Collection"): OMGUS Headquarters Records, 1938–1951, Roll 31.

"First, it is *my* orders" . . . "Dear Bunjes" . . . "let me worry about that" Bunjes letter presented at Nuremberg trials, March 20, 1946, in *Trial of the Major War Criminals before the International Military Tribunal*, vol. 9 (Nuremberg, 1947): 547–49.

Posey chose to push back Kirstein, "The Quest for the Golden Lamb," 183.

a large bound album Kirstein, *The Poems of Lincoln Kirstein*, 265.

He then started pointing Ibid., 265–66.

"It is here" Ibid., 266–67.

CHAPTER 13: GAINS AND LOSSES

entered Siegen's ghostlike ruins Hancock, "Experiences of a Monuments Officer in Germany," 291.

A well-placed German source Ibid., 290.

"Around a hole" . . . "Throughout we walked" . . . "We were the first" Stout to Margie, April 4, 1945, George Leslie Stout Papers.

"They are afraid" . . . "The radio threatened" Hancock, "Experiences of a Monuments Officer in Germany," 291.

Stout noticed a boy Ibid.

Herr Etzkorn George Stout daily journal, entry April 2, 1945, George Leslie Stout Papers.

over four hundred paintings Hancock, "Experiences of a Monuments Officer in Germany," 292.

a stack of crates, forty in all Ibid.

Stout believed George Stout daily journal, entry April 2, 1945, George Leslie Stout Papers.

His work at the Aachen Cathedral Rhona Churchill, "Elderly Germans Being Used to Restore Aachen," March 12, 1945, n.p. *The Journal News*, Newspapers.com (162391017).

"It may seem strange" Ibid.

"Aachen Cathedral belongs" Ibid.

Reaching Recklinghausen around 3:00 p.m . . . On the smooth road . . . Seeking directions . . . All Keck could see . . . "Your captain is dead" . . . "Head wound" . . . "He's white as snow" Sheldon Keck, handwritten memo, "Statement Regarding the Incident Involving the Decease of Captain Walter J. Huchthausen, AC," NARA, MFA&A: Personnel: Officers—U.S.: Personal Histories.

After about forty-five minutes Ibid.

"The buildings that Huchthausen hoped" Hancock to Saima, November 25, 1945, Walker Hancock Papers.

CHAPTER 14: SURPRISES

Early that cold and rainy morning Ralph G. Rush, "Holocaust: Confirmation and Some Retribution," http://www.89infdivww2.org/memories/pstory2.htm.

"It seemed that" Ibid.

TOP SECRET. NO PRESS. Carlo D'Este, *Eisenhower: A Soldier's Life* (New York: Henry Holt, 2002), 685–86.

more than a thousand soldiers in all Lincoln Kirstein, "The Mine at Merkers," Robert K. Posey Papers.

Two days earlier, MPs stopped two women "Report covering the discovery, removal, transporting and storage of gold, silver, platinum and currency, fine arts treasures and German patent records from salt mines in the Merkers and Heringen area," April 1945, NARA, RG260, DN1924: Records relating to the administration and operation of the Foreign Exchange Depository Group within the Office of the Finance Advisor, OMGUS, 1944–1950, Roll DN1924_0140.

550 bags of Reichsmarks Greg Bradsher, "Nazi Gold: The Merkers Mine Treasure," *Prologue: Quarterly of the National Archives and Records Administration* 31, no. 1 (Spring 1999): n.p., www .archives.gov/publications/prologue/1999/spring/nazi-gold-merkers-mine-treasure.html.

It wasn't until engineers . . . Before stepping Ibid.

"stay-behind SS men" Kirstein, "The Mine at Merkers," Robert K. Posey Papers, n.p.

Kirstein stepped through the opening Ibid.

The space measured Bradsher, "Nazi Gold: The Merkers Mine Treasure," n.p.

Almost every period of civilization Kirstein, "The Mine at Merkers," Robert K. Posey Papers, n.p.

After returning to the surface Bradsher, "Nazi Gold: The Merkers Mine Treasure," n.p.

"If that clothesline should part" . . . "Okay, George" . . . "No more cracks" D'Este, *Eisenhower*, 686.

two hundred common suitcases Bradsher, "Nazi Gold: The Merkers Mine Treasure," n.p.

code name Task Force Hansen Greg Bradsher, "The Monuments Men and the Recovery of the Art in the Merkers Salt Mine April 1945," *The Text Message Blog*, National Archives, January 27, 2014, https:// text-message.blogs.archives.gov/2014/01/27/the-monuments-men-and-the-recovery-of-the-art-in-the -merkers-salt-mine-april-1945/.

General Patton refused D'Este, *Eisenhower*, 686.

"We are told" Ibid.

His friend, a Jewish chaplain Hancock with Lathem, *Sculptor's Fortunes*, 158.

"I have one here" Ibid.

"the people weeping" Ibid.

CHAPTER 15: ON THE MOVE

walks in the countryside Ettlinger, *Ein Amerikaner*, 44.

three of his eight friends Ibid.

the owner of Castle Warsberg Rorimer, *Survival*, 240.

had prompted French First Army Valland, *Le Front de l'art*, 222.

eight large buildings Robert Posey, "Semi-Monthly Report on Monuments, Fine Arts and Archives, Period Ending 15 April, 1945," April 17, 1945, NARA, RG 260, M1941, Roll 31.

At Schloss Ellmann Robert Posey, "Semi-Monthly Report on Monuments, Fine Arts and Archives, Period Ending 30 April, 1945," April 30, 1945, NARA, RG 260, M1941, Roll 31.

Bunjes also named names Ibid.

Tens of thousands Earl F. Ziemke, *The U.S. Army in the Occupation of Germany, 1944–1946* (Washington, DC: Center of Military History, United States Army, 2003), 52–53.

despite mold growing Hancock to Saima, April 4, 1945, Walker Hancock Papers.

"desperate for need of help" George Stout daily journal, entry April 20, 1945, George Leslie Stout Papers.

"repos out of hand" George Stout daily journal, entry April 23, 1945, George Leslie Stout Papers.

"when the stampede begins" "Visit to Switzerland," March 26, 1945, NARA RG 331, 10000 / 145 / 297.

"good state" Alessandro Cagiati to Hartt, "Removal of Works of Art by Germans," April 3, 1945, Frederick Hartt Papers, Box 3, Folder 16.

"It is feared by the Germans" Pietro Ferraro, "Memo," signed Antonio, April 10, 1945, Giovanni Poggi Archive, Serie VIII, n. 155, 5.

"Coming into town" . . . "houses on fire" . . . "smell of death" Keller to Parents, April 25, 1945, Deane Keller Papers, Box 5, Folder 27.

the works of art Teddy Croft-Murray, "Displaced Works of Art from Florence," April 27, 1945, NARA, RG 331, 10000 / 145 / 401.

CHAPTER 16: THE BEGINNING OF THE END

"Very urgent matter" George Stout daily journal, entry April 29, 1945, George Leslie Stout Papers.

an army captain Hancock with Lathem, *A Sculptor's Fortunes*, 158.

four hundred thousand tons of explosives George Stout daily journal, entry May 1, 1945, George Leslie Stout Papers.

As the squad searched George Stout daily journal, entry May 2, 1945, George Leslie Stout Papers; Greg Bradsher, "Monuments Men and Nazi Treasures: U.S. Occupation Forces Faced a Myriad of Problems in Sorting Out Riches Hidden by the Third Reich," *Prologue: Quarterly of the National Archives and Records Administration* 45, no. 2 (Summer 2013): 14.

Regimental banners Hancock with Lathem, *A Sculptor's Fortunes*, 159–60.

Someone had hastily written Ibid., 160.

More than 270 priceless paintings Bradsher, "Monuments Men and Nazi Treasures: U.S. Occupation Forces Faced a Myriad of Problems in Sorting Out Riches Hidden by the Third Reich," 14.

"fighting till his last breath" radio broadcast transcript, "Death of Hitler in the Berlin Chancellery," May 2, 1945, *Guardian*, https://www.theguardian.com/world/1945/may/02/secondworldwar.germany.

representatives of Nazi SS Allen W. Dulles, *The Secret Surrender: The Classic Insider's Account of the Secret Plot to Surrender Northern Italy during WWII* (Guilford: Lyons Press, 2006), 176–77.

On May 4 Field Report, May 12, 1945, Deane Keller Papers, Box 21, Folder 33.

The message Memo from Newton, May 4, 1945, NARA, RG 331, 10000 / 145 / 401.

For the time being Field Report, May 12, 1945, Deane Keller Papers, Box 21, Folder 33.

In full dress uniform Nicholas, *Rape of Europa*, 379.

Rorimer quickly cornered Rorimer, *Survival*, 163.

According to her notes Ibid.

Looted Renaissance and eighteenth-century furniture Ibid., 164.

D.W. Ibid., 163–64; Nancy H. Yeide, Konstantin Akinsha, and Amy L. Walsh, *The AAM Guide to Provenance Research* (Washington, DC: American Association of Museums, 2001), 300.

more than 150 paintings Rorimer, *Survival*, 182.

"Works of art" Ibid., 115, 182.

"romantic and remote" Ibid., 183.

Christoph Wiesend Ibid., 184.

thirteen hundred paintings Ibid.,185.

The room—more like a vault Ibid., 185–86.

Rorimer grabbed a poker Ibid., 186.

file cabinets containing Ibid.

The custodian confirmed Ibid., 186–87.

Several hours later . . . "dogs and fiends" . . . By 7:00 p.m. James Rorimer typescript journal, entry May 4, 1945, James J. Rorimer Papers, Box 1-1, 183.

"I hear you speak German" Monuments Man Harry Ettlinger, in an interview with the author, 2008.

"Are you the new translator?" Ibid.

"What a wheeler-dealer" Ibid.

CHAPTER 17: SALT MINES AND JAIL CELLS

Over the next three days Hancock with Lathem, *A Sculptor's Fortunes*, 162.

Using the back Hancock to Saima, May 4, 1945, Walker Hancock Papers.

"Dear Saima" Ibid.

Hancock directed the men . . . With more than half the day gone . . . A radio installed in the mine office Hancock with Lathem, *A Sculptor's Fortunes*, 162–164.

felt as if *they* were the prisoners Kirstein, "The Quest for the Golden Lamb," 183–84.

Weeks earlier . . . Soon the miners Ibid., 184–85.

Kirstein inadvertently bumped Ibid., 184.

"How long will it take" Ibid.

An army clerical error Field Report, May 12, 1945, Deane Keller Papers, Box 21, Folder 33.

"Bomb hit of August 1943" Ibid.

"shell holes, and mountainsides" Hartt, *Florentine Art Under Fire*, 103.

Finding a hotel . . . The following morning . . . With the jingling Ibid, 103, 105.

three hundred paintings Edsel, *Saving Italy*, 289.

aside from one painting Field Report, May 22, 1945, Deane Keller Papers, Box 21, Folder 33; Hartt, *Florentine Art Under Fire*, 104.

CHAPTER 18: CLOSURE

Poggi recounted how Poggi, "Relazione sui Monumenti e le Opere d'Arte di Firenze durante la Guerra 1940–1945," 12.

"greatest single art-looting operation" Hartt, *Florentine Art Under Fire*, 105.

A curious mix Ibid.

When the SS colonel Ibid.

The carriage house was packed Ibid.

Laboring through the night Kirstein, "The Quest for the Golden Lamb," 184.

From the other side . . . The two Monuments Men Ibid.

"By our flickering acetylene lamps" . . . "the miraculous jewels" Ibid., 186.

Off to the side Kirstein, "The Quest for the Golden Lamb," 186; Thomas Carr Howe, Jr., *Salt Mines and Castles* (New York: Bobbs-Merrill, 1946), 159.

Then Posey learned Ibid., 186.

Mineralienkammer Ibid., 189.

Springerwerke Ibid.

Kammergrafe Ibid., 198.

"Monte Cassino" Ibid.

To prepare for Stout's arrival Ibid., 184.

CHAPTER 19: GOING HOME

According to the logbook Max Eder, Zusammenfassung der mir bekannten Einlegerungen im Salzbergwerk Altaussee, Max Eder Papers, DÖW 10610, Dokumentationsarchiv des österreichischen Widerstandes, Vienna, Austria, 4.

"This looks like a good day" Howe, Jr., *Salt Mines and Castles,* 159.

"I think we could bounce her" Ibid.

"Remember how crowded" . . . "You don't" Memo to Col. Arthur Sutherland, May 16, 1945, Deane Keller Papers, Box 21, Folder 33.

ten paintings "Inventory Check of Works of Art Removed by Germans," May 31, 1945, NARA, RG 331, 10000 / 145 / 401.

109 crates of paintings "Fine Arts Section," Deane Keller Papers, Box 19, Folder 10, 74.

"art treasures" . . . "Extreme care necessary" Freight Waybill, Frederick Hartt Papers, Box 3, Folder 19.

"$500,000,000" "Fine Arts Section," Deane Keller Papers, Box 19, Folder 10, 72.

The following day Hartt, *Florentine Art Under Fire*, 109–10.

Driving up the same winding road Valland, *Le Front de l'art*, 225; Rorimer, *Survival*, 190.

EPILOGUE

29,436 railroad cars Nicholas, *The Rape of Europa*, 139.

more than 70,000 French Jews David Downing, *The Nazi Death Camps* (New York: Gareth Stevens Publishing, 2006), 11.

"This gentleman saved" Letter to Mr. Kenneth Balfour, October 1, 1954, Papers of Ronald Edmond Balfour, Misc. 5.

Frieda van Schaïk van Schaïk to "Cambridge University," October 16, 1945, Harvard University Archives, Harvard University, Cambridge, MA; Marlie Schouteten (grave caretaker) in discussion with the Monuments Men Foundation, 2017.

Extremely proud of his military service Thomas Hoving, *Making the Mummies Dance: Inside the Metropolitan Museum of Art* (New York: Simon & Schuster, 1994), 19.

"a good start" Arthur A. Houghton, Jr., "James J. Rorimer," *The Metropolitan Museum of Art Bulletin* (Summer 1966, Part Two): 39.

"a leader" Smyth, *Repatriation of Art from the Collecting Point in Munich after World War II*, 16.

"George Stout was the greatest war hero" Duberman, *The Worlds of Lincoln Kirstein*, 403.

"Keller tried to hide his humanity" Leonard Fisher (friend of Deane Keller) in an interview with the author, December 23, 2010.

"I revere women" Leon Goldensohn, *The Nuremberg Interviews: An American Psychiatrist's Conversations with the Defendants and Witnesses* (New York: Alfred A. Knopf, 2004), 132.

"They tried to paint" Ibid., 128–29.

"Heil Hitler" Edsel with Witter, *The Monuments Men*, 404.

"minor offender" Kerstin von Lingen, "Conspiracy of Silence," *Holocaust and Genocide Studies* 22, no. 1 (Spring 2008): 93, http://hgs.oxfordjournals.org.

Deane Keller answered Edsel, *Saving Italy*, 340; Keller, "Sectional History—Fine Arts," Deane Keller Papers, Box 23, Folder 56, 30, 32, 38.

"in areas torn" . . . "To safeguard" . . . "To safeguard" . . . George Stout, "Protection of Monuments: A Proposal for Consideration during War and Rehabilitation," n.d., W. G. Constable Papers, Smithsonian Archives of American Art, Washington, DC, Section 6a.

PHOTOGRAPH AND MAP CREDITS

JACKET

Jacket photos ©: cover Hitler: Everett Historical/Shutterstock; cover center paper: Ridkous Mykhailo/Shutterstock; cover painting: A. Burkatovski/Fine Art Images/Superstock, Inc.; cover frame: WitthayaP/Shutterstock; cover spine: National Archives and Records Administration; back cover: Documentation Archive of the Austrian Resistance; cover back flap: Shauna Carranza.

BOOK

Photos ©: cover Hitler: Everett Historical/Shutterstock; cover center paper: Ridkous Mykhailo/Shutterstock; cover painting: A. Burkatovski/Fine Art Images/Superstock, Inc.; cover frame: WitthayaP/Shutterstock; cover spine: National Archives and Records Administration; back cover: Documentation Archive of the Austrian Resistance; cover endpapers: Robert M. Edsel Collection; iv: National Archives and Records Administration; xi Keller: Robert M. Edsel Collection; xi Hartt: Robert M. Edsel Collection; xi Stout: National Archives and Records Administration; xi Hancock: Archives of American Art, Smithsonian Institution, Hancock Collection; xi Posey: Robert Posey Collection/Monuments Men Foundation; xi Kirstein: Lincoln Kirstein © 2019 by the New York Public Library (Astor, Lenox and Tilden Foundations); xi Rorimer: National Archives and Records Administration; xi Valland: Archives diplomatiques du Ministère de l'Europe et des Affaires étrangères; xi Balfour: King's College, Archive Centre; xi Huchthausen: Frieda van Schaïk Gumn Collection/Monuments Men Foundation; xi Ettlinger: Harry Ettlinger Collection/Monuments Men Foundation; xii Mussolini: ullstein bild Dtl./Getty Images; xii Hitler: ullstein bild Dtl./Getty Images; xii Goering: REX/Shutterstock; xii Wolff: Walter Frentz Collection; xii Langsdorff: Mareile Langsdorff Claus Collection; xii Ronsenberg: Harvard Law School Library/Wikimedia; xii Behr: Archives diplomatiques du Ministère de l'Europe et des Affaires étrangères; xii Lohse: Landesarchiv Berlin; xii Bunjes: Rheinische Friedrich-Wilhelms-Universität Bonn Archiv; xvi: Robert Posey Private Collection; xix: Library of Congress; xx: Photo 12/Getty Images; xxii: Arianna and Elisa Magrini/Edizioni Polistampa, Firenze; xxiii: Bayerisches Hauptstaatsarchiv; xxiv: Library of Congress; xxvi: Monuments Men Foundation; 1: Monuments Men Foundation; 2: Robert M. Edsel Collection; 4: William Keller Collection; 10, 11: National Archives and Records Administration; 12, 14: DeaneKeller Papers (MS 1685). Manuscripts and Archives, Yale University Library; 17: Wellcome Collection; 20: Library of Congress; 21, 25, 30: National Archives and Records Administration; 36: Antonio Quattrone/age fotostock; 37: Frederick Hartt Papers. National Gallery of Art, Washington, D.C., Gallery Archives. 28MFAA-D8_13994_002; 38, 39: Civico Archivio Fotografico Milano; 41, 43: A. S. Pennoyer Collection, Department of Art and Archaeology, Princeton University; 44: DeaneKeller Papers (MS 1685). Manuscripts and Archives, Yale University Library; 48: Hulton Archive/Getty Images; 60: A. S. Pennoyer Collection, Department of Art and Archaeology, Princeton University; 61: Eugene Markowski Collection; 62: Ministero per i Beni e le Attività Culturali; 66, 68: National Archives and Records Administration; 75: Paul Almasy/akg-images; 77: Ministère de la Culture/Médiathèque du Patrimoine, Dist. RMN-Grand Palais/Art Resource, NY; 78 top: National Archives and Records Administration; 78 bottom: Robert M. Edsel Collection; 82: Roberto Cerruti/Shutterstock; 87: Erich Lessing/Art Resource, NY; 94: DeaneKeller Papers (MS 1685). Manuscripts and Archives, Yale University Library; 96 top and bottom: Ministero per i Beni e le Attività Culturali; 100: Vincenzo Fontana/Getty Images; 101: Wikimedia; 106, 108: National Archives and Records Administration; 110 top: Wikimedia; 110 bottom: CEphoto, Uwe Aranas/Wikimedia; 111: Walker Hancock Papers/Monuments Men Foundation; 115: James J. Rorimer Papers. National Gallery of Art, Washington, D.C., Gallery Archives; 125: Frieda van Schaïk Gumn Collection/Monuments Men Foundation; 127: Lincoln Kirstein © 2019 by the New York Public Library (Astor, Lenox and Tilden Foundations); 135 top: Bayerische Staatsbibliothek München/Bildarchiv; 135 bottom: A. Burkatovski/Fine Art Images/Superstock, Inc.; 136: Archives diplomatiques du Ministère de l'Europe et des Affaires étrangères; 137: James J. Rorimer Papers. National Gallery of Art, Washington, D.C., Gallery Archives. 28MFAA-J9_17269_I14F; 140: Eric Bernholz Private Collection; 142, 143: DeaneKeller Papers (MS 1685). Manuscripts and Archives, Yale University Library; 148, 152, 154: National Archives and Records Administration; 157, 158: DeaneKeller Papers (MS 1685). Manuscripts and Archives, Yale University Library; 162: Library of Congress; 163: Archives diplomatiques du Ministère de l'Europe et des Affaires étrangères; 181 top and bottom: National Archives and Records Administration; 182: Florian Monheim/age fotostock; 184, 189, 193, 194: National Archives and Records Administration; 195: Walter I. Farmer Papers. National Gallery of Art, Washington, D.C., Gallery Archives. 28MFAA-C7_13670_001; 197, 198, 199, 201, 203: National Archives and Records Administration; 206: Dale Ford Collection/Monuments Men Foundation; 207: National Archives and Records Administration; 218: Archives of American Art, Smithsonian Institution, Hancock Collection; 219: Archives of American Art, Smithsonian Institution, Hancock Collection; 221: Peter Horree/Alamy Stock Photo; 227: Charles Parkhurst Papers. National Gallery of Art, Washington, D.C., Gallery Archives. 28MFAA-F8_14255_2; 228, 230 top and bottom, 231, 232: National Archives and Records Administration; 233: Monuments Men Foundation; 236: Archives of American Art, Smithsonian Institution, Hancock Collection; 239: National Archives and Records Administration; 241: Robert Posey Private Collection; 242: Walter Frentz Collection; 245: DeaneKeller Papers (MS 1685). Manuscripts and Archives, Yale University Library; 247: National Archives and Records Administration; 249 top: Frederick Hartt Papers. National Gallery of Art, Washington, D.C., Gallery Archives. 28MFAA-D8_13990_013; 249 bottom: Frederick Hartt Papers. National Gallery of Art, Washington, D.C., Gallery Archives. 28MFAA-D8_13992_011; 252: Frederick Hartt Papers. National Gallery of Art, Washington, D.C., Gallery Archives. 28MFAA-D8_13990_014; 253: Bundesarchiv, Berlin, Bild R 58/9362; 256: Robert Posey Private Collection; 257: TopFoto/The Image Works; 258: Craig Hugh Smyth Papers. National Gallery of Art, Washington, D.C., Gallery Archives. 28MFAA-G7_14427_02; 259: Documentation Archive of the Austrian Resistance; 260: Topham/The Image Works; 261: Archives of American Art, Smithsonian Institution, Thomas Howe Collection; 264: National Archives and Records Administration; 266, 267, 268: DeaneKeller Papers (MS 1685). Manuscripts and Archives, Yale University Library; 269: National Archives and Records Administration; 270: Archives diplomatiques du Ministère de l'Europe et des Affaires étrangères; 272: William Vandivert/Getty Images; 273: G. R. and G. A. Walden Collection; 277: Robert M. Edsel Collection; 278: Wikimedia; 279: George Bush Presidential Library and Museum; 282 top: Eric Bernholz Private Collection; 282 bottom: Robert M. Edsel Collection; 283: Monuments Men Foundation.

INDEX

Note: Page numbers in *italics* refer to illustrations.

ACKNOWLEDGMENTS

Writing a book requires a tremendous commitment of time. Like any undertaking of excellence, it demands discipline and sacrifice, and in this instance on the part of not just the author but also his wife and two young sons. Anna shared my excitement about introducing the story of the Monuments Men to young readers. Without her understanding, support, and encouragement, I could not have written this book. Whatever success attends this effort belongs in equal measure to her.

In 1996, while crossing the Ponte Vecchio in Florence, I wondered how so many of the works of art and cultural monuments of Europe survived the most destructive war in history, and who were the people who saved them. Driven by curiosity, I located and interviewed twenty-one Monuments Men and Women. I thank each of them, and their family members, for entrusting me with their legacy, in particular S. Lane Faison, Jr., and my dear friend Harry Ettlinger. Gathering their stories, a journey that has now consumed more than twenty years, has been the privilege of my life.

While my name alone appears on this book as author, others helped me along the way. Dr. Seth Givens, a gifted military historian and teacher, has been invaluable to me throughout the writing process. This is a much better book because of his involvement. My wife and lead researcher, Anna Bottinelli, helped assemble the many photographs and read the manuscript throughout the writing process. The candor of her counsel and her thorough knowledge of the material helped me beyond measure. Casey Shelton has done an outstanding job sorting through my extensive files at the Monuments Men Foundation for the Preservation of Art to stay ahead of my research needs. Her meticulous work has been essential to a project of this scope and magnitude. Finally, the day-to-day support of Michele Brown, my executive assistant, in handling many of the business and personal matters that constantly threaten the completion of a writer's task enabled me to finish the book on time. Thank you, Michele.

I am particularly pleased to have had the opportunity to tell these heroes' wartime experience in Italy and northern Europe in one book. It is a new telling of the Monuments Men story made possible by more than fifteen years of research. For that reason, I want to recognize and thank members of my previous research teams, including Bryce McWhinnie, Dorothee Schneider, Christy Fox, and Elizabeth Hudson. I also want to tip my hat and thank Bret Witter, coauthor of my second book, *The Monuments Men*. Special thanks also to Michelle Rapkin and Tom Mayer, both of whom helped me become a better writer.

Lisa Sandell and her team at Scholastic have been enthusiastic supporters of this project from the outset. An author benefits greatly from an engaged editor; Lisa has been that and more. Our frank exchanges of views benefited this book in many ways. And I would like to thank the rest of the Scholastic team: Jael Fogle, Keirsten Geise, Olivia Valcarce, Crystal McCoy, Emily Heddleson, Jasmine Miranda, Matthew Poulter, Lizette Serrano, Danielle Yadao, Tracy van Straaten, Rachel Feld, Isa Caban, Vaishali Nayak, Mindy Stockfield, David Levithan, Ellie Berger, the entire Sales force, and the Scholastic Book Clubs and Book Fairs.

Finally, I want to express my appreciation to some of the people whose work behind the scenes has enabled me to remain focused on bringing visibility to the Monuments Men and their remarkable legacy. Robert and Patty Hayes have been longstanding supporters of my efforts to honor these men and women. No amount of praise for their assistance would be too great. Similarly, I want to thank the generous donors who have sustained the Monuments Men Foundation in ways both large and small. My attorney and friend, Michael Friedman, has been with me from the start of my career as an author. I continue to benefit from his wise counsel. Thanks also to my agent, Richard Abate.

The Archivist of the United States, David Ferriero, and his outstanding team at the National Archives in College Park, Maryland, in particular Greg Bradsher, have been an important part of my success. They continue to share my commitment to see this important part of our nation's history broadly known. The National WWII Museum and its cofounder Dr. Nick Mueller, now president and CEO emeritus, recognized the importance of the Monuments Men story at an early stage. With the backing of its dedicated trustees, the Museum will soon begin construction of a permanent exhibition honoring the Monuments Men and Women that will preserve these scholar-soldiers' contribution to civilization for all time.

This is my fourth book about the Monuments Men, but my first book for young readers. I have long wanted to share this exciting and noble story with a young audience, the Monuments Men and Women of tomorrow. Preserving our shared cultural heritage for future generations depends on them.

ABOUT THE AUTHOR

A former nationally ranked tennis player and pioneer in the oil and gas exploration business, Robert M. Edsel is recognized as one of the world's foremost advocates for art preservation and the recovery of cultural treasures missing since World War II.

Mr. Edsel is the author of three other books about the Monuments Men, including the number one *New York Times* bestseller *The Monuments Men*, which Academy Award recipient George Clooney adapted into a feature film, and *Saving Italy*, also a *New York Times* bestseller. He is also the coproducer of the Emmy-nominated documentary film *The Rape of Europa*. In 2007 he founded the Monuments Men Foundation for the Preservation of Art, recipient of the National Humanities Medal, the United States' highest honor for work in the humanities.

Mr. Edsel has received numerous awards, including the Anne Frank Human Writes Award from the Anne Frank Center; the Texas Medal of Arts; the Hope for Humanity Award, presented by the Dallas Holocaust Museum; and the Records of Achievement Award from the Foundation for the National Archives, which recognizes an individual whose work has fostered a broader national awareness of the history and identity of the United States through the use of original records. Previous recipients have included Tom Hanks, Ken Burns, David McCullough, and Steven Spielberg.

Mr. Edsel has served as a trustee on numerous not-for-profit organizations, including the National WWII Museum and St. Mark's School of Texas.

He lives in Dallas, Texas, with his family.

Robert M. Edsel is a dynamic and passionate public speaker who has introduced the Monuments Men to audiences throughout the United States and worldwide. Using a mix of photographs and film clips, Mr. Edsel shares his experiences locating and interviewing some twenty Monuments Men and Women, working with George Clooney to bring these heroes' legacy to film, and the ongoing discoveries by the Monuments Men Foundation of priceless works of art and other treasures missing since the end of World War II. He has educated and inspired sold-out audiences at schools and community centers, and many of our nation's most prominent universities and museums.

To inquire about inviting Mr. Edsel to your school or organization, please contact David Buchalter at David.Buchalter @unitedtalent.com.